The marketing casebook

The marketing casebook is specifically designed to illustrate the key concepts in marketing theory through a series of case studies and theory notes. By looking at the way marketing works in practice, the reader is drawn into the problems and questions that face marketers and managers in their everyday lives.

The marketing casebook has been designed to be used as an all round resource to help develop the skills of the reader in discussions and examinations. The book is divided into two main parts:

- 15 CASES
  - detailed case studies
  - a selection of key issues for analysis and oral discussion
  - cross-referenced with material in theory notes
- 15 THEORY NOTES
  - concentrated summary of key marketing principles
  - further reading

The marketing casebook also includes:

- full glossary of key terms
- master bibliography
- a major section on 'how to use cases' to develop a full understanding of marketing

The marketing casebook is the ideal resource for students of marketing whether at undergraduate, MBA or executive level. It is intended to work as a learning resource in its own right which can be used for distance learning or self-tuition, as well as being a good comprehensive revision guide. The cases are from a variety of well-known companies in Europe which should be of interest to anyone involved in the marketing process, be it for consumer goods, services or for industrial products.

The marketing casebook

Cases and concepts

Sally Dibb and Lyndon Simkin

London and New York

First published 1994 and reprinted 1996
by Routledge
11 New Fetter Lane, London EC4P 4EE

Simultaneously published in the USA and Canada
by Routledge
29 West 35th Street, New York, NY 10001

Typeset in Times by Leaper & Gard Ltd, Bristol
Printed and bound in Great Britain by
Biddles Ltd, Guildford and King's Lynn

British Library Cataloguing in Publication Data
A catalogue record for this book is available from the British Library

ISBN 0–415–08950–6

Library of Congress Cataloging in Publication Data
has been applied for.

The comments pertaining to specific companies and organisations are
supported by media and/or trade opinion and are not intended to reflect
badly on those companies and personnel concerned. These cases
hightlight the practices of modern marketing management and strategy.

Contents

Part III Theory notes

Figures

Tables

About the authors

In 1991 Sally Dibb and Lyndon Simkin joined with US colleagues Bill Pride and O.C. Ferrell to produce *Marketing: Concepts and Strategies* (published by Houghton Mifflin). In its first season this foundations of marketing textbook dominated the UK market for business school mainstream texts. Since then, the text has established itself as the major publication for European business schools, broadening its customer base to Eire, the Netherlands, Norway and Sweden, and attracting sales from in-company trainers for management development programmes. Married with two children – Becky and Jamie (who encouraged visits to Chester Zoo, TGI Friday's and various hotels for background to these cases!) – Sally and Lyndon have both been lecturing to MBAs and undergraduates at Warwick Business School since the mid-1980s.

Sally has a BSc (management science) and MSc (industrial marketing) from UMIST in Manchester, and a PhD (consumer marketing modelling) from Warwick. Lyndon was once an economic geographer (BA) at Leicester, before switching to marketing (PhD) at Bradford's Management Centre. Their current publications are in the areas of marketing modelling, market segmentation, marketing planning and services marketing. Consultancy is diverse, ranging from car parts, diggers and cameras to burgers, in the UK and Europe! Some of these experiences, with permission, are shared with you in these cases.

Acknowledgements

As with any text, this project has been supported by a number of colleagues, students, publishers and companies. Their comments, material, co-operation and encouragement have proved invaluable. Special thanks must go to our students – past and present – at Warwick Business School; to Chris Vere at Chester Zoo; John Bradley and the team at JCB; O.C., Bill and all at Houghton Mifflin; and to Francesca Weaver and Routledge for producing this book.

COMMENTS AND VIEWS

John Saunders   Gordon Foxall
Robin Wensley
O.C. Ferrell

MATERIAL AND IDEAS

Caroline Farquhar – Heineken, ABN AMRO
Peter Wingaard   – Electrolux
Leslie Tunbridge   – Stabburet, Kodak Norge
Jens Maier   – Stepcan

Gillian Skoulding   Adsearch
Peter Doyle   Rodney Gudger
Tim Grinnell   Mark Derry
David Harris   Cogent/John Wringe
Bill Pride   Countrywide/David Lake
Chris Vere   Esprit
Helen Baxter   John Bradley
Pat Menard   Greg Tobin
Peter Jackson

Sources

Company annual reports, companies' promotional material; Adsearch; Mintel; Euromonitor; KeyNote; Retail Business; Salomon Brothers; Barclays de Zoete Wedd; Christiana Bank og Kreditkasse; *Business Week*; *Financial Times*; *Institutional Investor*; *Marketing*; *Marketing Week*; *Campaign*; *Packaging News*; HMSO *Social Trends*; HMSO *Employment Gazette*; *Hoover's Handbook of American Business*; *AA Members' Handbook*; *Major Companies of Europe*; *The JCB Experience*, JCB; *Chester Zoo Life*, Chester Zoo; Norges Markedsdata; Marketpower; Target Group Index/BMRB; Henley Centre; British Tourist Authority; ABLCRS; NTC Publications; Chartered Institute of Marketing; Textline; Harvest; Warwick University's Business Information Service; Statistisches Bundesamt; Gesellschaft für Konsum; Markt und Absatzforschung; Statistisk Arbok; Statistisk Sentralbyra; *Marketing: Concepts and Strategies*, Houghton Mifflin Company.

Part I

General

Chapter 1

Introduction

As with many tasks in marketing, this book is presented to you in a very different format from the project first initiated in 1991. The original intention was simple: to produce an up-to-date strategic marketing case-book, containing cases focused on the UK and Europe suitable for MBA and undergraduate business school teaching. Our full-time students were seeking cases which were topical, multi-themed and suitable for exploring various scenarios in discussion. Our distance learning students were requiring cases which 'told a story', with supporting theory and explanation contained in one book. The finished result, it is believed, matches these goals, but in addition contains much more. There are cases targeted at executive teaching and in-company training. There is a full glossary defining key marketing terms. Most of the core topics within strategic marketing are summarised and included as theoretical overviews, complete with suggestions for further readings. All-in-all, the original casebook concept has been expanded to become a full teaching resource – one-stop strategic marketing.

Our experience with teaching marketing at all levels – executive courses, full-time and distance learning (correspondence) MBAs, and under-graduates – has highlighted the very different teaching and learning requirements of these target audiences. Business executives prefer prac-tical, 'real', lively cases. Undergraduates and full-time Master's students expect a variety of short, one-issue cases plus multi-faceted cases which permit separate syndicate groups to tackle separate issues. Giving each syndicate group its own questions to discuss adds to the depth of seminar sessions and reduces repetition for both students and staff. Distance learning or correspondence students typically have only a few weekend seminars or a summer school; they are left more to their own devices and require a text which is a resource – cases, readings, with supporting explanatory theory. Most of the cases published here have been well tried and tested by our students at Warwick Business School and with many com-panies. The results have been highly positive and led us to develop this text.

THIS CASEBOOK

The marketing casebook: cases and concepts presents a variety of cases in terms of topics, markets, countries and types of marketing, with guidance on their use and theory overviews of the key concepts of strategic marketing. It is hoped students will use this text for self-tuition, and that lecturers will appreciate the flexibility for teaching formats presented by this material.

- Teach yourself: cases, lessons, and explanation.
- Variety of styles: short/long; simple/complex; single issue/ multi-themed.
- European focus: UK 6, pan-European 2, Dutch 2, Irish 1, French 1, Swedish 1, Norwegian 2.
- All arenas: industrial marketing, business-to-business, services, and consumer marketing.
- Case themes: basics and marketing strategy; topical issues; successes and failures; practical insights.
- A complete resource: cases, readings, theory, references, glossary, instructions for tackling cases.

For lecturers and trainers

- Instructor's Manual
  – additional notes/solutions
- Multi-themed cases
- Various case lengths/styles
- Short 'revision' cases for discussion
- Suggestions for teaching formats
- Lesson notes for use as handouts
- Overhead transparency masters for key points

CONTENT

Most of the cases cover several marketing concepts and issues, although each can be used by the tutor or the student to examine only one topic if so desired. Table 1.1 summarises the main issues featured in each of the 15 cases. Table 1.2 explains the differing teaching styles and case lengths.

Case lengths and styles need to vary to give variety in teaching application and to assist in motivating student involvement. Certain sessions will require short, punchy cases concentrated on one or two issues, especially early in a course or term. Other seminars will benefit from discussion of more complex issues with full supporting market and company information as background. Cases with several core themes lend themselves to lively debate with little classroom repetition. For self-learning students, they

Table 1.1 Core marketing topics highlighted by case

	Harris	Waterford	Stepcan	Electrolux	Stabburet	Forte	Lucas	Heineken	Sketchley	TGI Friday's	Kodak	JCB	ABN AMRO	EuroDisney	Chester Zoo
Positioning	M					M									
Targeting									X				X		
Segmentation						M	X		M		X		X		
Buyer behaviour	X	M										M			
Marketing research	X								M		M				X
Competitive strategy	X					M				X					
Branding	M		M			M		M					X	X	
International marketing		X	X	M				M					X	M	X
Marketing channels	X			X		M					X				
Differential advantage		M			X										
Product management		X								X			X		
Marketing environment		X		M			X								
Marketing planning			X									X			
Services marketing			X						M				M	M	
Industrial marketing							X					X			
Marketing mix				X											
Promotional mix											M		M	X	M
Pricing	(X)		(X)												
Marketing assets													M		

Note: This is ruthless, only including key issues from each case. M = primary theme.

Table 1.2 Case lengths and case teaching styles

	Harris	Waterford	Stepcan	Electrolux	Stabburet	Forte	Lucas	Heineken	Sketchley	TGI Friday's	Kodak	JCB	ABN AMRO	EuroDisney	Chester Zoo
Length															
Extensive						X				X			X		X
Medium		X	X	X	X		X	X	X				X		
Short	X										X			X	
Style															
Scenario	M		M			M						(X)	(X)		
Focused		X	X	X	X			X	X	X	X			M	X
How to do	X								M			X			
Discussion	X	M			M	X	X	X	X	X	M	M	M	X	M

illustrate how the core elements of strategic marketing inter-relate in the realms of true-life marketing.

Case lengths

- *Extensive* = 10+ pages, considerable data/information on a variety of topics and issues.
- *Medium* = 5–8 pages, including data, tending to be focused on fewer, core issues.
- *Short* = 2–3 pages narrowly angled discussion style or 'how to do' cases.

Case styles

- *Scenario* cases are detailed; they include information enabling many aspects to be taught or examined, with different students or syndicate groups tackling separate issues.
- *Focused* cases concentrate on one or two issues only, permitting classroom discussion but within specific, narrow topic parameters.
- The '*how to do*' cases force students to apply specific techniques and thought processes to real problems: they have to investigate how to use basic tools and concepts of marketing and research.
- Discussions are often essential for exploring core issues in cases and for identifying optimum courses of action. These *discussion* cases lend themselves particularly well to wide-ranging and challenging debate.

CONTENT SUMMARIES

Harris Queensway was highly successful during the early 1980s, but with the repositioning of its Queensway chain came disaster. This case illustrates the problems of positioning, and of understanding and responding to consumer buyer behaviour. In addition, the case highlights aspects of marketing research and competitive strategy.

The *Waterford Crystal* case examines the current marketing of Ireland's Waterford Wedgwood group, one of the world's leading suppliers of fine china and crystal. The case focuses on consumer buyer behaviour, branding, international marketing and channel (distribution) management.

Stepcan, created by Metal Box, is a rare example of creating a differential advantage through packaging innovation. The retailers which test marketed Stepcan quickly realised its potential, but where is Stepcan today? This case concentrates on creating a differential advantage across national frontiers; controlling the marketing channel; and the impact of the broader marketing environment.

Sweden's *Electrolux* is a major force worldwide in white goods and electrical appliances, but faces an ever more aggressive challenge from

Whirlpool. Competition and competitive strategies in an international arena form the basis for this case, which additionally examines brand management (particularly brand positioning), the role of customer service in the augmented product offering, and the importance of marketing planning.

Stabburet dominates many of its markets and has ridden the economic recession in Norway quite effectively. The company has developed a successful marketing mix emphasising good value, desirable food products, tightly controlled distribution, and well-planned promotional activity. Norway's entry into the EC, with the removal of protective trade barriers, will create a radically more competitive trading environment. The changing marketing environment is playing a significant role in Stabburet's marketing.

Branding, market segmentation and positioning are complex issues. For a service provider such as *Forte*, identifying a branding strategy which matches the company's varied portfolio of hotels with the market's segments has been costly and perhaps risky. Rival operators have adopted similar approaches, but by no means all. This case concentrates on the segmentation, targeting, positioning process, as well as the associated branding strategies and competitive reactions.

Lucas is one of the largest suppliers of car parts, both to car manufacturers and to garages/repair shops. The *Lucas Aftermarket* case illustrates the importance of identifying – and of controlling – effective marketing channels. The problems of implementing true market segmentation are apparent, as are the implications of adopting any compromise.

As a company *Heineken* is active throughout the world. As a brand, Heineken is familiar to consumers in North America, Africa, Australasia and most of Europe. The company, though, takes account of the needs of local consumers and has a portfolio combining local with international brands.

Dry cleaner *Sketchley*'s market is highly competitive, with owner-operated independents a major threat to all of the national chains. Opportunities to expand the market are limited. The case illustrates the practicalities of conducting marketing research and for targeting market segments.

TGI Friday's is an American import into the UK. It is a leader in the branded, themed restaurant sector. Services marketing is different partly because of the intangibility of the product and the extended marketing mix – particularly the role of personnel. These characteristics of services marketing are well illustrated with Whitbread's TGI Friday's.

Kodak Norge (Norway's arm of the Kodak empire), as for most organisations, has incomplete marketing information and marketing intelligence. The company is highly successful but faces strong local and international competition. It is important for Kodak Norge to understand its market segments and to control effectively its marketing channels. Kodak Norge may need to instigate marketing research.

The *JCB* story is one of success for a large, privately owned UK engineering company. The case highlights reasons for this success as a major international supplier of construction equipment; featuring JCB's branding, positioning, marketing planning and promotional strategies. The difficulties of selling and marketing in industrial markets are highly evident.

Dutch *ABN AMRO Bank* recognises, with its *internal* and *interactive marketing*, the importance of personnel and the interaction with customers in a service business. The bank has global ambitions, but has not lost sight of local needs and the importance of establishing an operating hierarchy which enables national managers to fully understand their markets.

Assets do not necessarily travel! US Disney assumed its brand reputation and success in America would automatically transfer to Europe. The company did not fully take account of cultural differences or the marketing environment in Europe when in 1992 it launched *EuroDisney* near to Paris.

Chester Zoo, in the North West of England, is one zoo which successfully understands consumer concerns and needs. Persuading consumers to value a service, here a leisure attraction, is the main theme of this case. Services marketing and the promotional mix are well ilustrated, along with aspects of marketing research and competition.

These cases are supported with a full glossary of marketing terms (pp. 252–60), a guide to studying with cases (pp. 11–24), and theory notes (pp. 153–251) covering:

- An introduction to marketing and marketing strategy
- The marketing environment
- Consumer and organisational buyer behaviour
- Marketing research
- Forecasting
- Market segmentation, targeting, positioning
- Competition
- Products and product management
- Distribution/marketing channels
- Pricing
- Marketing communications/promotion
- Services marketing
- Industrial marketing
- Marketing planning
- International marketing

HOW TO USE THIS BOOK

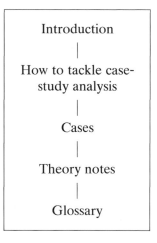

Introduction

|

How to tackle case-
study analysis

|

Cases

|

Theory notes

|

Glossary

How to tackle case-study analysis

Following this introduction is a set of guidelines aimed to assist those students new to the world of case-study teaching. There are basic rules designed to aid your assimilation of material in the cases, your analyses and the presentation of your solutions or responses. These guidelines cannot be definitive as every tutor, and each student, has a personal approach, but until you are comfortable with your own case strategy, these notes will enhance your use of these cases.

Cases

Immediately after the 'how to do' chapter are 15 strategic marketing cases, of varying lengths, styles, degrees of complexity and subject areas. Tables 1.1 and 1.2 in this introduction highlight these differences. Each case ends with an *issues* section. Each *issues* section includes (a) an overview of the core themes in the case; (b) suggestions for the most pertinent questions to be considered; (c) cross-referencing with the relevant theory notes presented later in this text.

Theory notes

Fifteen summaries of the fundamental subjects of strategic marketing are included in this text. Each is designed to introduce the subject and explain its main features. These overviews are included to reduce the annoyance of students who desire 'one-stop' reading. Additional texts will only need to be consulted to follow up and develop deeper understanding of these central themes. Each theory note concludes with our suggestions for further reading: UK, US and practitioner texts. Each theory note is referenced at the end of cases when the theory may assist the student's understanding of the case. Lecturers may use these theory notes as handouts.

Glossary

The text ends with a glossary containing explanation of over 100 terms, with full cross-referencing for their appearance in the associated theory notes.

AND FINALLY ...!

If you are a student, we hope you find at least some of these cases to be of interest and of help in enhancing your understanding of marketing. If you are a lecturer or trainer, we hope to have made your work a little easier.
    Good luck!

Sally Dibb
Lyndon Simkin
University of Warwick

Chapter 2

How to tackle case-study analysis

At undergraduate, postgraduate and practitioner level, the case study is a well-accepted and widely used learning tool. The established popularity of case studies in marketing management education is primarily linked to the technique's ability to bridge the gap between marketing theory and practical situations. This capacity to make the connection between standard textbooks and real business problems allows students to practise applying the theoretical concepts they have learnt. This is achieved by providing students with appropriate background and market information, then asking them to take responsibility for making key marketing decisions.

Success in providing case-study solutions, as in real life, is largely determined by the nature and quality of the analysis carried out. Learning how to make decisions about case studies in a logical, objective and structured way is an essential part of the education process. Such decisions must take into consideration all relevant aspects of the marketing and competitive environment, together with an appreciation of the company's resources. In developing their decision-making and analytical skills, students should become more familiar with different corporate structures and philosophies, achieve a better understanding of the implementation of a range of marketing tools, and become increasingly comfortable with real business situations. In addition, the learning process should allow the student to witness, at first hand, the risks and problems associated with decision-making at managerial level.

Working in seminar or syndicate groups is a popular approach to case-study learning. This helps develop group as well as individual skills; a very positive contribution given the extent to which real business situations require individual managers to work together towards a solution. Developing group skills takes time as individuals learn to cope with the expression of differing opinions and views, allocating roles to different group members. However, this closely emulates real work situations where a working consensus must be reached.

Preparing cases on an individual basis may appear to be simpler than having to consider such a range of disparate group views. However, there is a risk that the analysis carried out fails to examine key alternatives which happen not to coincide with the individual's views. It is important to be especially vigilant in generating case solutions when working individually. Nevertheless, tackling cases by yourself also builds up analytical and decision-making skills. If a written solution to the case is required, the opportunity to develop report-writing skills also arises.

STEPS FOR TACKLING CASE-STUDIES

There have been many attempts to summarise the case-study approach into a sequence of steps or a process. The following five stages are often cited:

I   Understand and analyse the problem
II   Derive alternative solutions
III Analyse alternative solutions
IV   Recommend the 'best' alternative
V   Implement the chosen solution

In order to be able to tackle these tasks, students need firstly to undertake a general overview of the key case issues and to conduct a *situational analysis* which is sufficiently detailed to provide the necessary inputs to the case tasks. Although this step is not usually listed, it is an essential element of the case approach and must not be omitted. For this reason, this situational analysis is reviewed ahead of the above five stages.

1: Situation analysis

Thoroughly examining the situation in which a business operates helps to put the problems in the case into context. A number of key areas warrant attention:

– Company position (financial, structure, marketing, etc.)
– Market analysis
– External environment, threats and opportunities
– Competitor situation

Company's internal position

An appreciation of the company's internal position, drawing attention to particular capabilities and resources, is an essential element in the situation analysis. This analysis should take into consideration company structure, the financial situation and marketing.

Company structure

The way in which organisations are structured impacts upon the opera-

tional and managerial decisions which are made. It is important to understand the nature and reasons for the organisation's structure. Remember
that every organisational structure is unique in some aspect. Students
should therefore undertake a thorough and careful analysis of this facet of
the company. Questions to be addressed can include:

- Is the organisational structure hierarchical or flat?
- Where does the balance of power lie?
- What is the company's mission statement?
- Does the company have particular philosophies?
- What are the key characteristics of the company?
- Is managerial activity delineated by function?
- Who are the key decision-makers for each functional area?
- How do the lines of communication operate?
- What formal and informal decision-making structures operate?

The answers to at least some of these questions help build up an overview
of the characteristics of the company. This understanding should be used as
a basis for assessing how realistic are the various case solutions eventually
recommended.

Company financial situation

A number of techniques can be used to assess the financial position of the
company. The first stage is usually to analyse the balance sheet and income
statement. This allows the student to achieve a quick understanding of the
company's financial performance and state of health. Comparing current
year figures with those from earlier trading periods is especially informative. This form of horizontal analysis allows students to map percentage
change in certain items over time.

    Provided that basic balance sheet and income statement information is
available, a range of simple financial ratios can be calculated (see Table
2.1). These ratios can be used to achieve greater financial insight into an
organisation. Once calculated, current ratios can usefully be compared with
ratios from competing organisations, or from the company's own earlier
figures. This enables a better understanding of the company's relative
position to be achieved, together with an appreciation of emerging trends.

    In some circumstances, it may be possible to further enhance the
financial view by carrying out break-even analysis and by trying to achieve
a greater understanding of the relationship between supply and demand.

    It is important to note that there are a number of potential difficulties
linked to the use of financial ratios. These difficulties centre on (a) the way
in which the ratios are calculated and (b) the context within which they are
applied.

    (a) Ratios represent a snap-shot of a company's financial state at a

Table 2.1 Key financial ratios

Profitability ratios
These ratios measure financial and operating efficiency by assessing the organisation's ability to generate profit from revenue and money invested.

Name of ratio	*Calculated*
i) Gross profit margin	$\dfrac{\text{Sales} - \text{Cost of goods sold}}{\text{Sales}}$

This shows the total margin available to meet operating expenses and generate a profit.

ii) Net profit margin	$\dfrac{\text{Profit after taxes}}{\text{Sales}}$

Sometimes referred to as return on sales, this ratio shows after tax profit per £ (pound) spent.

iii) Return on assets	$\dfrac{\text{Profit after taxes}}{\text{Total assets}}$

This ratio measures the company's return on total investment.

iv) Return on net worth	$\dfrac{\text{Profit after taxes}}{\text{Total shareholders' equity}}$

Also referred to as return on stockholders' equity, this ratio gives a measure of the rate of return on shareholders' equity.

Liquidity ratios
These ratios are used to demonstrate the company's ability to meet current liabilities and to ensure solvency.

Name of ratio	*Calculated*
i) Current ratio	$\dfrac{\text{Current assets}}{\text{Current liabilities}}$

This demonstrates the company's ability to satisfy short-term liabilities.

ii) Quick ratio	$\dfrac{\text{Current assets} - \text{Inventory}}{\text{Current liabilities}}$

Also referred to as the acid-test ratio, this demonstrates the company's ability to meet current liabilities, in the period in which they are due, without resorting to the sale of stock.

iii) Inventory to net working capital	$\dfrac{\text{Inventory}}{\text{Current assets} - \text{Current liabilities}}$

This indicates the degree to which company working capital is tied up in stock.

Leverage ratios
This group of ratios helps in the assessment of the company's responsiveness to
debt and ability to meet repayments as scheduled.

Name of ratio	Calculated

i)   Debt to assets ratio

$$\frac{\text{Total liabilities}}{\text{Total assets}}$$

This indicates the extent to which borrowed funds have been employed to
finance the company's operations.

ii)   Debt to equity ratio

$$\frac{\text{Total liabilities}}{\text{Total shareholders' equity}}$$

This shows the balance of equity provided by the owners, and funds provided by
creditors.

iii) Long-term debt to equity ratio

$$\frac{\text{Long-term liabilities}}{\text{Total shareholders' equity}}$$

This ratio allows the balance between owners' equity and liabilities to be viewed
in context of the company's overall capital structure.

Activity ratios
These ratios are used to gauge how effectively the company generates sales
and profit from assets.

Name of ratio	Calculated

i)   Total assets turnover

$$\frac{\text{Sales}}{\text{Total assets}}$$

This ratio, which signals the level of sales productivity and utilisation of total
assets, can be compared with the industry average to show whether the volume
of business generated justifies the level of asset investment.

ii)   Fixed assets turnover

$$\frac{\text{Sales}}{\text{Fixed assets}}$$

This measures both sales productivity and utilisation of equipment and plant.

iii) Inventory turnover

$$\frac{\text{Sales}}{\text{Inventory}}$$

This measure of inventory turnover can be compared with the industry norm to
show whether the company carries too large or small an inventory.

particular point in time. When comparing the results from more than one
ratio, it is therefore necessary to ensure that the figures applied are from
the same time period and calculated according to similar accounting
conventions.

(b) The way in which ratios are interpreted and used is more important
than the figures in isolation. In order to understand the significance of a

particular ratio, it is essential to fully understand the factors, both internal and external to the company, which have caused the financial position reflected in the figures. Properly understanding the cause of the figures puts the company in a better position to suggest remedial action.

Once the financial analysis has been completed, it is necessary to pull together the different strands of the overall financial picture. At this stage, the student needs to make a simple assessment of the company's position, highlighting issues which are likely to significantly impact upon the case solutions which are recommended.

Company marketing organisation

Evaluating how the company handles its marketing should systematically cover all aspects of the marketing strategy and programmes. This will include marketing research processes and marketing information systems, maintenance of the product portfolio including new product design and development, pricing strategies, distribution policy including the policing and management of distributors, all aspects of communications policy from above the line activity through below the line promotions, publicity and personal selling, and after sales service.

Market analysis

Understanding market structure and customer requirements is a funda-mental stage in any case analysis. The following key questions should be addressed:

Market structure
- What is the market size?
- What are the trends in market size? E.g. is it increasing or decreasing? How quickly?
- How is the market structured? E.g. what evidence is there of segments?
- Which segment(s) or customer group(s) is the company targeting?

Customers
- Who are the customers?
- What are the customers like?
- For what purpose do they buy the product/service?
- What features do they look for in the product/service?
- What is the buying process?
- What factors impact upon them as they buy?
- How do they feel about the product/service?
- How do they feel about alternative suppliers?

Clear and thorough insights into the customers who make up a particular market are essential to organisational success. Having conducted the *market analysis*, it is necessary to assess how effectively the company is reaching its target customers and whether it is geared for expected changes in customer needs and/or market structure. This analysis will impact on the solution(s) which are selected.

External environment

A wide range of factors from the external environment impact upon the well-being of an organisation [cf. Chapter 19]. These include economic, political, social, cultural, technological, legal and regulatory issues. These environmental factors continually change, moulding the conditions in which companies operate. Sometimes these changes can have a major impact on a company's business dealings. Recognising the significance of such changes at an early stage can help companies to maximise the positive benefits and minimise the detrimental effects.

Early warning of the effects of environmental factors can be achieved by assessing the potential opportunities/threats presented by any observed changes. In case-study analysis, as in real life, it is often necessary to extrapolate trends and make predictions regarding the level of future change. It is helpful to remember that most potential threats can also be viewed as opportunities should an organisation have the resources and interest to pursue them.

Competition

Understanding the competitive structure of markets helps companies put their marketing options into perspective [cf. Chapter 24]. The strengths on which companies hope to build can only be realistically appraised when placed within this context. From the customer's viewpoint, buying decisions are based on the strengths and weaknesses of a particular player relative to other available choices. There are a number of key questions which should be considered if an organisation's competitive situation is to be fully understood:

- Who are the key players?
- How is market share divided amongst competing organisations?
- What competitive positions do the players occupy? E.g. who is market leader, which companies are challengers, followers and nichers?
- How aggressive are the competing organisations and what are the trends? E.g. is it possible to identify fast movers?
- On what basis are the key competitors competing? E.g. what are their differential advantages, are these sustainable and how are they supported with marketing programmes?

The competitive stance which companies adopt impacts on their current and future actions. Understanding the answers to these questions allows the case analyst to fully appreciate the relative competitive strengths and weaknesses of the company and to assess whether or not different case solutions are realistic. It is sometimes helpful to try to predict likely competitive responses to different case solutions. This would involve asking how a named competitor would be likely to react to a defined set of action on the part of the company. The competitive information outlined can make a strong and reliable contribution to these questions.

2: The case-study process

I. Understand and analyse case problem areas

After the situational analysis has been conducted, it is necessary to develop a clear view of the problems/key issues set out in the case study. Although the use of specific case questions will impact upon exactly where the key areas lie, the company and market analysis will usually have revealed a range of problem areas which the company (or market as a whole) needs to address. Formally listing these issues helps to ensure that no omissions are made when alternative scenarios are considered. Any specific questions can be tackled once these problem areas have been identified.

One way to make this assessment of the case material and the core issues is to carry out a *marketing audit* (see Kotler, 1991). The marketing audit offers a systematic way of considering all aspects of the company's marketing set-up, within a pre-determined structure (see Table 2.2). The marketing audit should aid the analysis by:

- describing current activities and results: sales, costs, profits, prices etc;
- gathering information about customers, competitors, and relevant environmental developments;
- exploring opportunities for improving marketing strategies;
- providing an overall database to be used in developing marketing strategies and programmes for implementation.

Not all cases require such a formal review, nor do they necessarily present sufficient information for such an audit. The initial *situational analysis* may well give adequate focus and understanding. In more complex cases covering dynamic and competitive markets, the marketing audit can assist in sifting through the market and company data to identify more thoroughly the most pertinent issues.

When drawing up a list of problem areas, it is necessary to make a distinction between symptoms of problems and the problems themselves. The difference is that symptoms are defined as the outward signs of an

Table 2.2 The marketing audit

Part I: The Marketing Environment Audit

Economic–Demographic	Markets
Technological	Customers
Political	Competitors
Legal–Regulatory	Distributors and Dealers
Cultural–Social	Suppliers
Ecological	Facilitators in the Channel
	Publics

Part II: Marketing Strategy Audit
Business Mission
Marketing Objectives and Goals
Strategy

Part III: Marketing Organisation Audit
Formal Structure
Functional Efficiency
Interface Efficiency

Part IV: Marketing Systems Audit
Marketing Information System (MIS)
Marketing Planning System
Marketing Control System
New Product Development System

Part V: Marketing Productivity Audit
Profitability Analysis
Cost-Effective Analysis

Part VI: Marketing Functions Audit
Products
Price
Distribution
Promotion
Personnel

---

underlying problem or problems. For instance, symptoms might include falling sales, declining profits, reducing market share and too much stock. The underlying problem may be poor understanding of customer needs in chosen customer segments, signalling a need for closer links with customers and regular marketing research and feedback from the marketplace.

The identification of symptoms and problems should start with the most major problem(s). The associated symptoms can then be pinpointed and listed. Minor difficulties, whether or not related to the major problems, should be kept until after the main problem(s) have been signalled. It is helpful to signal whether the problems are impacting on the company's position in the short, medium or long term. This makes it easier to predict the likely effect of the problems on the company's objectives and plans.

II. Derive alternative solutions

Selecting an appropriate case solution is an iterative process. The starting point should be to generate as many different alternatives as possible. Each potential solution must relate to the key problem area(s) in the case and offer a realistic way of solving it. Make sure that the alternatives suggested are distinct and different. Spending time reviewing many similar solutions can be counter-productive. Such detailed fine-tuning can be carried out at a later stage, once a selection has been made.

In some circumstances it is helpful to frame the generation of alternatives around the following questions:

- Where is the company now?
- How did it get to its current position?
- Where does it want to go/what does it want to achieve?
- How can it achieve what it wants, and head to where it wants to go?

The understanding of the organisation's current position should have been achieved through the *situational analysis*, but explicitly framing the first two questions helps ensure that these issues from the earlier analysis are not overlooked.

At this stage it ought to be possible to exclude the more unrealistic solutions, so that the more likely options can be analysed further.

III. Analyse alternative solutions

The next step is to critically evaluate the suitability of the alternatives which have been identified. This is a key part of the analysis and should involve a formal assessment of the advantages and disadvantages of every alternative. Each proposal should be considered within the context of the company, market, competitor and environmental analyses which have already been carried out. Conducting a form of 'What if ...?' analysis – where attempts are made to predict the likely outcome(s) of alternative solutions – can provide a meaningful and positive input. It is helpful to formally list each advantage and disadvantage with, if possible, a ranking of the relative importance of each. This ranking should help identify the most appropriate alternative.

IV. Recommend the 'best' alternative

Providing that the case analysis has been thoroughly carried out, selection of the appropriate solution should not be too complicated. Whichever solution is ultimately chosen, it is important to double check through the environmental, competitor and market analyses that the chosen solution is consistent with the prevailing market conditions.

It is unlikely that a course of action will be identified which is ideal in all respects. It will therefore be necessary to consider both the acceptability of the various options as well as the associated risks. Understanding such risks will be inevitably constrained by limited data availability and/or ambiguous market conditions which make it difficult to make clear decisions. However, it should be remembered that in real life situations decisive decision-making is required in comparable circumstances, with associated compromises.

Once a decision has been made, arguments should be prepared supporting the choice(s). In some circumstances, part of the recommendations may be based on the success of initial actions. Some flexibility will be required in responding to the differing circumstances which may arise. It may be helpful to develop *decision 'trees'* which show different routes to the final objectives, depending on the short-term reactions to the recommendations.

V. Implement the chosen solution

Ensuring the design of plans and marketing programmes to implement the chosen solution is as fundamental to case-study learning as the analyses and choice of the 'best' solution:

- At which target groups is the solution aimed?
- How will the company's offering be positioned?
- Exactly how will the solution be implemented?
  - Marketing mix proposals (product, people, price, promotion and distribution).
  - What processes will the company need to set up to ensure that implementation occurs?
- Which departments/individuals will take responsibility for the day-to-day implementation?
- When will the solution be implemented?
- What will be the likely cost implications of implementing the solution?
- What are the expected benefits of implementing the solution? E.g. revenues, cash flow, competitive position, customer perceptions, etc?

In real situations, implementation rarely runs according to plan. This is largely due to the number of interacting factors, some unforeseen, which impact on the organisation and its markets. For this reason, it is helpful to recommend a back-up plan of action – a *contingency plan* – to be followed in the event of the initial recommendations being unsuccessful. These back-up suggestions should be limited to the key recommendations and should not go into too much detail.

PRESENTING THE CASE-STUDY FINDINGS

Once the case-study analysis is complete students are usually asked to report on their findings. The format of the reporting back may include a combination of an informal discussion, a structured presentation, or a written report. Learning how to present case solutions, like the analysis itself, takes time. While there is a strong personal element in presentational style, the following guidelines are intended to help students develop their effectiveness in this area.

Formal presentations

There is a tendency for case-study presentations to become turgid, clumsy and monotonous. With care and imagination there is no reason why such sessions should not be transformed into lively and interesting experiences which encourage debate. The following simple suggestions should assist in this process:

- Keep repetition of the basic case facts to a minimum. If presentations are being made to a group of students, it is likely they will all have read the case study anyway. There is nothing worse than hearing five or more different syndicate groups each presenting the same basic material over and over.
- Try to maintain a degree of eye contact with the audience. This can be achieved by not talking to the overhead projector screen/overhead projector/board.
- Avoid the use of fully scripted notes. Prompt cards inserted between overhead transparencies or 'key word' notes made on paper copies of the transparencies can be helpful. Using these types of prompts becomes easier with practice.
- Keep any visual material as simple and direct as possible. An audience will have difficulty taking in highly complex tables or slides which are covered in text. Clever use of colour and diagrams can make visual material more interesting and easy to follow. Presentation slides or transparencies must *never* be too 'wordy' or detailed.
- Use lively material, add the occasional touch of humour and try to involve the audience. Try to vary the presentation format: don't always opt for the formal approach with the stand-up 'lecture' style.
- Do not try to include too much material in the presentation time allocated.
- Do not use too many presenters: hand-over time is wasteful and boring for the audience.
- Rehearse! Presenters should never be surprised by material they encounter in their own presentation. Think through, in advance, the points which need making at each stage of the presentation. Also check any electrical equipment, know where the on/off buttons are, etc.

Writing reports

It is difficult to generalise exactly how case-study analysis should be written up. The most appropriate structure will depend partly on the student's or tutor's objectives as well as on individual style and any organisation constraints regarding format. Report writing is a skill which takes practice to properly develop, but which also offers considerable rewards when mastered.

The purpose of the case-study report is to present analyses and recommendations: demonstrating that a full and thorough understanding of the situation has been achieved. The emphasis should be on reasoned argument to support the key recommendations and should not merely reproduce the information and figures presented in the case. This needs stressing because there is a tendency for students to quote verbatim from the source material and present raw data without giving consideration to their interpretation.

Much has been written about report structure. This should be an area of concern for student and tutor alike. Too often reports are submitted with imperceptible structure, verbose paragraphs and no sense of direction or clear recommendations. While it is not realistic to present a standard report format which can be applied in all circumstances, certain generalisations are possible. Essentially, the report is presenting the following:

Background to the case study. This should give a simple overview of the company/industry and may include an indication of the nature of the market.

Understanding of the underlying problem(s). This will probably focus on the areas highlighted in any questions or areas which have been indicated by the tutor. The problem should be briefly reported rather than discussed in detail at this stage.

Analysis of case-study material. The analysis part of any case study is likely to involve the most extensive and detailed discussion. This is where the student reports back on the analyses undertaken of the company, market, competition and environment. The length of this part of the report will probably mean that a series of sub-headings is used to add structure and clarity to the discussion.

Recommendations with justifications. Although the recommendations represent the outcomes of the case-study analysis, they should fall naturally out of the discussion which has already taken place. At this stage, there should not be any surprises in the course of action which is being recommended. In this respect, the report itself should have '*told a story*' about the case study, leading logically to the recommendations.

Every report is different but the following simple check-list of section headings may be helpful to consider when structuring the final report document:

Executive/management summary
Contents
Introduction (including objectives)
Background to the problem
Analysis (divided into relevant sections)
Conclusions and recommendations
Bibliography/references
Appendices (supporting data and facts)

Points to remember

- The executive summary should provide a short and succinct account of the entire report. It should explain the background to the case, discuss the key issues and themes, report on the analysis and list the recommendations. All in a page or so.
- Make the report as user-friendly as possible. It helps to number sections, pages and provide a contents list. References should be sourced as appropriate within the main body of the report and then listed in the bibliography. Diagrams and tables should also be properly labelled and referenced.
- Make the writing style as clear as possible. Avoid long sentences and jargon. If jargon is unavoidable, use a glossary to explain terms which are not in common usage.
- Take care to support arguments with appropriate sources (references, statistics, quotes, examples, comparisons etc.), as available. This does a lot to add credibility to the discussion.
- Use data from the case with care. If possible interpret the information: this may involve extrapolating trends or making predictions regarding the likely outcome of certain activities. Only use data which are relevant to the point being made.
- Appendices should include any relevant material which would clutter the main body of the document. Each appendix should be referred to from within the main body of the report.

Part II

Cases

Chapter 3

Harris Queensway
Discounter supreme

BACKGROUND

In 1957 Philip Harris's family had three carpet shops in London. By 1986 there were 440 carpet shops/stores throughout the UK with sales of £109.2 million and operating profits of £12.36 million. Carpets were sold by Harris Queensway from 128 vast edge-of-town discount warehouses (retail sheds), branded as Carpetland or General George. In town centres there were Harris Carpets shops – once the mainstream operation for the company as a whole – and Vogue concessionary departments in Debenhams department stores (selling carpets and furnishings). At the time, Allied Carpets, the major competitor, had sales of £125 million.

DIVERSIFICATION

The company diversified into the retailing of furniture with the acquisition of Queensway Discount Warehouses Limited in the mid-1980s. By 1987 the furniture division had grown to 410 stores with a total of 4.6 million square feet of retailing space (very large by any retailer's standards), 60 per cent of which was in edge-of-town superstores (retail sheds), branded predominantly as Queensway. The remaining floor space was taken up with Times Furnishings, acquired in 1986, and concentrated in traditional town centre downtown shopping centres. Initially the furniture division contributed to profits, mainly from the budget-orientated Queensway chain. In 1986 the group further diversified with the addition of the Ultimate electrical chain (never profitable) and Harvey's soft furnishings. Ultimate ran the electrical departments as concessions within the Debenhams department stores, operated a handful of concessions within Queensway furniture stores, and had a small number of freestanding traditional electrical stores in the high street. Harvey's was re-focused as discount sheds on retail parks. In 1987 the total group's pre-tax profits peaked at £42.1 million.

THE BUBBLE BURSTS

In 1988 the bubble burst. For three years running profits crashed. The founder, Sir Phil Harris, knighted in the height of the 1980s retailing boom and once the 'golden boy' of UK retailing in the City and in the media, left the company. Ultimate electricals and Harvey's soft furnishings were sold off and there were major property disposals throughout the group. Sir James Gulliver, supermarketer supreme, was brought in by the City to lead the company to recovery. In 1990, however, the renamed Lowndes Queensway (concentrating purely on carpets and furniture) went into receivership, and – despite attempts to rescue the company – ceased trading.

High interest rates and reduced UK consumer spending contributed to the company's problems. Furniture and carpets are infrequently bought merchandise. They are expensive items to purchase and in most households are replaced only when deemed to have worn out. Indeed, research showed that Harris Queensway was competing for consumers' disposable income more against packaged holidays and used cars than against rival furniture/carpet retailers such as Courts, Cantors, MFI or Allied Carpets.

The end of the 1980s brought an economic recession: major items of consumer spending, such as Lowndes Queensway's merchandise, are purchases which tend to be postponed when times are hard. Competing retail groups became even more price driven, offering greater discounts, attractive credit and interest-free deals, with intense supporting promotional spends. Lowndes Queensway traded on price, with already rock-bottom prices. The company could not viably reduce its price points further; it had few resources for high promotional activity and only limited credit lines with its already anxious suppliers.

CONSUMERS HAD MOVED ON

The company's problems, however, were much more deeply rooted. Phil Harris was a discounter – 'pile it high, sell it cheap' – with low-cost retail outlets. Throughout the 1980s, led by companies such as Body Shop, Next, Burton Group, Oddbins and Habitat, the British consumer had been experiencing a revolution in retailing practices. Retailers increasingly devoted more time and expenditure not only to the design of the merchandise, but also to the retail stores – lay-out and ambience – and to the quality and service levels offered by their personnel. The UK furniture industry was the only sector of retailing which had seen no real growth. Low product and design innovation did not prompt frequent changes of furniture by consumers. The company's philosophy was sales led – the antithesis of modern marketing. Low-cost product was poorly displayed in hanger-like sheds, or in cramped, poorly laid out town centre shops. The consumers' needs and expectations were not taken into account, nor were they identified.

Industry marketing research showed that consumers did not perceive a need to change carpets or furniture unless they moved to a new house. Consumers tended to fall into, therefore, one of five categories:

- *first-time house buyers* – modern starter homes or older terraced housing (small rooms, low budgets; but still often design/image conscious)
- *newly weds/cohabiting couples* – slightly larger housing, more rooms, but still relatively small properties (small rooms, low budgets; but design conscious)
- *growing families* – by necessity, larger properties, more bedrooms, gardens (higher disposable incomes, but greater demands upon spending; furniture often not a priority until children older and more controllable!)
- '*just the two of us again*', where children have grown up and left home – larger houses, more affluent suburbs (larger and more rooms, greater disposable income, higher expectations, and more leisure time).

However, this category often realises that the property in which they are living is too large, and is totally unsuitable for impending retirement, which leads to a fifth category:

- *newly retired* – flats/bungalows (smaller properties, smaller rooms, much leisure time; initially reasonably high disposable income, reducing with age).

No retailer – except perhaps for the niche appeal of Habitat – had really attempted to persuade consumers to purchase carpets and major items of furniture on a regular basis, unless consumers were moving house. Consumers, though, were used to the innovative electrical goods retailers and fashion clothing companies which throughout the 1980s provided stylish, ever-changing merchandise, and stores with an appealing ambience.

The product-led discounting tactics of the Queensway group were deterring many customers rather than providing the right product in suitably designed stores with professional assistance, price points and merchandise to appeal to the growth segments of the market. The company ignored the principles of marketing: it did not consult customers and differentiated itself purely on price (see Figure 3.1); there was no full marketing research undertaken and no marketing department. Indeed, when times became hard for Phil Harris, all senior management in non-operational areas were immediately sacked, including all marketing and planning executives.

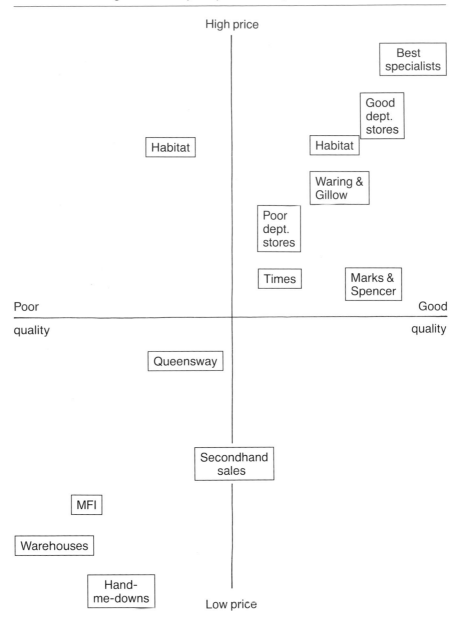

Figure 3.1 Perceptual map – the furniture retailers
Note: This is derived from consumer views: 'price' of furniture and 'quality' were identified as being the key considerations of the bulk of UK consumers, followed by design/image, utility, durability and delivery lead-times. The emphasis was on 'value for money' – price/quality. At the time of this research in 1988, safety of furniture/carpets was not an issue of concern to most consumers.

A NAME

The rise of the Harris Queensway group and its flagship, the Queensway chain, had been phenomenal during the 1980s. The company had been price driven, targeting budget-conscious consumers while keeping operating costs to a minimum. Three events linked to pull the company down. There was a hefty reduction in consumer spending, Queensway and its sister chains had done little to keep abreast of changing retailing fashions, but in addition the group altered the focus for two of its mainstay chains.

Times Furnishings, based on the high street with a conservative, traditional image, had for decades been staunchly middle market in focus. Instead, once acquired by Harris Queensway, the chain was re-focused as a high street discounter. With no name change or re-branding, this alienated current customers without attracting new ones: existing customers did not want the cheaper merchandise and price-driven selling, and the new target segment did not realise Times had moved 'more down market'. Simultaneously, the popular and clearly positioned discount chain Queensway was taken further up market to appeal to the less price-conscious middle market consumer. Merchandise did improve; store layout was researched and room-sets, colour co-ordination and service points were introduced; while greater attention to customer service was evident. Unfortunately, the cash-strapped group had not the resources to roll out nationally its new store proposition. This resulted in there being significant merchandise, service and layout differences between various Queensway stores. For the consumer, there was additional confusion as the discount brand Queensway sought to re-position itself away from being a price-driven discounter.

ISSUES

Harris Queensway was highly successful during the 1980s, but with the repositioning of its Queensway chain came disaster. This case illustrates the problems of positioning, and of understanding and responding to consumer buyer behaviour; plus the case highlights aspects of marketing research and competitive strategy.

Positioning

What were the market segments? How did Harris Queensway as a group of companies and retail brands target its segments? How could Harris have targeted additional market segments?

Buyer behaviour

What is the likely buying process in this market? What are the main influences on the decision?

Marketing research

How could consumer needs best be researched? How could consumer perceptions of rival furniture retailers be researched and explained?

Competitive strategy

Which were the main threats facing Harris Queensway? How has Sweden's IKEA entered the UK market? As a new entrant how could the market best be researched in order to determine the ideal target segments and product positioning? How could a new entrant best challenge the market leader?

THEORY NOTES

Chapter 23, Market segmentation, targeting, positioning, pp. 189–96
Chapter 20, Consumer and organisational buyer behaviour, pp. 165–72
Chapter 21, Marketing research, pp. 173–80
Chapter 24, Competition, pp. 197–204

Chapter 4

Waterford Crystal
A brand for any occasion

Irish crystal manufacturer Waterford Glass Group acquired the famous chinaware manufacturer Josiah Wedgwood in 1986. The china division has since become profitable, but the crystal operation suffered an immediate 73 per cent drop in profits and has yet to recover. Nevertheless, Waterford Wedgwood is the world's leading manufacturer of high quality china and glassware. The company is particularly strong in North America, with expanding markets in Japan and Europe. Its products, premium-priced giftware, are bought for special occasions or as notable gifts; emotional purchases supported by its strong, reputable brand names: Waterford, Wedgwood and Johnson's.

CRYSTAL IN RECESSION

Expensive giftware items are anything but recession proof: with the deepening recession in 1992, the company planned to lay off 750 of its 3,000 crystal workers, primarily at its Waterford base in Eire. In total, the group employs 10,000. Crystal sales have been hard hit, falling from IR(£) 43.1m to IR (£) 30.6m in 1991. Sales in the USA and Ireland, a large proportion of which are to American tourists, fell by 29 per cent to IR(£) 25.9m. Sales outside the USA and Ireland, handled by Wedgwood's distribution, fell by 30 per cent to IR(£) 4.7m. Sales of ceramics have held up better, with only a 4.5 per cent decline to IR(£) 4.7m. In 1992 there were total group sales of IR(£) 130.6 million and a record loss of IR(£) 1.762 million.

The marriage of the two famous names has benefited significantly distribution and brand awareness, although the two companies still independently manufacture and design. Wedgwood's presence in Japan and Waterford's in the USA have given a spring board for each other in Australia and Canada. However, all profits (see Table 4.1) are presently made in the UK, mainly through Wedgwood china tableware, with the crystal operation still to return to profitability. Range developments in North America are expected to improve the fortunes of the crystal division.

Table 4.1 Financial summary, Waterford Wedgwood

Wedgwood Group	1987	1988	1989	1990
Sales IR(£) m	169.9	190.0	220.3	204.1
Operating profits IR(£) m	25.1	27.5	20.9	17.3
Operating margin	14.8%	14.4%	9.5%	8.5%
Waterford Crystal	*1987*	*1988*	*1989*	*1990*
Sales IR(£) m	76.4	93.7	111.8	87.0
Operating profits IR(£) m	−18.3	−20.5	−21.6	−5.0

In 1990 the group was reorganised, merging crystal operations and ceramic manufacturing to form two new divisions: crystal and ceramics.

Ceramics Division	1990		1991	
	IR(£) m			
	Sales	Profits	Sales	Profits
Wedgwood & Johnson Brothers	96.1	7.4	92.7	5.0
Waterford	6.8	−1.6	4.7	−0.65
Non-group	7.8	−1.5	6.2	−1.15
Total	110.7	4.3	103.7	3.2

Crystal Division	1990		1991	
	IR(£) m			
	Sales	Profits	Sales	Profits
Waterford Crystal	36.3	−3.0	25.9	−1.65
Other	1.2	−1.0	1.17	−0.5
Total	37.5	−4.0	27.07	−2.15

Source: Business Information Service, University of Warwick

PRODUCT INNOVATION

To grow their markets, major manufacturers have introduced new products to take advantage of the growing popularity of crystal giftware. Some have moved away from conventional bowls and platters with lines as diverse as salt and pepper mills to individual designer pieces – a new wave in crystal: candlesticks, animal figurines, personalised items. Crystal giftware, according to the US consumer magazines, now outshines traditional stemware. US demand for Waterford's handcrafted crystal has outstripped supply in the large department stores such as Bloomingdale's.

Table 4.2 Sales by territory, 1990

	Crystal	Ceramics
	IR(£) m	
USA	58.1	32.1
UK	7.8	91.9
Ireland	11.9	1.4
Europe	0.8	26.4
Far East	2.3	28.5
Other	6.1	23.8

DEVALUING A BRAND?

With its new *Marquis* line, the venerable crystal maker has taken a new approach to manufacturing and marketing. Waterford has moved its production into Europe and scaled down its price points in the USA, which now start at $30 for smaller pieces, on average 30 per cent cheaper than traditional Waterford lines. This is seen by some US observers as risky: introducing a line for 'the less well healed', manufactured in Germany, Portugal and the former Yugoslavia, and leading to labour unease at Waterford's Irish plants.

In America, where Waterford has 28 per cent of the luxury crystal market, '*Marquis* by Waterford Crystal' is positioned in the $30 to $40 niche – although larger platters and bowls retail at $135 – in order to compete more directly with crystal suppliers Mikasa, Lenox, Miller Rogasks and Gorham. The 1991 launch into 30 stores proved immediately profitable, but it is unclear how the range can be taken into other territories. *Marquis* is a huge gamble, moving away from the 'finest handcrafted Irish' traditions, and away from the Waterford brand heritage, which in the USA and Japan puts it alongside names such as Rolls Royce and Rolex.

CUSTOMER TARGETS

The Wedgwood and Waterford ranges, on the whole, are not intended to be day-to-day functional lines. They are premium priced and intended as 'special', lasting purchases. This is an image well-cultivated by the company's advertising, public relations, and refusal to become involved with discounting and retailer promotions. Carefully controlled distribution through only leading china/crystal showrooms and department stores further enhances the exclusive branding. The core market is the giftware sector, which its ceramics and glassware share with cutlery, jewellery (by far the dominant gift category), toys and games, and leather goods (see

Table 4.3). Within crystal giftware there are five distinct segments:

- *General giftware* for formal, informal and special occasions: anniversaries, retirements, birthdays, romantic interludes, public holidays and festivals.
- *Weddings*, a distinct market where young couples often gain entry into the market for expensive 'home adornments', particularly in America where the *wedding chest* (registry) at specific stores is so popular.
- *Investment giftware*, where items are bought both for their intrinsic beauty and for their latent, accruing value; a market exploited to great effect by Lalique's range of glass sculptures.
- *Business gifts* and *incentives* or promotions; £30 million is now spent annually in the UK on china and glass for promotional purposes.
- *Specials*, such as the growing market for glass and crystal sporting trophies; particularly important in Europe and Canada.

EMOTIONAL APPEAL

The continuing success of crystal, despite the recession of the early 1990s, is due in part to the manufacturers' broadening ranges and innovative designs, and to their marketing and image-building activities. The emotional appeal of giftware – especially of crystal – is, though, the dominant force. Once the domain of weddings and women consumers, the appeal of crystal has grown. One-off special purchases have become recognised as family heirlooms, collectors buy for longer-term investment, married couples add piecemeal to growing collections, and companies – for promotions and special gifts – have recognised the longevity and appeal of crystal, china and silver: *fine giftware.*

The giftware market depends on emotions. The selection of a gift, no matter the occasion, is a personal, subjective and often risky action. Nowhere are individual consumer tastes and social influences more to the

Table 4.3 Retail gift market, UK

Retail market size (£m)	1987	1988	1989	1990
Glassware	120.7	132.0	151.3	151.1
Ceramics	391.1	435.3	490.9	439.7
Cutlery	30.1	33.3	34.4	26.1
Jewellery	–	789.5	928.2	931.5
Toys and games	821.8	831.6	1,007.4	1,012.9
Leather goods	41.4	45.4	51.9	52.1
Total	–	2,267.1	2,664.1	2,613.4

Source: KeyNote, 1992

fore. Innovative, individually crafted, expensive crystal is a difficult, agonised-over purchase. High ticket prices and the very 'personal' nature of the merchandise often extend the buying process as family and friends' opinions are sought. Will the choice be liked? Is it right for the intended home? Is it correct for the occasion? Is it value for money?

WATERFORD IN THE 1990s

Waterford has an enviable reputation worldwide, but one built upon a heritage of handcrafted superior workmanship at its Irish birthplace. The company has been able to command premium prices in expanding international markets. The giftware market is idiosyncratic and very much consumer driven. In an economic recession, premium-priced crystal is not top of every consumer's shopping list. Waterford is striving to build on its roots, while taking its wares into more countries and to a wider audience with its new ranges and lower pricing. In each segment, customers have specific needs and expectations, not always matched by the premium-priced Waterford products. To expand the appeal and sales of a deluxe product without alienating the core target market is no easy task, particularly for such an emotive product as crystal.

ISSUES

The main focus is consumer buyer behaviour, but the case illustrates aspects also of branding, international marketing, and channel management (distribution).

Buyer behaviour

How important is the understanding of consumer tastes, buying practices and peer groups in this premium giftware market? What is the likely buying process? How might this vary in different circumstances?

Branding and buyer behaviour

Does *Marquis* risk devaluing the Waterford name?
What are the risks to the branding of Waterford?

International marketing

Can one company really target the idiosyncratic giftware markets in so many territories? Is the marketing of crystal and china, premium-priced giftware, similar in Japan, Canada, Australia, USA, UK and Europe? Will local differences devalue global marketing activities? What are the potential opportunities and threats for Waterford?

Marketing channels

Waterford places great importance on carefully selecting and controlling its channels of distribution. Should these channels be the same country to country? What alternative approaches to distribution are there? Is Waterford using appropriate channels? How can Waterford control its channels to safeguard its premium branding and customer service levels?

THEORY NOTES

Chapter 20, Consumer and organisational buyer behaviour, pp. 165-72
Chapter 25, Products and product management [branding], pp. 205-13
Chapter 32, International marketing, pp. 246-51
Chapter 26, Distribution/marketing channels, pp. 214-18

Chapter 5

Stepcan

Competitive advantage through packaging

For several decades, fruit products had been tinned by canning companies or fruit producers for sale as predominantly manufacturer brands such as Del Monte, or as voluntary group brands such as Spar or VG. With the success of retailer own labels, fruit producers and canning companies had to satisfy the merchandisers of the large retailers with their own-label packaging requirements. In the mid-1980s, retailers such as Tesco, Sainsbury and Marks and Spencer (M&S) in the UK, or Carrefour in France, were seeking to differentiate their products not purely through quality, value or taste, but increasingly with the packaging and appearance of merchandise. Visual appeal of items on shelves was seen to increase purchase rates, and potentially ticket prices, too. For the suppliers of cans and packaging materials, however, it was still very much a price-driven commodity business: high volumes, low prices, and small returns. But then came Stepcan.

THE INTRODUCTION OF STEPCAN

'M&S adopts clear plastics STEPCAN for premium fruit pack presentation' screamed the news headline in *Packaging News*. According to Metal Box (MB), the developer of Stepcan, this form of food packaging benefited from numerous advantages:

- clarity
- high quality image
- long ambient shelf life
- lightweight
- shatterproof
- easy open ends
- stackable
- re-usable
- interchangeable on canning lines.

The feature in *Packaging News* elaborated:

> Marks and Spencer has nationally launched satsumas, grapefruit, and red grapefruit in clear plastic cans following successful test markets last year. A particular advantage of the can is that the shopper can see the contents at a glance and the clarity of the pack enhances the eye appeal of the fruit. M&S has further enhanced this high quality image by including a gold colour ldpe overcap on top of the metal ends.
>
> Metal Box has developed this patented style of container – Stepcan – over a number of years, and it is manufactured by the *s*tretch *t*ube *e*xtrusion *p*rocess in pet. The metal ends are conventionally double seamed on, but importantly they feature an easy ring pull. Additional benefits include less rusting, no shattering and of course distinction on shelf. It is also lighter and easier to handle and the ring pull makes it a highly convenient pack to use. 'Stepcans present the ideal image for premium products in the quality sector of the convenience foods market,' says Steve Thomas, business development manager at MB.

In fact, Marks and Spencer had test marketed Stepcan-contained products in several stores, examining price points ranging, for example, from 60 pence to £1.30 for a 330 gramme 'can' of peach slices. It was found that even where Stepcans were placed on shelves immediately adjacent to tin cans of similar weight and content, the Stepcans heavily outsold the tin cans. Even where the price differential between the two types of containers differed by three to one, Stepcan still outsold the cheaper tin cans, often by up to four times!

CONSUMERS PREFERRED THE VISUAL APPEAL

Tracking research revealed the visual impact of the peaches or fruit cocktail, plus the shatterproof container, outweighed higher prices. The packaging enhanced the product's appeal and gave a genuine competitive advantage in a previously unexciting commodity-based market for containers. The consumers interested in Stepcan wanted high quality products: the visibility of the fruit implied safety in the purchase; quality was taken for granted. They were reasonably affluent, 'up-market', educated shoppers, making purchases not out of necessity but by choice, and not too constrained by price.

The result was heavy demand for MB's Stepcan, with several major retail groups – including Waitrose, Sainsbury and M&S adopting Stepcan, and wanting exclusivity of supply.

AN UNKNOWN 'COMMODITY' WITHIN MB

For Metal Box, Stepcan's success was something of a problem. Initially developed on a side line as a whim of certain engineers and a couple of middle managers, the product was 'too successful' too quickly in that production could not be geared to meet demand immediately. There was a lead over competitors of approximately two years, but the company had many difficult decisions to make.

Stepcan, unlike the company's staple packaging products, was not a cheap, easily discounted commodity item. Retailers were charging premium prices because of the perceived quality and safety expectations of their customers. Unfortunately, the MB salesforce, used to selling tin cans at so many pence per thousand, found it difficult to grasp that they should be seeking higher returns from the Stepcan product. This was a problem inherent in MB; many senior managers seemingly were unaware of Stepcan's potential for higher unit prices and profit margins. Although a slight price advantage was gained from Stepcan over tin cans for the company, the bulk of the price premium gain was going to the retailers. There was, perhaps, a need to set Stepcan up as a self-contained operation within MB, with a product champion, bespoke production and separate distribution. The real risk was that MB would fail to recognise the potential of the product, allowing only the retailers to gain from the higher retail prices.

DIFFICULT DECISIONS

Retailers were seeking Stepcan supplies, but so were the fruit growers. MB needed to have clear priorities. Stepcan's positioning – 'The Choice is Clear' – was based on a quality image and the opportunity presented to retailers to premium price previously low-margin commodity food stuffs. Were distribution coverage to be too diluted, this quality, high price base would quickly be eroded. MB needed to concentrate either on retailers or on growers, but probably not both. The company had limited production capacity and needed to maximise returns. Particularly in countries dominated by the large grocery retail chains, MB had to tie in retailers before competitors' products appeared. Partners needed to be selected with caution. Various avenues were explored, ranging from the existing structure and approach, to the establishment of a separate operating company within MB, to a joint venture with a grower or major retail group. Ultimately, with a few minor changes, the existing situation was allowed to continue: there was no joint venture or separate operating division within MB.

THE EUROPEAN DIMENSION

Outside the UK, Stepcan was gaining a following, but not with the enthusiasm as demonstrated by the UK retail groups. MB subsidiaries had mixed feelings, with some seeking the right to produce and sell Stepcans, but with others more reluctant, instead desiring to focus on metal-based containers and other plastics. Opinion within the industry was also divided; some rivals were envious, but there were those which were cautious, believing that Stepcan would find general acceptance difficult. However, certain competitors were known to be researching and developing similar products, and the general consensus was that Metal Box had a winning product in Stepcan, but not on the scale implied from the UK market.

Consumer reaction differed between countries. The company commissioned marketing research which, through personal interview and focus group discussions, sought consumer reactions in several countries. Interviews with supermarket managers and merchandisers (buyers) gained the retailers' views. In most of Europe, particularly France and Scandinavia, the consumers perceived the shatterproof containers to be a real advantage, which when coupled with their liking of the transparency of the Stepcan, seemed to auger well for Stepcan. However, in certain areas of Scandinavia and particularly in Germany, the raw material – plastic – was a significant drawback. The recyclability of glass was preferred over any container made from plastics. At the time (1988), however, there was no indication that the strength of the German 'green consumer' would spread to France, Britain or the Mediterranean countries. The ring pull lid was seen, during the European research, to be more of a disadvantage than a product benefit, often proving difficult to remove from the container.

Table 5.1 The canned fruit market – brand shares in the canned fruit market, UK

| | % of volume | |
Manufacturer	1987	1990
Del Monte	16	17
Princes	12	9
John West	3	3
Gerber Pride	4	3
Dole	–	2
S & B	–	2
Australian/Premier Gold	4	1
Own label (retailer)	32	47
Others	29	16
Total	100	100

Source: Retail Business

Table 5.2 Retail distribution of canned foods, UK, 1988

	% of volume
All grocery multiples	73
Co-operatives	15
Independent grocers	12

Source: Euromonitor

Table 5.3 Major grocery retailers, UK, Denmark, France and West Germany

UK: major grocery retailers	% market shares	
	1987	*1989*
Sainsbury	10.7	13.0
Tesco	11.1	12.3
Argyll	7.6	9.0
Asda	5.9	8.6
Gateway	8.8	6.7
Others	55.9	50.4

Denmark: major integrated food retailing groups, 1987–8		
	Net turnover (DK m)	No. stores
Co-op Group:		
FDB	8,457	442
Independent Societies	7,863	865
Fakta (discount)	1,237	76
Bonus (discount)	392	20
Irma	3,979	190
Dansk Supermarket Group:		
Salling	85	2
Bilk (hypermarkets)	2,025	5
Foetex	3,052	39
Netto (discount)	1,733	76
Aldi (discount)	1,742	88
Jaco Group:	317	5
Alta Discount	300	15
ABC Laupris (discount)	100	5
Loevbjerg:		
Loevbjerg (incl. Normann)	832	22
Prisa Discount	305	22

France: leading groups of supermarkets and hypermarkets, ranked by sales area, 1989–92	
	'000m
ITM Enterprises	1,829
Leclerc	1,279
Promodès (excl. co-ops)	1,094
Carrefour	671
Casino	592

West Germany: Top 10 food retailers, 1988

	Retail sales DM bn
Aldi	19.7
Rewe Leibbrand	16.3
Tengelmann	14.6
Co-op AG	11.4
Asko-Schraper	9.4
Spar AG	7.9
Edeka	7.6
AllKauf	4.5
Massa	4.0
Lidl & Schwarz	3.9
Market share of Top 10	58.8%

West Germany: food sales by organisation type, 1987–8

	1987	1988
	%	
Multiples	23.5	23.2
Co-operatives	11.4	13.9
Edeka	17.0	16.7
Rewe	15.7	15.6
Spar AG	7.6	8.1
Others	24.8	22.5

Sources:
UK: *Retail Business*
Denmark: Euromonitor
France: Euromonitor
West Germany (food retailers): Euromonitor; company reports; statistisches Bundesamt
West Germany (food sales): Gesellschaft für Konsum; Markt und Absatzforschung; Euromonitor

WHERE NEXT?

Stepcan had many inherent product benefits. Consumers – on the whole – were favourable and so were the large retail groups. There were problems, however. Costs of producing the Stepcan were higher than for rival tin cans. The ring pull was not functioning correctly, and in certain territories plastics were not *de rigueur*. In addition, within the Metal Box company, Stepcan posed some fundamental questions. How should MB have proceeded with the development of the Stepcan and its market? The choice was not clear.

ISSUES

Creating a differential advantage or competitive edge is never simple; packaging is often an option neglected. The retailers which test marketed Stepcan quickly realised the container's benefits, but not so every one at Metal Box. The case also illustrates the role of the marketing environment, the problems of marketing across international frontiers, and of controlling the supply chain.

Creating a differential advantage

Why is a differential advantage important? How can one be achieved? Did Stepcan give MB a competitive edge? Could Stepcan's apparent advantages be defended?

International marketing

Stepcan was researched in various countries. Reaction was mostly favourable, but not totally so. Why were there some warning signs in the negative reactions? Were these unusual in marketing a product across national borders? Could they be addressed with the marketing mix?

The marketing environment

Social, cultural and regulatory changes may mean that if MB test marketed Stepcan today, the product would receive the thumbs down from the European consumer. Why? Is this change of heart surprising?

Pricing

The retailers tested Stepcan at various prices: it was successful at all levels, including the highest. Why was this so? What should have been the implications to MB and its sales force?

Product management

Metal Box had problems defining a role for Stepcan in its portfolio. What were the options available? Which could have given the company the best rewards? Were there any obvious problems with this 'best' approach?

THEORY NOTES

Chapter 18, An introduction to marketing [differential advantage], pp. 155–60
Chapter 32, International marketing, pp. 246–51
Chapter 19, The marketing environment, pp. 161–4
Chapter 25, Products and product management, pp. 205–13

Chapter 6

Electrolux

Gearing for Whirlpool's challenge

A GLOBAL BUSINESS

With a market share of 20 per cent, Sweden's Electrolux is amongst the world's largest manufacturers of white goods and market leader in Europe. The company's ownership of White Consolidated gives it the number three position in the American market. The Electrolux group comprises more than 600 companies in over 40 countries. Worldwide, it has 150,000 employees and a turnover (1990) of SEK 82 billion.

During the 1980s the Electrolux strategy for growth was through acquisition. In only 10 years the company bought in excess of 200 companies, collectively worth US$ 4.25 billion. These acquisitions were particularly pervasive in terms of the markets covered, including Granges (Sweden), Zanussi (Italy), Corbero and Domar (Spain) and White Consolidated (USA). Electrolux management clearly saw establishing a global presence as the way to tackle the keen competitive pressures which the company was facing.

In the words of Electrolux President and CEO, Anders Scharp, 'There are global trends today. We are getting a more universal user. We realised some years ago that the market was becoming more and more global, and we see it; it is not enough to have a quality national or regional presence – you have to have a world presence.'

To attain economies of scale required heavy investment during the 1980s, involving Electrolux setting up networks around the world linking similar parts of its empire to cut out any overlap in manufacture, design and marketing, and minimise inefficiencies. In America, the company hit problems when it spent around $250 million building and upgrading plants. In the words of US CEO Donald C. Blasius, 'The new plants have not come quite as quickly as we would have liked.' These difficulties were compounded by an aggressive price war at the end of the 1980s in which some retailers dropped Electrolux brands in favour of cheaper alternatives. The combined effects of these problems left the company facing a very difficult situation at the start of the 1990s.

The company has misread its competition, been hurt by weak markets, and tripped up in bringing expensive plants on line while closing old ones. In late August, bosses in Stockholm reported that second-quarter pretax profits tumbled by 56 per cent to $87 million, on a slight drop in sales.

(*Business Week*, September 1990)

Electrolux has moved forward by concentrating its efforts on the core appliance business where it is especially strong. By divesting unprofitable areas and cutting products out of the portfolio, there are more resources available to develop new products in the key areas. This, senior management hopes, will help to create the right conditions for the next expansion phase.

THE COMPANY TODAY

The Electrolux organisation concentrates its efforts in five key business areas (see Figure 6.1):

- Household Appliances (accounting for 54.4 per cent of sales)
- Commercial Appliances
- Industrial Products
- Outdoor Products
- Commercial Services

Household appliances
White goods
Floor-care products
Leisure appliances
Room air conditioners
Sewing machines
Kitchen and bathroom appliances

Commercial appliances
Food-service equipment
Industrial laundry equipment
Commercial refrigeration
Commercial cleaning equipment

Outdoor products
Forestry equipment
Garden equipment
Agricultural equipment

Industrial products
Granges
Materials handling equipment
Equipment for car safety
Components

Commercial services
Environmental services
Laundry services and goods
   protection

Figure 6.1 Nineteen product lines in five business areas
Source: Electrolux Annual Report

Over the last few years sales have fallen to SEK 82.4 billion. Profits have also plummeted, with the biggest drops in the Household Appliances and Industrial Products areas, which in one year fell 43.7 per cent and 57.4 per

Table 6.1 Sales and operating income by business area

Division	Sales (SEK bn)		Profit before tax	
	1990	1989	1990	1989
Household Appliances	44.9	45.1	1.19	2.12
Commercial Appliances	8.7	7.7	0.64	0.55
Outdoor Products	8.7	8.4	0.66	0.70
Industrial Products	15.8	19.8	0.49	1.15
Commercial Services	4.3	3.9	0.26	0.50

Source: Electrolux annual reports

cent respectively (see Table 6.1). Amidst the gloom, the only positive trend in profits has been in the Commercial Appliances sector, which has seen sales increase by 13 per cent with a corresponding rise in profits of 16 per per cent.

THE COMPETITIVE ENVIRONMENT

The white goods industry is characterised by large global corporations and increasing supplier concentration. During the 1980s a new global player emerged with the merger of Whirlpool and Philips which married their expertise in the USA and Europe. Since then, Whirlpool has overtaken General Electric and Electrolux to become the largest manufacturer of appliances. Whirlpool's CEO David Whitwam masterminded the company's transformation, spending an estimated $175 million to improve quality and profitability. The strategy was three-fold:

1 Pursue manufacturing efficiencies through product improvements.
2 Use the company's clean balance sheet to finance a series of component manufacturer acquisitions.
3 Engage a new management team to direct the company's new structure.

Within this arena, the main competition which Electrolux faces comes from Whirlpool and General Electric in the US and the Whirlpool–Philips alliance and General Electric–GEC joint venture in Europe. In Germany, Electrolux attentively watches Bosch-Siemens which provides especially strong opposition at the upper end of the market while Miele, in France, does what it can to exploit its reputation of quality and social esteem.

There is also an indication that Japanese activity in the white goods market is set to increase, following successful forays into the microwave oven market by Panasonic and Toshiba. However, the barriers to entry are likely to be high.

• The industry relies on economies of scale which take time and expertise to develop.

- Japanese companies would need to invest heavily in European production facilities as shipping costs from Asia may prove prohibitive.
- Opportunities for new types of product are small. The microwave oven is the only new product category in the last 20 years.

The continual search for a differential advantage drives the competing players to seek new and better ways of developing and maintaining an edge. For Philips-Whirlpool, pan-European market penetration is sought by building up customer and retailer service levels, concentrating on the augmented product (see Figure 6.2). This increased service level guarantees a replacement machine if product failure occurs in the first 12 months of use. This guarantee operates regardless of where in Europe the machine was originally purchased. In the UK the company has established a customer care telephone line, offering the customer a fixed point of contact. Customers are also offered a 10-year spare part guarantee, based on a once-only premium payment. The service is backed with the assurance of a refund if service engineers fail to arrive within two working days of being called out.

Philips-Whirlpool is not losing sight of retailers' needs. Through Whirlpool Financial Corporation the company offers a range of financial services, including extended payment terms, financing of display stock and store inventory.

1 = Core product
2 = Tangible product
3 = Augmented product

Figure 6.2 Three levels of the Philips-Whirlpool product

THE ELECTROLUX MARKETING PRINCIPLES

The stated marketing objective of Electrolux is to operate as a global competitor and become the largest supplier of white goods and one of the three largest of appliances. This is to be achieved by making the most of economies of scale and using the resulting competencies to the maximum.

Within this scenario, Marketing Director Christer Forsstrom sees the product as central to all aspects of the marketing programmes. Company culture dictates that excellent, high quality and suitable products should be the focus; new product development should be a joint effort between marketing and research and development. Overall Electrolux's Forsstrom considers the main keys to marketing success to be:

- a strong product and brand
- competitive pricing
- effective command of logistics

To direct the company to success there are three-year strategic marketing plans, with an emphasis on market share objectives. These consist of a detailed two-year plan, containing finely tuned and carefully calculated targets, with a broad statement of likely trends for the third year.

The company's marketing decisions are based on an ongoing market research programme which aims to identify and monitor customer groupings, anticipate changes in customer behaviour due to environmental trends, and provide a continuous monitoring of retail market shares. These combined activities help Electrolux closely monitor and control its marketing programmes.

THE ELECTROLUX POSITIONING

The company's positioning is based on the principle of achieving technological and quality leadership in the market for white goods. In building a differential advantage, Electrolux takes care to focus on the retailer as well as the consumer. For the consumer, the emphasis is on producing products which offer the real technology and quality benefits which Electrolux believes will help create and maintain a strong brand. Like Philips-Whirlpool, the company also recognises the importance of offering reliable after-sales service. The benefits offered to the retailer appeal to the needs for quick and secure delivery and low-cost finance.

Typically, four brands are offered in each market; international brands such as Electrolux and Zanussi as well as regional brands like Husqvarna in the Nordic area. This brand structure allows the company to cater for both national and regional differences while maximising the use of the international brands. Electrolux takes care to avoid cannibalisation by positioning different brands at different end user segments. Organisation of the marketing activities is through brand management, with one manager acting as a 'General' for each brand. These brand managers are responsible for controlling brand identity issues as well as managing the product and promotional mixes.

MARKET SEGMENTATION

Segmentation of the European white goods market is complicated by the many cultural and regional variations. Manufacturers need to cater for the differing requirements which result. For example, in England, where customers like front-loading washing machines the product is physically different than in France, where the top loader is preferred. In Italy, spin speeds on washing machines are much lower than in Germany: more hours of sunshine in Italy allow wetter clothes to dry much faster. How much these regional differences will converge over time is the subject of debate and the outcome hard to predict. It is also unclear what the impact of the developing 'green' movement will be on the white goods industry. Certain constraints are inevitable though, with the outlawing of freon gas in fridges and freezers and the likelihood that washing machines will be required to use less water.

Electrolux sees market segmentation as a top priority and uses marketing research to help gain a better understanding of the issue. The company employs the *global scan* method which asks a series of questions to establish the values, opinions, attitudes, expectations and behaviour of customers, thereby identifying similarities and differences between them. It is then possible to identify pan-European customer groups, based on benefits sought and consumer values, by assigning customers to different customer groups on the basis of their answers. The underlying intention is to be able to match customer attitudes and behaviour and make comparisons across national boundaries, thus reducing company marketing costs by using fewer marketing programmes.

MARKETING PROGRAMMES

Product

The marketing department co-operates with research and development, to produce products which offer customers the user benefits they really want. Traditionally this has required a combination of good quality, economy of use and appropriate size. More recently, the fashion-conscious customer has demanded appliances that look good, as well as do the job effectively. This has placed greater demands than ever on the design element of new product development.

Price

Apart from Miele, which prices at between 10 and 15 per cent above the others, the major manufacturers adopt a reasonably uniform pricing structure. However, the segmentation of the market means that Electrolux, like its key competitors, targets different segments with different levels of pricing. Electrolux usually has three or four brands in every market, each aimed at a different user group with different price points, collectively offering full market coverage.

Distribution

Electrolux management is keenly aware of its dependence on a close working relationship with its distributors. Co-operation and the building of close working partnerships with members of the distribution channel are seen as important components of the company's marketing success. After all, the customer is a customer of the complete channel, not just of the manufacturer. It is therefore insufficient merely to concentrate on the customer; the co-ordination of the complete chain of supply, from point of manufacture to point of consumption, is essential if a differential advantage is to be maintained at all levels of distribution.

The choice of distribution channel is closely linked with the positioning of the products concerned. For instance, Electrolux must choose channels which allow the company to be responsive to customer requirements, fitting in with changing needs and market trends as appropriate. In many markets, with a trend towards increasing retailer concentration, it is necessary for Electrolux to build close and adaptive relationships with a relatively small number of retailers (in the UK, six retailers control around two-thirds of the white goods market).

Promotion

The company's promotional strategy is centred around its individual brands, rather than at a corporate level. Local advertising, such as co-operative deals with retailers, is favoured. This allows the company to respond to cultural and local differences. This localised approach to communications is typical of the programmes implemented in this market. Only Whirlpool-Philips has attempted to implement advertising at the pan-European level. Many countries' consumers dislike 'Americanisms' in advertising style, while messages can be interpreted in different ways in various markets.

FACING THE COMPETITION

The white goods and appliance market is highly price competitive, dominated by three global manufacturers. Electrolux has responded to the threats posed by Philips and Whirlpool by establishing a more efficient manufacturing base across the globe, with internationally recognised brands such as Zanussi supported by locally produced national brands. A commitment to understanding the consumer results in a marketing planning process geared to offering specific marketing programmes in each market, targeted at the company's core market segments. Whether the company can maintain its support of so many brands and markets in the face of the new challenge from Whirlpool remains to be seen. Electrolux believes it is well placed to expand its market share and respond to changes in the marketplace. The emerging threat from the Far East, coupled with the penetration of the Whirlpool name, pose even more problems for the still consolidating Swedish company.

ISSUES

Competition and competitive strategies in an international arena form the basis for this case, which additionally focuses on brand management, particularly brand positioning; the role of customer service within the augmented product offering; and the importance of marketing planning.

International competition

Philips with Whirlpool has upstaged Electrolux and the other major manufacturers, becoming a major force in the white goods market. The companies have established themselves globally, but each has adopted slightly different strategies in order to compete successfully. What are these strategies? Internationally, what are the main threats posed by the Philips–Whirlpool tie-up? How realistic is the pan-European identification of customer segments which cut across national borders?

Branding and positioning

Electrolux in its own right is a major brand name. The company's acquisitions throughout the 1980s gave it control over leading international and regional brands. How has the company used its brands? How and why do their positionings differ?

Marketing planning

Electrolux has placed great emphasis on its two to three year marketing plans. Why, for a company as large and complex as Electrolux, is formal marketing planning so important? What are the likely difficulties in undertaking such a planning exercise? Which core marketing assets form the basis for Electrolux's marketing planning?

Augmented product

Whirlpool has included a major customer service and guarantee scheme within its product package. Why? How can Electrolux compete and gain an advantage?

THEORY NOTES

Chapter 24, Competition, pp. 197–204
Chapter 23, Market segmentation, targeting, positioning, pp. 189–96
Chapter 32, International marketing, pp. 246–51
Chapter 31, Marketing planning, pp. 239–45
Chapter 29, Services marketing, pp. 231–4
Chapter 30, Industrial marketing, pp. 235–8

Chapter 7

Stabburet
Change and competition

BACKGROUND

From chilled and cured meats to canned goods, jams, pizzas and frozen foods, Norwegian food producer Stabburet AS specialises in a diversity of products. The selling effort is organised and co-ordinated through two company divisions. Fresh Meat controls distribution of chilled meats from the point of manufacture to retailer, while the Wholesale arm distributes Stabburet's range of foodstuffs via an extensive wholesale network to retailers and caterers mainly in Norway.

Stabburet is wholly owned by the 8.1 billion Kroner turnover Orkla Borregaard. Formed in 1986, out of a merger between Orkla and Borregaard, Stabburet's parent is the 15th largest Norwegian organisation (by turnover). The dynamism of the organisation has continued into the 1990s with Orkla Borregaard becoming involved in negotiations with Nora Industriers AS. The goal for such talks: another merger which would give Orkla Borregaard ties to other food manufacturers, offering complimentary product lines to its subsidiary Stabburet.

The changing face of Orkla Borregaard has impacted on Stabburet itself. In the second half of the 1980s, during a period of industry recession, major restructuring at Stabburet, involving acquisitions and rationalisation, was to change the face and fortunes of the organisation.

ENVIRONMENTAL TRENDS

Historically, the Norwegian economy has been heavily dependent on trade in goods and services. Primary customers have been Denmark, France, Germany and the UK, accounting for around two-thirds of all trade. Sweden and Finland receive a significant 14 per cent of Norwegian exports.

Around half of all imports originate from the EC with Sweden and Finland providing just under 20 per cent. Given Norway's high buying power, the trend is towards high-value-added products, such as machinery and equipment. Table 7.1 illustrates the trade trends.

As a source of income, the sale of North Sea Oil has been very bene-

Table 7.1 Norway's trade in goods (visible trade), 1984–90

Year	Imports Kr m	Exports Kr m	Surplus Kr m	Exports % of GDP
1984	113,102	154,035	40,933	34%
1985	132,563	170,733	38,169	34%
1986	150,052	133,847	−16,205	26%
1987	152,041	144,543	−7,498	26%
1988	151,101	146,166	−4,935	25%
1989	163,380	187,146	23,766	30%
1990	169,998	211,579	41,581	32%

Source: *Statistisk Arbok 1991*, Statistisk Sentralbyra, Norway, 1991, Table 339.

ficial to the economy, particularly during the mid-1980s. Not surprisingly, recent declines in oil prices have led to a fall in Norway's economic growth – currently in the region of 1.2 per cent (see Table 7.2). In 1988 the rate per head of GDP was around $US 21,272. Estimates for 1991 are $US 27,830. This projection puts Norway behind Sweden and Finland, but ahead of Japan.

Politically, Norway is a country of centre-line coalitions. Although this has resulted in frequent changes in government, the Norwegians have grown used to reasonably consistent economic policies as coalition partners strive to maintain the status quo.

One particular characteristic of the Norwegian political system is the high level of intervention, regulation and state control to which business is subjected. The main impact on food producers such as Stabburet is from the stated policy that Norway aims to be self-sufficient in food production. Heavy subsidisation has resulted in high prices for the consumers while acting as a barrier to trade from other countries.

Table 7.2 Gross domestic product and rate of growth for Norway, 1985–91

Year	GDP Kr m	Growth Volume	Prices
1985	500,200	5.3%	5.0%
1986	513,718	4.2%	1.4%
1987	561,480	2.0%	7.2%
1988	583,278	−0.5%	4.4%
1989	622,991	0.4%	6.4%
1990	662,445	1.8%	4.5%
1991		3.0%	−

Sources: *Statistisk Arbok 1991*, Statistisk Sentralbyra, Norway, 1991, pp. 340, 346, 347
Estimate for 1991: *Economic Review*, Christiana Bank og Kreditkasse, Issue 5, 14 May 1991

Opinion within Norway on whether to join the EC is divided. Historically the country has been closely linked and has actively traded with other
Scandinavian states through its membership of EFTA. Indeed, in certain
markets the Norwegians have not been particularly resentful of competition
from further afield. However, while many politicians believe that the way
forward for Norway is through full EC membership, some of the electorate
is less convinced. It is generally accepted that despite such reservations, the
decisions of Sweden and Finland to join the EC will probably mean that
Norway follows in time.

FINANCIAL PERFORMANCE AND THE COMPETITIVE
ENVIRONMENT

Within this changing environment Stabburet has seen its sales turnover cut
by almost 30 per cent in only 14 years. This is partly a reflection of the cut
in food consumption from 29 per cent of total consumption in 1978 to 15
per cent in 1990. In 1988 alone, at the height of the recession in Norway,
Stabburet's sales fell by 12 per cent. Despite this apparently gloomy
picture, more recently profits have improved. The restructuring of the
company, following the acquisition of a number of food manufacturers in
1987 (see Figure 7.1), did involve short-term sales reductions as the
product portfolio was rationalised. Since then profits have steadily risen
(see Table 7.3).

Viking Askin AS
Smak's Salater
Stabburet Marine Produkter AS
Viking Frys AS
Norfisk Delicatessen GmbH

Figure 7.1 Recent Stabburet acquisitions

On the basis of market share Stabburet is a dominant market leader in
all sectors in which it has a presence. Taking 5 per cent of the total
Norwegian food market (worth 40 billion Kroner in 1988) the company's
stake ranges from 32 per cent in fruit juices up to 65 per cent in frozen
pizza. This overall market share is particularly impressive when considered
within the context of what, overall, is a highly concentrated market. Only
two other market suppliers can claim a product market share of greater
than 10 per cent (see Tables 7.4 and 7.5).

Table 7.3 Stabburet results, 1986–90

Year	Current prices	Turnover Kr m 1985 prices	Real growth	Profit Kr m Before tax
1986	2,051.7	1,913.9	–	33.9
1987	2,045.9	1,755.1	−8%	2.5
1988	1,912.2	1,537.7	−12%	33.6
1989	1,900.2	1,461.3	−5%	51.0
1990	1,869.8	1,381.3	−5%	81.7

Source: *Orkla Borregaard annual report, 1990*

STABBURET'S CUSTOMER BASE

In general, control over grocery retailing is more fragmented than in some other parts of Europe. For instance in the UK, Sainsbury and Tesco dominate, accounting for around 60 per cent of the market, while the names of the followers, Safeway and Asda, are probably equally well-known. In Norway, the picture is different. The Co-op (Norges Koopera-tive Landsforening – NKL) is clear market leader with 22.8 per cent of the market but has a host of smaller chains contesting the remaining market (see Table 7.5).

Table 7.4 Competing shares of selected food product sectors

Product	% market shares			
Frozen pizza	Stabburet 65%	Saether 13%	Frionor 10%	Others 12%
'Foie gras' paste	Stabburet 64%	FS 15%	TPC 12%	Others 9%
Canned mackerel	Stabburet 49%	Norw. Foods 15%	TPC 12%	Others 24%
Jams/preserves	Stabburet 39%	Lerum 24%	Wandelbo 10%	Others 24%
Frozen vegetables	Stabburet 37%	Frionor 31%	Findus 14%	Others 18%
Frozen potatoes	Stabburet 36%	Frionor 28%	Hoff 20%	Others 16%
Fruit juice	Stabburet 32%	Forma 28%	Meieriene 18%	Others 22%

Table 7.5 Grocery retailers' market shares in Norway

Company	% market share
Norges Kooperative Landsforening (Co-op)	22.8
Hagen-gruppen (Arena, Rimi)	10.2
FM Norge	7.9
Kjopmannskjedene	7.3
Norgeskjeden	7.1
Reitangruppen (Rema)	5.7
Matmestern	4.6
Vivo	3.5
Matringen/Focus	2.3
Sparemat	1.7
Others	26.9

Source: Norges Markedsdata AS

The supermarkets themselves tend to be small. Nearly 80 per cent are less than 1000 m², while the remaining 20 per cent are superstores of more than 2500 m². The small size of outlets means that only a very limited number of brands, in many cases only one, can be offered to shoppers. Retailer 'own-label' brands, so strong in the UK, are almost unknown in Norway. Only the Co-op follows this branding approach, selling simply packaged, cheap, staple items.

In a market where so few brands are stocked, the need to maintain control over distribution is paramount. Stabburet ensures its hold on the market by close, regular contact with both the retailing and wholesaling ends of the distribution network. A system of bonuses helps ensure that it is Stabburet's lines which consistently appear on the shelves.

THE STABBURET OFFERING

Stabburet's control over distribution, with its own delivery fleet, allows direct delivery to retail outlets all over Norway. Combined with Stabburet's wholesale operation this is probably the most powerful way the company has of creating a competitive advantage over rival manufacturers.

Distribution is not the only aspect of the marketing programme which management puts under careful scrutiny. Promotional strategy combines personal selling incentives which 'push' products from the point of manufacture to the point of sale, with newspaper, television and magazine advertising designed to create consumer demand and 'pull' goods through distribution channels. Stabburet's products are positioned throughout as 'good Norwegian food', emphasising taste and quality and they are produced to have mass market appeal. The company also promotes its corporate identity through publicity and sponsorship of some sporting events.

For Stabburet, high reputation and awareness of its brands permit a premium pricing strategy to be followed. Despite the frequent use of price advertising by supermarket outlets, the benefits offered by Government protection of Norwegian producers allows the company an 8 per cent profit margin on turnover.

THE WAY FORWARD

For Stabburet, with its entrenched hold on the food products market, times may be about to change. If Norway joins the EC, the competitive situation will inevitably intensify. The removal of trade barriers, which currently protect Norwegian companies, will result in lower food prices at home. In time, Norway will have to come into line with other EC countries as import restrictions are lifted and competition from the rest of Europe enters the market. Even now, the Norwegian Government is looking at ways to bring legislation into line with EC countries. Food hygiene laws, packaging regulations, selling techniques, plus consumers' awareness of tastes, styles and trends outside Norway – all will change, perhaps dramatically.

With the prospects of falling food prices, Stabburet's hopes lie with the specialist Norwegian foods which account for around 50 per cent of its turnover, and which could not easily be offered by competitors from EC countries. How effective Stabburet is at maintaining this part of the market will depend on whether Norwegian tastes become less conservative and more similar to those in the rest of Europe. Senior company management accepts that market share in the remaining product sectors will be more closely fought and that Stabburet will need to become more price competitive. The prospects are that the company will lose market share as larger European organisations compete more strongly on a cost leadership basis.

ISSUES

Stabburet AS dominates many of its markets and has ridden the economic recession in Norway quite effectively. The company has developed a very successful marketing mix, emphasising good value, desirable food products to the mass of the Norwegian population, with a well-planned promotional strategy and tightly controlled distribution network. Entry into the EC, with a removal of protective trade barriers, will create a radically more competitive trading environment.

The marketing environment

What are the main macro and micro marketing environment elements currently impacting on Stabburet and its markets? How will entry into the EC alter this situation? What can the company do to pre-empt any of these changes?

Marketing channels

What are Stabburet's principal channels of distribution? How does the company control and protect its channels?

Marketing mix

What are the main strengths and weaknesses of Stabburet's marketing? What aspects of the marketing mix could be improved; how and why?

THEORY NOTES

Chapter 19, The marketing environment, pp. 161–4
Chapter 26, Distribution/marketing channels, pp. 214–18
Chapter 28, Marketing communications, pp. 224–30
Chapter 24, Competition, pp. 197–204

Chapter 8

Forte Hotels
Branding in Services

The hotel business is complex and highly competitive. Branding is hampered by the uniform look of most hotel bedrooms and restaurants. Services are notoriously difficult to both brand and differentiate from competitors' offerings; the hotels sector is a prime example. Recently, having traded as THF or Trusthouse Forte for several decades, the leading international hotelier Forte, based in the UK, underwent a well-publicised and expensive re-branding of all its diverse activities, including its expanding hotels division.

Founded by Charles Forte, Forte plc is one of the world's leading hotel operators and catering companies. In 1992 the company had a turnover of £2,662 million and, despite the Gulf War which affected business travel and tourism in the key markets of Europe and the Middle East, profits were £73 million. In 1990 profits had peaked at £291 million. Measures of size for hoteliers include turnover, number of hotels, distribution coverage of hotels, number of beds, plus the real indication of success, occupancy of beds. Irrespective of the criteria adopted, Forte's hotel division is the market leader in the UK, one of the top three within Europe, and one of the world's top operators (see Table 8.1).

NO SMOOTH RIDE

The hotel business is a difficult industry in which to thrive. Research reveals that the bulk of the UK population never stays in a major hotel, a trend echoed around the world. There is always the need, therefore, to promote the generic form of the industry to pull in these new category users. For most users of hotels, the destination is selected first, either for business or for vacation, with the choice of hotel a secondary decision. Very few people are brand loyal to a particular hotel chain. Even in the company market, where leading hotel operators attempt to tie-in major companies with discount deals for large numbers of reservations and frequent repeat bookings, few hotel operators genuinely offer a hotel in every town, city or international location. Hotel users tend to experience

Table 8.1 Leading hotel groups

Major hotel groups: UK Company	*Hotels*	*Bedrooms*
Forte	334	30,000
Mount Charlotte Thistle	105	14,000
Queens Moat Houses	104	10,790
Rank Hotels	22	3,159
(incl. Butlins/Shearings)	58	7,129
Ladbroke (Hilton & Associates)	35	7,137
Bass (Holiday Inn & Toby)	78	6,668
Vaux (Swallow)	30	3,672
Stakis	29	3,565
Jarvis	39	3,020
Greenalls (De Vere)	25	2,900
Seibu Saison (Forum/Intercontinental)	6	2,454
Whitbread (incl. Lansbury)	74	2,400

Major hotel groups: Europe (excluding UK operators)

	No. hotels	*No. Rooms '000s*
Accor (F)	688	69
Club Méditerranée (F)	178	40
Sol (E)	139	35
Grupos Hoteles Unidos (E)	140	26
Golden Tulip (NL)	144	25
Pullman (F)	100	20

*Major hotel groups: USA (excluding UK operators: Hilton, Holiday Inn)**

	No. hotels
Marriott – worldwide	
Marriott, Courtyard	639 in 1990
Fairfield Inns	new 57 in 1991
Carlson Hospitality – worldwide	
Radisson Hotels	250
Colony Hotels & Resorts	70
Hyatt – worldwide	
40% owned and operated, 60% managed	
Hyatt, Grand Hyatt	
Hyatt Regency, Park Hyatt	160
ITT Sheraton – worldwide	
Sheraton, Sheraton Towers	120

Sources:
UK: companies concerned, 1991
Europe: Salomon Brothers
USA: *Hoover's Handbook of American Business*, 1992
*UK brewer Bass purchased Canadian/US Holiday Inn and UK leisure operator Ladbroke purchased Hilton

rival companies' hotels; few are brand loyal when compared to, for example, fmcgs (fast-moving consumer goods) or financial services.

Research also reveals the personal nature of the product. People are away from home, often uncertain of their surroundings and looking for a certain level of re-assurance and comfort. The hotel and its amenities are a short-term substitute for home. For management, it is very much a 'people business'. At the core of the business, hotel employees personify the establishment: their proficiency, attitude and attention to detail augment the basic service offer of bedroom, restaurant and conference/leisure amenities.

Experience has shown the hotel industry to be highly prone to outside influences. IRA terrorist activity in London has ruined the Annual General Meetings of many hotel groups, as tourists cancel trips and companies or trade associations re-locate conventions. The Gulf War caused air travel, business conventions and tourism to drop in parts of Europe by an estimated 80 per cent. Economic recession in the early 1990s has forced companies to curtail conferences, seminars, product launches – all previously lucrative business for the major hotel operators – as well as business travel and expense accounts. Consumers, too, are hit in times of recession, cancelling or postponing holidays, weekend breaks and overnight stays in hotels.

MARKET SEGMENTS

In general, the hotel industry orientates its activities around five broad market segments. The relative importance of these segments varies for different operators and locations.

Domestic business travellers

These customers usually do not pay personally for their accommodation and subsistence as their employers will meet their expenses. Some employers may have negotiated preferential rates with certain hotel companies. For this segment, amenities in bedrooms are important, as are restaurant and bar facilities. Where longer stays are involved, sports and recreational facilities are also desirable. Business support services, such as secretarial provision, fax and computing, are increasingly important. These customers are in the hotel for business meetings or to attend conferences and seminars.

International business travellers

Many of these customers view airport hotels as their prime destination, rather than city centre or downtown hotels. On the whole they expect a wider range of in-room amenities, including mini-bars, air conditioning, satellite TV; extensive business facilities (secretarial, telecommunications, audio-visual aids), plus extensive leisure facilities (sauna, gymnasium, swimming pool), as well as adequate bars and restaurants. The longer the duration of their stay, the greater the emphasis placed on leisure facilities and the less important are in-hotel restaurants and bars. These customers rarely pay their own bills, with employers picking up the tab. It is also unusual for them personally to make their own travel arrangements and hotel bookings.

British/domestic tourists

Unless attending a weekday theatre show at a major London theatre, these customers aim to take advantage of the lower weekend room rates offered by most hotels. Business users are the focus during the week, with higher rates, but at weekends hotels offer heavy discounts to fill otherwise empty rooms. These weekend 'bargain-breakers' are rarely interested in extensive sports or leisure facilities (unless in the countryside for a weekend away from city stress), and clearly are not users of a hotel's business services. Their focus is on value for money, comfortable bedrooms, adequate catering facilities, and locations convenient for shopping, theatres and leisure attractions.

International leisure travellers

For some of this segment's customers, an airport hotel is the first destination, but in general they wish to be based centrally in the city close to the main theatres, shopping areas and tourist attractions. The hotel is a base, providing comfortable bedrooms with good amenities, coffee shop and snack facilities, and room service. Within reason, these customers will not be interested in too many hotel amenities: rarely do they dine in hotel restaurants, choosing instead to eat while out sightseeing. Sports facilities and business services are not used. Their focus is on getting out into the city to experience the sights, attractions and restaurants on offer.

Banqueting and functioning

Most international city hotels offer extensive ballroom and banqueting facilities. During the week these may be used by businesses for conferences, conventions, trade shows and seminars. At weekends they tend to focus on social functions: wedding receptions, anniversaries, reunions, etc. Most hotel operators treat their bedroom and banqueting functions totally separately, with different management teams and sales forces.

THF VERSUS FORTE: THE NEED TO RE-BRAND?

An advertisement in the *AA Members' Handbook* in the early 1980s stated the case for 'thf':

> Stay Trusthouse Forte: Britain's widest choice.

> Trusthouse Forte have more than 200 hotels throughout Britain. In London, internationally renowned hotels such as Brown's, the Hyde Park and the Grosvenor House. In the rest of the country, modern Post House Hotels near main highways, airport hotels and city centre hotels – such as the Albany Hotels in Glasgow, Birmingham and Nottingham. And traditional inns, and resort hotels such as the famous Imperial in Torquay. Trusthouse Forte restaurants, also, are very varied: superb luxury restaurants such as London's splendid Café Royal and The Hunting Lodge. And in our hotels, the convenient Coffee Shops or the ever popular Carverys.

Yours faithfully, Trusthouse Forte

No matter which hotel they stayed in, the visitor would be left in no doubt that it was a 'thf'-owned hotel: branding ran through from stationery and literature to signage and flags. The situation, though, was confused: the acquired chain of hotels from Strand Palace was dual-branded: Strand Palace in name, but with 'thf' branding. Similarly, the Post House chain was promoted separately under the Post House brand, but also clearly signed for visitors under 'thf' and included in all Trusthouse Forte brochures. The more exclusive hotels, such as Oxford's The Randolf or London's The Hyde Park combined separate identities (their own logos on all signage and printed matter) with the 'thf' brand. In the 1980s, this diversity of 'thf' branding was further complicated as the company attempted to group hotels under various banners: Exclusives (for hotels such as London's The Hyde Park or The Grosvenor, the George V in Paris or Milan's The Ritz), Forte Hotels and Post Houses. The expansion of the budget chain Travelodge added another brand. The Exclusives and Forte hotels all had separate hotel identities. Simultaneously all 'thf' hotels were clearly branded as belonging to 'thf'.

The problem was the clear identification with the 'thf' name. A poor meal, delayed check-in, slow room service, or a dilapidated room may have been the exception to the rule but potentially could tarnish a particular customer's perception of the particular 'thf' hotel or restaurant. The customer might associate such a poor experience generally with the 'thf' name and even with the company's other hotels and services. The company faced a problem of quality control common to many service providers.

In the late 1980s, Trusthouse Forte carried out a major review of its branding with the assistance of management consultants and design houses. The company re-grouped and re-branded its hotel portfolio. The aim was to have clearly defined product offers with similar hotels targeted at like-minded consumers grouped together. Within each category, hotel image, facilities, pricing and service levels were to be of a similar standard. Each category, however, was still to be linked to the parent company's name – and to the controlling family – with the inherent risks of cross-branding any poor perceptions of a particular hotel in the consumers' eyes. Trusthouse Forte as a company was renamed Forte plc, with the familiar 'thf' logo and brand name dropped totally. From airport catering, through motorway service areas, to Little Chef roadside restaurants, all operating divisions were re-branded as Forte. For hotels, including the recently acquired Crest chain, five groups were identified (in addition to the roadside Travelodge operation) described by Forte in its brochures as:

Forte Posthouse

Our UK chain of accessible, straightforward modern hotels providing good facilities at competitive prices for the business or leisure traveller.

Forte Crest

Our chain of high quality modern hotels offering personal recognition and service. Most of the properties are situated in major city centres throughout Europe.

Forte Heritage

Our collection of traditional British inns offering a unique combination of comfort, hospitality and character, spanning a wide range of individual properties.

Forte Grand

Our collection of hotels in the grand tradition, where service and quality rub shoulders with timelessness and elegance.

Exclusive Hotels of the World

The finest collection of hotels in the world, each offering discreet service within exquisite surroundings.

These hotel groupings were supported with a whole host of promotional brochures and offers, including:

Forte Europa, featuring 27 superb hotels for the independent traveller in Europe.
Forte Leisure Breaks, the only complete guide to UK short breaks at 230 Forte Hotels in the UK.

Forte Hotels Xmas & New Year, seven exciting packages for getting away during the festive period.

Forte Showcase, an exciting new idea in Hotel and Entertainment services from Forte Hotels: tickets with accommodation for sports, theatre and events across the UK.

Forte Leisure Select, containing a selection of the very best hotels in Britain.

RIVAL APPROACHES

National and international competitors to Forte have adopted a variety of branding and segmentation options. From the small Copthorne group, to UK focused Lansbury and Europe-orientated Queens Moat Houses, to the internationally recognised hotel brands of Hilton and Holiday Inn, the targeting of specific customer segments is central to performing successfully against rival operators.

Copthorne

With over a dozen hotels in Britain, France and Belgium, Copthorne has opted for a more uniform marketing approach. The physical attributes of the hotel properties vary from modern purpose-built hotels such as the Charles de Gaule Copthorne or Birmingham's Copthorne, to the traditional Hotel Copthorne Commodore in Paris and the former stately home, The Copthorne Effingham Park. 'Each individual hotel has a style and ambience of its own, whilst boasting a wealth of 4-star facilities to make your stay a truly memorable one.' Each hotel may indeed be unique, but the Copthorne branding is strong and consistent, with service levels and quality maintained consistently across the chain.

Holiday Inn

Until a few years ago, Holiday Inn (formally Commonwealth Holiday Inns of Canada, now owned by UK brewer Bass) opted for a similarly uniform product concept and branding for all its 5,000 hotels worldwide. Recently, to enable the company to cater for several segments of the market, Holiday Inn has developed several sub-brands, described by the company:

Holiday Inn

Holiday Inn hotels have a worldwide reputation for providing a consistently high standard of product and service, whilst offering good value for money across the globe. Guests, whether travelling on business or for pleasure, appreciate the spacious, well appointed bedrooms with large beds, luxury bathrooms and 16-hour room service. Every hotel has a variety of meeting and conference rooms and most hotels offer leisure facilities, a swimming pool and free parking.

In order to meet the ever-increasing needs of the traveller, in many different locations, we have introduced three brand extensions to the Holiday Inn name:

Holiday Inn Crowne Plaza

Holiday Inn Crowne Plaza hotels are superior Holiday Inn hotels, located mainly in major city centres. They offer superb amenities and facilities.

Holiday Inn Garden Court

Holiday Inn Garden Court hotels are located mainly in smaller European towns and cities. They are 3-star hotels, very competitively priced and offer an intimate reception area, bistro-style restaurant and bar, and also provide the traveller with superb Holiday Inn bedrooms, as well as meeting rooms and a fitness area. A stylish concept designed for today's busy traveller.

Holiday Inn Express

For people who want a comfortable room but have a limited need for restaurant, recreational facilities and service amenities, Holiday Inn Express hotels in the United States are a welcome alternative. They offer bright, comfortable guest rooms, a buffet breakfast; and a Great Room/ lobby with comfortable seating and a large-screen television. Small meeting rooms and fax services are also available.

Hilton

When Ladbroke plc bought the world-famous Hilton Corporation, the DIY to betting-shops company was faced with a dilemma. It already operated one of the UK's major hotel chains – Ladbroke Hotels – which had a varied portfolio of properties, including modern purpose-built hotels, some 4-star in city centre locations, but mostly 3-star hotels on trunk roads. The prestigious Hilton group comprised mainly 5-star deluxe and 4-star hotels. Ladbroke initially bought the European Hilton operation, returning to the market a year later to purchase the Hilton company (excluding the Conrad hotels) worldwide. To mix its existing UK hotels with the newly acquired Hilton hotels, under the same brand name, risked diluting the real marketing asset of the Hilton brand. Not to merge operations seemed to admit to shortcomings in Ladbroke Hotels and added significantly to operating costs, management and marketing expenses. The solution was to develop sub-brands:

Hilton Hotels

The deluxe originally Hilton Corporation hotels, plus the best of the Ladbroke Hotels.

Hilton National

The more modern 3-star (some 4-star) trunk road hotels.

Associate Hotels

The small residual of hotels, one or two city based, but mostly rural, mainly more traditional hotels, which did not sit correctly within the two main brands of Hilton and Hilton National.

Queens Moat Houses

For Queens Moat Houses the way forward has not been so clear. The fast-growing international hotel group has close to 180 hotels in the UK, Belgium, the Netherlands, Germany and Switzerland. Already expanding under the Moat House brand, the company has acquired several hotels through one-off acquisitions, such as the Chester International Hotel. It also bought out Norfolk Capital Hotels which itself had expanded quickly during the early 1980s.

The majority of Queens Moat Houses plc's hotels had traded as Moat Houses, but by no means all. Few of Norfolk Capital's hotels had been under one brand, most having freestanding, separate trading identities. The confusion is exaggerated in Belgium where the company operates one IBIS hotel, two Ramada hotels and 20 Holiday Inns. Within the UK portfolio the range of product and service offerings is quite diverse, including a few 2-star properties right up to The Royal Crescent Hotel in Bath, one of 'The Leading Hotels of the World'. Most of the Norfolk Capital hotels are older, more traditional properties. The Moat Houses tend to be modern constructions. The bulk of the portfolio is made up of 3- and 4-star business-orientated hotels. Branding is not uniform, nor are products and services.

Lansbury Hotels

Occupying the middle ground in the UK, Whitbread's 43 Lansbury Hotels are all 3-star standard, mainly small town or trunk road located, with typically between 35 and 45 bedrooms. Husband and wife pairs are preferred as resident management teams for each hotel. These managers have strong profit/bonus incentives, with the objective of encouraging them to run their hotel to the optimum of efficiency with a focus on staff attitudes and customer service. Bedrooms have full 4-star amenities, but most hotels offer only excellent local-cuisine based restaurant, bar and free car parking. Although the 'Lansbury' name features on signage and the full list of hotels is promoted at each location, the emphasis is strongly on the individual hotel's name and identity. Many are old coaching inns in market towns where the hotel has long been a household brand name. Whitbread gives its chain of hotels the support of a large hotel group, but focuses customers on each hotel's separate facilities and reputation.

THE LONDON HOTEL BUSINESS AND COMPETITORS' APPROACHES

The hotel business has attracted major international corporations, such as ITT with its Sheraton chain, Carlson with Radisson Hotels, Ladbroke's Hilton and Bass with Holiday Inn. There are major European competitors, plus quickly emerging Japanese and Pacific Rim operators. In the UK, there are rivals to market leader Forte, including Queens Moat Houses, Hilton, Whitbread, plus US Marriott which in 1992 took over the franchise of half of the UK's Holiday Inns. Most of these hotel groups have brands and marketing programmes designed to attract the key market segments. Nowhere more than in London is this plethora of branding and targeting more apparent.

Whether for business or pleasure, London features in the top three cities worldwide for visitors. Heathrow and Gatwick airports are two of the busiest in the world. There are over 130 3-, 4- and 5-star hotels, with more than 30 more in the suburbs. Additionally, there are 10 out at Heathrow airport and four at Gatwick. Competition is severe, with 80 per cent bed occupancy rates difficult to achieve: many hotels are pushed to achieve 55–60 per cent occupancy. The market is prone to seasonal peaks – summer tourism, or Christmas shopping trips – and troughs. These lows may result from economic recession, exchange rates temporarily deterring overseas visitors or from IRA terrorist activity.

Forte has 16 London hotels including:

3 Exclusives: Brown's, The Hyde Park, The Grosvenor House;
4 Forte Grand Hotels: The Waldorf, The Westbury, St George's, Hotel Russell;
3 Forte Crest;
1 Forte Posthouse.

In addition there are three hotels at Heathrow airport, and two at Gatwick.

Hilton has six Hilton Hotels in central London, three Associate hotels, and one Hilton National at Wembley. Holiday Inn has two hotels in London and one each at Heathrow and Gatwick airports, none of which is a Crowne Plaza or Garden Court – they are all trading under the original Holiday Inn brand. For Copthorne there is only one London location: the Kensington Copthorne Tara. Within central London there are no Lansbury hotels, only one in the suburbs. Queens Moat Houses has three hotels in central London: Drury Lane Moat House, Norfolk Hotel, Royal Court; plus airport hotels the Gatwick Concorde and Gatwick Moat House.

Each company has taken a slightly different approach to serving and competing in the important but at times volatile London hotel market. The emergence of sub-brands for the large operators gives the customer more choice, but the marketer more segments to monitor and numerous marketing programmes to control. For Forte, the problem is how to market its hotels, promoting to so many customer segments. Forte has such a diverse portfolio of varyingly branded sub-groups of hotels competing against numerous UK hotel groups, individually owned hotels, plus all of the major international operators. The re-branding under *Forte* has given the company renewed resolve to remain as the UK's leading hotels group; the initiative has additionally brought the company's name increasingly to the attention of the consumer. In this competitive market it has been a bold move, echoed by the branding activities of some direct competitors, but by no means all of the industry's key players.

Table 8.2 Travel and tourism

	Overseas visitors to UK		Visits abroad by UK residents	
	000	%	000	%
Total all visits	17,338	100.0	31,030	100.0
Area of residence (inward) or visited (outward)				
Europe EC	8,960	51.7	22,424	72.3
W. Europe non-EC	1,728	10.0	3,704	11.9
N. America	3,481	20.1	2,218	7.1
Other countries	3,168	18.3	2,684	8.6
Mode of travel				
Air	11,829	68.2	21,925	70.7
Sea	5,509	31.8	9,105	29.3
Purpose of visit				
Holiday	7,286	42.0	21,847	70.4
Business	4,363	25.2	4,505	14.5
Visit friends/family	3,497	20.2	3,485	11.2
Miscellaneous	2,193	12.6	1,193	3.8

Source: *HMSO Employment Gazette*, 1991, International Passenger Survey

Table 8.3 Forte plc selected financial highlights

Activities: hotels, public and contract catering, airport services
SIC codes: 66401   66111   66112   66402   66501

Year ended	1992 12 months Cons.	1991 12 months Cons.	1990 15 months Cons.	1988 12 months Cons.
Sales – turnover (£m)	2,662	2,641	2,983	2,044
Profit before tax (£m)	73	190	291	232
Net tangible assets (£m)	3,985	3,790	3,472	3,027
Share funds (£m)	2,916	2,961	2,712	2,245
Profit margin (%)	2.74	7.19	9.76	11.35
Return on share funds (%)	2.50	6.42	8.58	10.33
Return on capital employed (%)	1.83	5.01	6.71	7.66
Liquidity ratio	0.54	0.48	0.51	0.57
Gearing (%)	50.34	41.54	40.60	44.63
No. of employees	89,500	92,100	92,900	79,800

Source: Business Information Service, University of Warwick

ISSUES

Branding, market segmentation and positioning are complex issues. For a service provider such as Forte, identifying a branding strategy which matches the company's varied portfolio of hotels with the market's segments has been costly and perhaps risky. Rival operators have adopted similar approaches, but by no means all. This case concentrates on the segmentation, targeting, positioning process, as well as the associated branding strategies and competitive reactions.

Branding

What is Forte's new branding strategy? How is this a new approach for the company? What are the apparent advantages and disadvantages? What other branding options were open to Forte?

Segmentation

What are the main market segments? How is Forte targeting them? What are the competitors' approaches? How could marketing research be used to examine and verify these market segments? Which bases are being used? Which other bases could be used? Why?

Positioning

What are the Forte brands' positionings? How are these geared to (a) the market's segments, (b) consumer behaviour in this market, (c) competitor brands?

Competitive strategies

With which marketing mixes and competitive advantages do competitors target the main market segments? Which approach is the most effective? Why?

THEORY NOTES

Chapter 25, Products and product management, pp. 205–13
Chapter 23, Market segmentation, targeting, positioning, pp. 189–96
Chapter 24, Competition, pp. 197–204
Chapter 21, Marketing research, pp. 173–80

Chapter 9

Lucas Aftermarket Operations
Finding the customers

> To strive to offer customers in our targeted markets products and service
> of a quality which is recognised as giving the best value available.

Such is the stated mission of Lucas Aftermarket Operations, the division of
Lucas Automotive charged with supplying the service needs of vehicle
users around globe. Offering a complete range of braking, electrical and
diesel products for all types of land transport, the division aims to give
parts and service back-up to the engine and vehicle manufacturers, its
original equipment (OE) customer base. In addition, Aftermarket Operations supplies the independent aftermarket worldwide through a distribution network serving specialist repairers and wholesalers which, in turn,
serve garages, retailers and end users. Aftermarket Operations is one of
seven divisions of the Lucas Automotive company. The full company
structure is shown in Figure 9.1.

Lucas Automotive is part of Lucas Industries plc, international supplier
to the automotive, aerospace and industrial markets, with sales of more

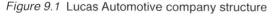

LUCAS AUTOMOTIVE

Finance	Marketing
Strategic planning	Technology

Divisions

Car braking systems	Diesel systems	Body systems	Aftermarket operations
Heavy duty braking systems	Engine management systems		Electrical products

Figure 9.1 Lucas Automotive company structure

Source: Lucas Automotive promotional literature

than £2 billion and in excess of 50,000 employees. The Automotive side of the business has benefited considerably from the large parent which has heavily resourced the Aftermarket division.

DISTRIBUTION CHANNELS

Lucas Aftermarket Operations has a global network of Lucas-branded and independent distributors and dealers. In addition to the UK there is manufacturing and re-manufacturing capability through centres in France, Germany, Portugal and Spain. Lucas distribution centres are based in 16 major centres (including Japan), worldwide:

Argentina	Greece	Japan	South Africa
Canada	India	Mexico	Spain
France	Ireland	Pakistan	UK
Germany	Italy	Portugal	USA

These Lucas distribution outlets are supplemented by numerous independent distributors in more than 100 countries around the world. In total, the distribution network gives Lucas a presence in 128 countries through 4,000 authorised outlets.

Two typical, yet contrasting distribution channels for a manufacturer, such as Lucas, are shown in Figure 9.2. Many other combinations of these elements are to be found in the diverse and complex systems of distribution in this market.

LUCAS PHILOSOPHY AND THE COMPETITIVENESS ACHIEVEMENT PLANS

Lucas's philosophy is well defined: the emphasis is on providing an extensive range of quality products for just about any type of vehicle imaginable. The company takes pride in its technological leadership which allows it to supply components for a diversity of vehicle brands, including those originally supplied without Lucas equipment. It strives to maintain its position at the leading edge of technological development with a research and development effort which spans fuel injection systems, anti-lock braking, engine management and automotive information systems. In the recession in the early 1980s, Lucas cut costs and held back on investment and R&D spend. This enabled international competitors to catch up with Lucas's technological and design leads. Despite the recession in the early 1990s, Lucas has no intention of cutting back its enviable R&D programme which has given the company a lead in so many of its markets.

As a player in a service industry, Lucas Aftermarket Operations recognises the importance of quality service provision. This is reflected in the company's stated mission. Throughout its promotional literature the

```
Channel A:                    Supplier

                    Manufacturer's factory
                    Original equipment manufacturer
          Vehicle manufacturer's (VM) service department
                    VM franchised garage
                    Service market

Channel B:                    Supplier

                    Manufacturer's factory
                    Parts and service department
                    Wholesale distributors
                    Cash and carry
                    Local parts shops
                    DIY market
```

Figure 9.2 Typical aftermarket distribution channels

company stresses its reliance on the skills of the individuals who fit the components it supplies. Efforts to ensure that personnel maintain the highest levels of technological know-how are supported by a heavy commitment to training and development at all levels in the organisation. This training effort extends to Lucas distributors and authorised outlets throughout Europe and the company's other main markets.

Despite current emphasis on quality, service and technological innovation, in the past the company was dogged by a poor reputation for quality. These difficulties, which prevailed right through the 1960s and 1970s, were compounded by the collapse of the UK automotive market in 1980.

In 1984, with the introduction of 'Competitiveness Achievement Plans' (CAP), management proposed a radical solution. The message to business managers was simple. Match the performance of the best UK or international rival, or face factory closure.

At the Lucas brake factory in Cwmbran, Wales, the benefits of the CAP programme have been felt widely. Originally opened in 1947, over the last five years the factory has moved from manual to automated assembly, and away from traditional assembly lines. Products are now handled in 'modules', with small groups of workers collectively responsible for producing a particular item. This has resulted in better morale, lower absenteeism, higher quality standards and a more positive attitude towards management. Innovations aimed at improving quality have included the use of quality circles and the development of 'total-quality' programmes. So far the signs are encouraging. Despite some problems with managers trying to accept the shift in power towards the factory floor, the new approach has been well received by the work force.

Table 9.1 Lucas financial performance

Lucas Trading Ltd
Manufacturer and distributor of a wide range of aerospace, automotive and
industrial systems and components
SIC codes: 36400   35300

Year ended	1991 12 months	1990 12 months	1989 15 months	1988 12 months
Sales – turnover (£'000s)	1,162,022	1,122,622	1,100,194	1,038,822
Profits before tax (£'000s)	14,451	65,029	84,849	98,960
Net tangible assets (£'000s)	197,382	242,216	194,256	192,449
Share funds (£'000s)	119,601	152,345	111,643	78,113
Profit margin (%)	1.24	5.79	7.71	9.53
Return on share funds (%)	12.08	42.69	76.00	126.69
Return on capital employed (%)	7.32	26.85	43.68	51.42
Liquidity ratio	0.63	0.68	0.67	0.66
Gearing (%)	304.53	213.31	326.75	407.21
No. of employees	27,857	30,642	31,784	36,616

Source: Business Information Service, University of Warwick

THE INSTALLERS AS CUSTOMERS

By definition, before an understanding of customers can be reached, it is
first necessary to identify them. In the automotive aftermarket this is not
necessarily as simple as it seems. Although the vehicle owner may appear
to be the ultimate target, the distribution channels which have developed in
this market are geared towards satisfying the product and service requirements of installers (the garages or workshops where parts are fitted to
vehicles). This, in itself, is unusual in that it is the installer, rather than the
end user (vehicle owner) which the manufacturer must satisfy, as the final
brand choice is most often made at the installer level. Although vehicle
owners may have some interest in the quality, availability and price of
parts, they are less likely to be interested in the branding. For this reason,
manufacturers tend to focus marketing and distribution on the installers.

Traditionally the industry has recognised a number of installer types,
each with particular characteristics (see Figure 9.3). Industry experts point
to historical reasons for grouping installers in this way. Amongst the more
important developments are the setting up of franchised dealerships by
vehicle manufacturers; the UK legal requirements for MOTs on all cars
over three years old; and trained mechanics responding to government
encouragement to start their own businesses. Towards the end of the
1980s, the expectations of vehicle owners changed. Increased emphasis on
speedy service and competitive prices resulted in the emergence of the fast-
fit and menu service operations.

Vehicle manufacturer's agents:
Garages or workshops franchised to sell, repair and service the cars of one or more manufacturers (Lex, Kennings).

Specialist repairers:
Garages or workshops which carry out work on either a limited range of components or car makes.

Fleet owners:
Local or national commercial operators. May carry out own repairs and servicing (British Steel, RAF, GEC).

Fast-fit:
Garages or workshops offering limited range of easy-fit parts at competitive prices (Kwik Fit).

Menu servicing:
Independent outfits offering repairs and servicing at fixed prices (Lucas Autocentres, Charlie Brown's).

Independent garages:
Independent operators, not affiliated to a particular vehicle manufacturer. These garages are often small in size and work generally on cars over three years old (Murco service bays, etc.).

Retailers:
Retail outlets which serve the market for DIY vehicle parts.

Breakdown organisations:
Crisis organisations such as the AA and RAC.

Figure 9.3 Key characteristics of installer types

Although the industry groupings which have resulted from these developments are well known and recognised as operationally useful, it is less clear whether they represent an effective way of *segmenting* customers in marketing terms. For instance, do the different groups contain customers with distinctive needs which are heterogeneous to those in other groups? Or do some customers in several groups share needs and usage characteristics?

This raises a number of interesting questions for Lucas Aftermarket Operations. Should the existing structure be maintained? After all, while the structure's development has been iterative, it has presumably been derived to satisfy market needs. If changes are to be made, is it possible that a more effective approach could be found? Would this put customer needs and market segmentation at the centre? Is it likely that the costs and practicalities of change would be unrealistic? If so, how might these costs be minimised and what would be the real cost for the installers?

ISSUES

The Lucas Aftermarket case illustrates the importance of identifying – and of controlling – effective marketing channels. The problems of implementing true market segmentation are apparent, as are the implications of adopting any compromise.

Marketing channels

What are the main distribution channels in the UK car aftermarket? How does Lucas take account of these with its channel management and marketing? What new channels might be worthwhile exploring for Lucas? Where are the priorities?

Market segmentation

How are the market's segments currently defined? On which bases? How could these segments be researched with a view to refining them? What other approaches to segmentation could be relevant in this market? What problems might arise from any such redefinition of segments? Why?

THEORY NOTES

Chapter 26, Distribution/marketing channels, pp. 214–18
Chapter 23, Market segmentation, targeting, positioning, pp. 189–96
Chapter 30, Industrial marketing, pp. 235–8

Chapter 10

Heineken
Global brands, local focus

Heineken is the third largest brewery group in the world. Operating in 150 countries, with many export, licensed and local production facilities, the company is clearly a well-established global organisation. Although Heineken's activities are centred predominantly in Europe, worldwide the company ranks behind only US-based leader Anheuser Busch and is quickly catching Miller, the US number two. Heineken as the brand is number three behind Budweiser and Miller Lite.

Financially, the Heineken group is solid and well established, with good growth of sales and profit in recent years (see Table 10.1). The company has taken care not to become overextended, ensuring solid return on assets and on equity ratios for its shareholders. Heineken adopts a pragmatic view to growth, balancing the need to expand with the need for caution when entering new markets. Growth takes place organically, as well as through acquisitions, joint ventures and alliances, depending on management's view of the appropriate route.

Table 10.2 illustrates how Heineken's beer sales can be broken down geographically, including export and licensed operations. There are strengths in many major European and world markets.

CHANGING PATTERNS OF CONSUMPTION

Europe is a major part of the beer industry, providing around 40 per cent of beer production globally. Changing patterns of consumption over the last decade have seen falling volumes in high-consuming Germany, Belgium, Denmark and the UK, with rapid growth of consumption in Spain, Italy, Portugal and Greece. Tourism is seen as a key contributing factor in these traditionally lower-consuming countries.

Overall, despite certain regional differences, there is evidence that tastes within Europe are gradually converging. Analysts predict the growth seen in part of southern Europe will continue, probably soon to be joined by rapid increases in consumption in former USSR countries. In the mature markets, the decline may be exacerbated by increasing social pressures, as

Table 10.1 Heineken financial summary, 1987–91

	1987	1988	1989	1990	1991
Net profit (Dfl m)	280	306	338	362	410
Beer sales (hl m)	42.5	47.0	48.0	54.0	52.5
Turnover (Dfl m)	6,658	7,290	7,820	8,210	8,696
Return on assets (%)	9.7	9.1	8.9	9.3	8.5
Return on equity (%)	12.2	11.6	11.0	10.5	11.6

Sources: Heineken annual report; Barclays de Zoete Wedd

Table 10.2 Geographic breakdown of Heineken's sales

	Hectolitres (m)	%
The Netherlands	6.9	13
France	5.3	10
Spain	4.7	9
Italy	3.4	7
Greece	3.2	6
Ireland	0.6	1
Rest of Europe	3.8	7
Total Europe	27.9	53
Western Hemisphere	13.1	25
Africa	8.1	16
Asia/Australasia	3.3	6
Total	52.4	100%

Source: Heineken annual report

consumers become more health conscious. Pressure on the brewing industry from governments is also set to increase, with interest focusing on a number of key areas:

- Efforts to reduce levels of alcohol consumption. Associated with this are limits on the nature and style of advertising. For example, beer advertising is banned in Austria, Denmark, Finland, Norway and Sweden. France announced that restrictions will be imposed from the start of 1993.
- The drive for legislation regarding environmentally friendly packaging. In Germany and Denmark, the importing of non-returnable bottles has been prohibited. In addition, by 1995, manufacturers must ensure that at least 65 per cent of packaging will be reusable. This is likely, in the short term, to increase the costs of packaging and distribution as new technology is introduced. Such costs will almost certainly be passed on to the consumer.

– More stringent drink-driving legislation is expected, reducing permitted consumption of alcohol when driving.

HEINEKEN IN EUROPE

As the largest brewery group in Europe, Heineken generates 53 per cent (1991) of its beer sales from this region. The Netherlands, France and Spain are particularly large contributors, accounting for well over half of all European sales. Heineken's geographic coverage is related to the company's historical development. Early involvement in, and domination of, the European market can be traced to the company's expansion from the Netherlands into countries close by.

During the Gulf War, the reduced numbers of tourists visiting Europe and travelling in general, meant lost sales, particularly in the café, restaurant and hotel sector. Despite this temporary set-back, Heineken's position remained strong, mainly due to improved margins and close control over fixed costs.

As Heineken increases its coverage of world markets, the company adapts its entry method to suit local conditions: direct investment, joint ventures or other alliances. A typical entry strategy would be to begin exporting via intermediaries, move into direct export, look at licensing and joint ventures with local brewers, with finally direct local production. Whatever the approach selected, Heineken has a reputation for making careful, well-considered decisions.

The Netherlands

With sales of 6.9 million hectolitres and market share of 53 per cent, Heineken is a strong market leader in the Netherlands. These figures far exceed the shares of rivals Grolsch (15 per cent) and Allied Lyons' subsidiary Verenigde Brouwerijen (15 per cent). Unfortunately, for Heineken the picture is not totally positive. The Heineken brand's 45 per cent market share in 1980 dropped to only 30 per cent in 1991. However, the company declared this decline to have been halted. The introduction of the Amstel brand and Buckler, the first non-alcoholic beer available on draft, compensated for Heineken's fall.

A 1992 cost-cutting exercise successfully increased the company's rate of return. The company also identified financial benefits in increasing its control over the distribution network. By bringing most of the wholesale of draught beers directly under its umbrella, production forecasts proved easier to supply, with improved margins.

France

The Heineken interest in France was developed when, in 1982, the company acquired Albra, which had an 8 per cent market share and owned two breweries. Heineken continued along the acquisition route when in 1984 it merged Albra with Brasseries et Glacieres International to form the Sogebra group. Sogebra now has a 25 per cent market share, challenging the first placed BSN Kronenbourg (50 per cent). Since the formation and successful reorganisation of the Sogebra group, Heineken's fortunes have continued to improve. The strong position of the French premium segment has been an important factor. However, the poor economic climate of the early 1990s was a threat to that position, as French sales figures fell. The situation has not been helped by the intensifying competition for limited shelf space in hypermarkets and supermarkets.

Italy

Heineken's presence in Italy started in 1960 when the company acquired a minority stake in a small brewing company. This minority stake was extended in 1974, when Heineken and Whitbread each bought a 42 per cent holding in the company, renamed Birra Dreher. By 1980, having acquired the Whitbread 42 per cent, Heineken was the sole owner of Dreher. As it moved towards its current one-quarter share of the Italian market (market leader Peroni takes around 40 per cent), Dreher was further strengthened by mergers with two former Henniger breweries.

The decline in the Italian beer market has been more marked than in some other European markets. Fierce price competition has meant that by maintaining its margins, Dreher has taken an overall cut in market share. Despite this gloomy scenario, the Heineken brand has retained its position while Buckler beer has benefited from the increasing growth of the non-alcoholic segment. Here, as in other European countries, Heineken, through Dreher, has increased its control on distribution by purchasing a number of drinks wholesalers. Furthermore, efforts to cater more effectively for the premium segment resulted in 1991 in the importing of other Heineken brands.

Spain

Heineken's entry into the Spanish market took place in 1984, much later than in other parts of Europe. At this time, the company was able to purchase a 37 per cent stake in the local El Aguila company. This stake has since been increased to 51 per cent, giving Heineken a controlling interest.

In order to make a success of its Spanish interests, Heineken had to instigate major changes at El Aguila, which suffered from outdated

Table 10.3 Spanish beer market shares by company, 1991

Company	Market share	Foreign partner
Cruzcampo	28%	Guinness/Carlsberg
El Aguila	18%	Heineken
Mahou	15%	BSN
San Miguel	14%	San Miguel Philippines

Sources: Heineken annual report; Barclays de Zoete Wedd Securities, February 1992

production techniques and poor branding. Heineken was forced to re-structure production, with inevitable redundancies and short-term losses. Branding strategy changes involved positioning the Aguila Pilsener brand in the standard segment, while introducing the new Adlerbrau brand, geared towards the premium segment. Heineken was offered in the top, premium segment. Further change occurred in 1991, when Aguila Master was introduced to replace the badly performing Adlerbrau in the premium segment.

Despite the problems with El Aguila, the Spanish market was a particularly attractive one for Heineken, with beer consumption the third highest in the EC, increasing from 51 litres per capita in 1978 to 71 litres in 1989. Not surprisingly, other companies have also been quick to compete for a slice of the market (see Table 10.3).

Greece

Greece is dominated by the Athenian brewery, which is owned by Heineken and Henniger Heblos. Heineken's involvement began with the acquisition of Amstel in 1965. Today, with a market share of approximately 70 per cent, Heineken has three production sites in Greece. This strong position has allowed the company to strengthen the Heineken brand, while importing Dreher and Coors beers.

Ireland

This market is dominated by Guinness and Heineken, with a combined market share of around 85 per cent. Heineken has been producing the Heineken brand under licence in Ireland since the 1970s, acquiring its own production site in 1983. Murphy's stout has been a particular success story, becoming the number two brand of stout (behind Guinness) in both Ireland and the UK. The brand is also now being sold in the US and France.

The Rest of Europe

This category includes the UK, Germany and Eastern Europe. The UK, which is the second largest market for beer in Europe, warrants special attention. Here, the pattern of beer consumption is different from the rest of Europe with more than 80 per cent being drunk in pubs, many of which are still linked or tied to breweries. Heineken's route to the market was through its connections with Whitbread, which allowed the company access to Whitbread's distribution network with a licensing agreement.

In the 1960s, when Heineken entered the UK market, the beer-drinking public was not familiar with the strong beer being drunk in other European countries. Instead, Whitbread brewed a weaker version of the Heineken brand which proved very popular with lager drinkers. In 1990 it was estimated that 10 per cent of all lager drunk in the UK carried the Heineken brand. Recently, as beer drinkers have become increasingly familiar with the continental brands, the company has introduced Heineken Export Strength to the UK market. This brand is also brewed under licence by Whitbread.

In 1993 Heineken began its entry into the German market. In consumption terms this is the largest beer market in the world. On average, each year Germans consume 142.8 litres of beer per head. Heineken's late entry to this market can be explained by historic German beer purity laws which have only recently been relaxed. Today, the attractions of the market are limited by very strong loyalty to the 1,200 local German breweries. The regional variations which result make it difficult for Heineken to achieve distribution on a national scale. One possible route is by introducing Heineken through top restaurants, hotels and cafés.

Opportunities for Heineken in the Eastern European market are potentially large. Beer is already accepted and enjoyed in these parts of Europe, although shortages due to production and distribution problems have deprived consumers of the product. The market potential in these countries, possibly through the direct export of the Heineken brand, is very attractive to the company.

Entry into Hungary, which is considered to be one of the more sophisticated markets, has already been achieved via a different route. Here, a majority interest has been acquired in Komaromi Sorgyar, a local brewery. Komaromi Sorgyar produces 350,000 hectolitres of beer a year and offers the consumer four brands: Talleros, Matros, Aranytaller and Kapsrciter. Together these brands account for around 4 per cent of the Hungarian market.

THE IMPACT OF EC LIBERALISATION

Heineken management is aware that convergence in the EC market and the liberalisation of boundaries present a mix of potential opportunities and threats. While the unification of excise duties across Europe will probably ease administration problems, the excise rate chosen will significantly impact upon the level of trade. For instance, if the rate is higher than that currently seen in most countries there will be a drop in sales. Despite these concerns, there is optimism that the EC will be discouraged from enforcing extreme excise duties on alcohol. Previous experience suggests that high duties can result in undesirable black market activities and attempts by producers to evade payment.

The beer industry relies on economies of scale in both production and distribution in order to be successful. The removal of trade barriers, with the chance to capitalise on economies of scale, will probably assist companies which currently operate in small domestic markets. The success of both Heineken and Carlsberg (Denmark) is, after all, due to the small size of their domestic markets requiring them to operate internationally in order to survive.

In view of the need for scale economies, it is not surprising that the beer industry has become more concentrated through acquisitions and mergers in recent years. Management at Heineken sees such activities as a continuing trend, but does not view such manoeuvres as being anti-competitive or monopolistic. Instead, the measures are seen as positive ways to buy in brand franchises or complementary distribution networks. For example, the alliance between Heineken's wine and spirits division and Bols in the Benelux countries helped maximise economies of scale in both distribution and complementary brands. However, it is true that a useful by-product was the reduction of costs and the elimination of price competition.

The reaction of EC and other government regulators to such industry convergence in light of the monopolies and mergers legislation is not clear. While the EC has published clear guidelines regarding both acceptable and unacceptable mergers and takeovers, the application of such principles in practice needs testing more widely.

The opportunity to exploit the liberalised EC market is not without its problems. The transport industry is a long way from being as liberalised as the EC's borders. Under a liberalised transport system, Heineken would be able to use one truck to despatch cargo to a destination, returning with a different load for somewhere else. Instead, because of current regulations and working practices, Heineken pays for a return trip, with trucks returning empty, when only a single load has been carried. This creates obvious barriers to the development of better scale economies.

BRAND STRATEGY

Flexibility is a key characteristic of Heineken's approach to market segmentation. Company philosophy suggests that it should be possible to target segments in each market with the company's own brands, such as Heineken, Amstel or Buckler. This, it is argued, is because there are segments which cross both national and regional boundaries.

Despite its interest in pursuing general, cross-boundary segments, Heineken is also realistic about the need to cater for the tastes of local, smaller segments. Each country is catered for by combining the use of global brands with those which are indigenous to the local market. This allows local brands, differing in taste, packaging and image, to be offered in conjunction with Heineken's own brands, which are not varied to suit local needs. This is usually achieved by targeting three segments in each market:

- A local, standard brand for the high volume market segment: 'Dreher' in Italy, '33' in France, and 'Tiger' in Singapore.
- A brand to occupy the higher middle segment of the market. This may be a local brand such as the Spanish Aguila Master, or the Amstel brand.
- The Heineken brand in the top premium segment in the market. This may be brewed locally or exported directly. The image and quality of this brand are always carefully controlled by the Netherlands head office. Only in the UK do the recipe and taste vary significantly from the original Heineken.

Heineken has successfully promoted its core brand names throughout the world. The company, though, recognises the differing expectations and tastes of each national and even regional market. The international brands are distributed in each territory, but alongside locally produced and sold beers.

THE WAY FORWARD

Heineken's strategy of giving autonomy to local operating companies in the markets it enters has resulted in the production of beers which appeal closely to local tastes and preferences. It has also enabled the company to use its foothold in the marketplace to understand and anticipate market trends. The use of a stratified segmentation approach, by offering brands to the lower, mid and premium segments in each market has prevented the company becoming trapped as a niche player.

With the stated aim of becoming the world's number one beer company, Heineken is continually seeking ways to spread into new markets while moving towards domination in those it already occupies. The company has a global philosophy and internationally known brands, but also an understanding and commitment to local markets and production.

ISSUES

As a company Heineken is active throughout the world. As a brand, Heineken is familiar to consumers in North America, Africa, Australasia and most of Europe. The company, though, takes account of the needs of local consumers and has a portfolio containing local with international brands.

Branding

Heineken as a brand is available throughout the world. In most countries, differing competitive positions and consumer tastes have led the company to offer locally produced brands alongside its mainstay Heineken. Why is this approach to branding necessary? How does it gain market share for the company's portfolio? What are the disadvantages with this multi-branding strategy?

International marketing

There are few genuinely global brands. Perhaps Heineken is one. How does Heineken deal with its different market territories? Why? Does the company have one standard product offer, branded as Heineken, for the whole world? How would you tackle such a complex international branding problem?

Marketing environment

Changes in EC regulations are expected to impact on all of the European brewers. How? Can these regulatory actions be predicted? Can they be included within a marketing strategy? Should they be considered when evaluating a market?

THEORY NOTES

Chapter 25, Products and product management [branding], pp. 205–13
Chapter 32, International marketing, pp. 246–51
Chapter 19, The marketing environment, pp. 161–4

Chapter 11

Sketchley

More dry cleaning

In the 1980s Sketchley operated a range of services to household consumers primarily through its chain of dry cleaning shops, and to industrial and commercial organisations with vending, catering and textile maintenance. It also rented and serviced a wide range of workwear and auxiliary items to industry. This case focuses on Sketchley the dry cleaner in the late 1980s. The UK dry cleaning industry: a market with no growth. Consumers who begrudge having to use a dry cleaner and who put off doing so unless really necessary. How could Sketchley build on its brand leadership in the UK dry cleaning market? Were there any customer segments which could be developed to grow the market? 1989 saw Sketchley facing difficult decisions.

COMPANY PROFILE

Sketchley plc was registered in 1916 and became a public company in 1949. It is the second largest dry cleaning chain in the UK, behind Johnson plc, but is widely regarded as the market leader. Most consumers believe Sketchley is the biggest operator, partly because Johnson Group trades under different brand names in separate regions: Smiths in Yorkshire, Johnson's in Lancashire, Harris in the Midlands, Bolloms in the South East. Sketchley's brand name is so strong that it is perceived by many consumers to be a generic term for dry cleaning.

Until recently, the company had four distinct areas of operation: *consumer services*, incorporating dry cleaning, laundry and removals; *business services*, incorporating workwear rental, contract cleaning; *vending equipment*; and *office equipment*, incorporating furniture, computer services and supplies. Problems and senior management changes in 1989 and 1990 led to the disposal of contract cleaning and office equipment, with a purchaser being sought for the loss-making vending operation. By 1992 only the dry cleaning and laundry divisions remained: Sketchley plc had returned – very successfully – to its roots. In 1989, however, dry cleaning was far from being the group's only focus.

Dry cleaning was the core business of the company's consumer division and it operated around 490 retail outlets (about 12–15 of which were reported to be franchised in 1988). Most of these shops were in the South East, South West, Wales, the Midlands and London; the company had not ventured further north than Harrogate in Yorkshire. Sketchley also owned Jeeves of Belgravia and Lilliman & Cox (with the Royal Warrant) – two prestigious, 'up-market' London-based chains of dry cleaners. Most Sketchley branches cleaned garments on the premises, sending bulky or valuable items to the Leicestershire headquarters at Hinckley. Jeeves and Lilliman & Cox were serviced by a new, purpose-built factory in north London.

Sketchley's performance had been quite impressive over the years in terms of gross profits growth and turnover. Towards the end of the 1980s, however, its dry cleaning business had witnessed a decline in growth rate in real terms as a result of problems which were symptomatic of the UK dry cleaning market. Sketchley reported in late 1987 that its dry cleaning shops were encountering problems. Profits had dropped and drastic cost-cutting measures were undertaken to maintain margins. Group pre-tax profits fell from £11.7 million to £10.7 million in 1987. In the year, up to 1 April 1988, the dry cleaning arm of the business made a profit of £5.07 million, up 18.5 per cent on a turnover of £50.63 million. Total 1988 group turnover was £181.2 million, up from £131.7 million, and pre-tax profits were £13.4 million, up from £10.7 million. City analysts believed the company was making inadequate profits.

The group reported that its new strategy was to build on strengths and seek out new opportunities that could be integrated into existing operations. Emphasis was to be given to consolidating and developing what the group saw as its core strengths (laundry work, workwear rental). The core dry cleaning business was to be maintained but other businesses were to be developed to reduce group dependence on dry cleaning. After unsuccessfully dabbling in dry cleaning in the USA and Canada, Sketchley decided to pull out of North America where profits were unsatisfactory.

Although not the holding company's priority, Sketchley was considering measures to expand its UK dry cleaning business; mainly through increasing its geographical coverage to build up a truly national chain, and by expanding its range of auxiliary activities. Most of its outlets were refurbished and some larger stores opened. Its franchise outlets were being extended with 40 new outlets planned for 1988/9. There were also plans to open branches within Sainsbury grocery superstores.

MARKET OVERVIEW

The dry cleaning sector experienced continuous gradual decline in real terms between 1977 and 1982, since when the trend was halted but hardly reversed. High street dry cleaners were affected by the increasing overhead costs resulting from rising rents, business rates and the increasing costs of utilities. The effects of the economic recession led people to reduce their expenditure on all non-essentials, including dry cleaning. The trend in fashion towards more casual clothing did not help the dry cleaners: such clothing required much less dry cleaning. The sector also faced competition from 'do-it-yourself dry cleaning' launderettes.

There were 4,500–5,000 dry cleaning shops operating in the UK, controlled by 1,000–1,500 companies (see Table 11.1). A gradual increase in the concentration of ownership has occurred over the years. The two largest companies – Johnson Group and Sketchley – account for some 40 per cent of the turnover of the entire sector. Between them they control 1,200 branches. The remaining 60 per cent of the industry consists of owner-occupied premises and small local chains, such as Brooks, with typically less than 40 shops. There has also been a reduction in the number of employees in the sector over the last 20 years, mainly due to the automation in the industry and the move from factory-based to in-shop cleaning of garments.

Turnover of the industry was believed to be between £180 million and £220 million per annum, a static picture at the end of the 1980s. Generally the UK has experienced low per capita spends on dry cleaning, as illustrated in Table 11.2.

Against this background Sketchley has been able to develop a strong brand name and strong image. Its performance has been quite successful.

The company's retail strategy had concentrated on being 'all things to all people', being uniform across all branches in the 'Sketchley' chain, and predominantly high street located. This tended to ignore certain key customers, particularly business executives and working housewives. Sketchley was vulnerable to niche competitors who targeted defined market segments or local catchments. Its single retail concept was considerably threatened by retail segmentation and niche marketing. Most successful retailers had identified specific target groups and developed retail concepts geared to their exact needs: Burton, Body Shop, IKEA, KwikSave, Next and Sainsbury's are examples.

Table 11.1 The dry cleaning industry: number of companies, outlets and employees, 1960–88

	Companies	Outlets	Employees
1960	2,300	6,000+	43,000
1970	1,500–2,000	5,000–6,000	30,000–35,000
1980	1,000–1,500	4,000–5,000	20,000
1988	1,000–1,500	4,000–5,000	20,000

Sources: ABLCRS; retail business estimates from *Retail Business*, No. 366, August 1988

Table 11.2 Per capita spend on dry cleaning

Country	£ per capita per annum
USA	22
W. Germany	12
France	11
UK	3

Sketchley realised it had to progress, but how? From where could growth come? Sketchley's marketing director for its dry cleaning operation commissioned a programme of marketing research and analyses to identify a strategy for market development and growth.

MARKETING RESEARCH

A qualitative research study was commissioned with the stated objective of establishing a 'consumer view of the dry cleaning market, leading to a development of market segment definitions'. The study had specific aims:

- To establish an understanding of consumer attitudes and behaviour in the market.
- To establish the services and communication messages to increase use of Sketchley.
- To establish the basis of Sketchley's future marketing strategy.

The research covered the following specific questions:

- Background attitudes to clothes, the home, cleaning, and the care of cloths and household items.
- The dry cleaning process; what did consumers think it was.
- The term 'dry cleaning services'; why did customers go/not go to dry cleaners?
- Reactions to specific features and benefits of dry cleaners (convenience, product/service range, quality, price, credit, service, process of dry cleaning, marketing communications). ·
- Comparison with competitors.
- Potential positioning statements for Sketchley.
- Usage and loyalty – how could customers be persuaded to use Sketchley in preference to competitors and to use Sketchley more often?

RESEARCH METHODOLOGY

The research was based on a series of nine extended group discussions of two and a half hours each, held with defined groups (see Table 11.3). These focus groups were from around the country expressing their views

Table 11.3 Extended focus group discussions

1 White collar	A: Male 25–39	AB Commute (Eastcheap)*
	B: Male 40–55	AB Commute (Hitchin)
	C: Female 25–44	ABC1 Exec/Sec (Bristol)
2 Working class	D: Female 25–44	C2 Wives/Skilled Working (Leicester)
3 Housewives	E: Female 35–40	AB Wives/Family (Leamington Spa)*
	F: Female 25–34	C1 C2 Wives/Family (Sheffield)
4 Young	G: Male 18–29	C1 C2 Independent (Ealing)*
	H: Female 18–29	C1 C2 Independent (Wellington)
5 Grocery shoppers	K: Female 25–44	BC1 C2 Shoppers (Winchester)

Notes: Recruitment included minimum 4 of 8 Sketchley users
           *Held in store

on dry cleaning in general, their hopes and fears, and their specific needs from dry cleaning outlets. Sketchley was compared with competing chains and independents. There were 73 respondents altogether, consisting of males and females of all ages and mixed social classes – white collar, blue collar, families, light users, heavy users – from the geographic areas covered by Sketchley's operations. Three of the group discussions were conducted in branches, four in hotels and two in private houses close to Sketchley branches.

RESEARCH FINDINGS

1. Attitudes to clothing and appearance
The research found that very few people enjoyed cleaning work and washing and even fewer accepted a need for dry cleaning. 'Housewives' saw it as an overflow of cleaning which they could not safely do themselves; businesspeople wore suits only due to corporate pressure and begrudged paying for their cleaning. Dry cleaning was regarded generally as a need-driven but begrudged activity.

Dry cleaning was viewed as not making clothes appear new but rather as bringing them back to life for a period. Dry cleaning was comparable to the necessity of the shoe repair process, and the formality of a visit to a new doctor or dentist; something which must be done but is not fun!

2. Prompts to dry cleaning
Customers had the following drives for using dry cleaners:

– Need driven; must clean clothes (but could not tackle dirt, stains, smells, creases).

- Technical factors (customers' inability to achieve results).
- Risk/fear (of harming a garment by washing, particularly for expensive items).
- Want driven (the need to look good and feel good).
- Special occasions (weddings, funerals).

3. Reasons why people deferred going to a dry cleaner

The key deterrents were expense, poor value, short-term effects, potential loss of items and potential damage. The main reasons why people used dry cleaners infrequently were cost and materials needing less care. This was linked to an increasing tendency among women to 'have a go' at washing dry clean items themselves, and avoiding the purchase of 'dry clean only' items in the first place.

4. Choice of outlet

Dry cleaning was prompted by necessity. People tended to choose (a) the most convenient location and opening times; (b) a big company like Sketchley which had the 'right' facilities and expertise; (c) one that had 'qualified', friendly staff, and provided an acceptable product at a reasonable price. Very often this meant the local independent rather than the more impersonal chains. Location of the shop and attitude of staff were key consumer choice criteria.

5. New ideas/services for the future

To sum up the findings, the dry cleaning process was avoided by most people and many, particularly young people, saw no use for it. They preferred to wash items themselves. This view was shared by women who are the key group in the dry cleaning transaction at present. Dry cleaning is begrudged, need/necessity driven and perceived as inconvenient. What the customer wants is a reliable, quality service; improved knowledge, expertise and friendly attitude of staff; a clean, professional but caring and personal atmosphere; reassurance possibly through guarantees; convenient outlets and opening times; value for money and a truly individual service.

ISSUES

Sketchley's market is highly competitive with owner-operated independents a major threat to all of the national chains. Opportunities to
expand the market seem limited. The case illustrates the practicalities of
conducting marketing research and for targeting market segments.

Marketing research

What research was undertaken by Sketchley? Was this the most effective
approach for the company to identify ways in which to grow its business? What would be the best marketing research programme to
develop, making the most effective use of resources?

Market segments

How important is the understanding of market segments to this
industry? Which are the main segments? How could each be effectively
targeted? Which would be the priorities? Why these?

Competition

Which are Sketchley's major competitors? What are the relative
strengths and weaknesses for these players versus Sketchley? How can
the independents compete against Johnson or Sketchley?

THEORY NOTES

Chapter 21, Marketing research, pp. 173–80
Chapter 23, Market segmentation, targeting, positioning, pp. 189–96
Chapter 24, Competition, pp. 197–204
Chapter 31, Marketing planning [SWOT], pp. 239–45

Chapter 12

TGI Friday's
Themed restaurants compete

As living standards have risen, the UK, as in much of Europe, has seen tremendous growth in the hotel and restaurant sector. In the latter half of the last decade, in real terms, expenditure on eating out rose by 51 per cent. This growth has been accompanied by the opening and development of thousands of hotels, restaurants, pubs (bars), and fast food outlets. The figures in Table 12.1 illustrate the scale of the catering outlet industry within the UK. The numbers of outlets in the particular categories disguise to some extent the near 25 per cent share of the market held by hotel restaurants, restaurants and public houses. For the last two decades, the brewery-run steak house and grill chains, led by Beefeater, Berni, Harvester and Porterhouse, have dominated the middle, mass market. Currently, Beefeater (which acquired the bulk of the Berni Inns estate) leads with close to 300 outlets, followed by Toby (120), Porterhouse (90), Harvester (80) and Aberdeen Steak Houses (30).

For many years the UK consumer who did not wish to eat at home was faced with simple choices: a fast food take-away such as a fish and chip shop or a burger bar, a snack bar café, a steakhouse, ethnic restaurant, upmarket restaurant, or hotel restaurant. The introduction to the UK of McDonald's, which now has close to 450 outlets, and the aggressive retaliation from Burger King, added a new dimension to the market during the 1980s. Within the restaurant sector, however, the steakhouse concept reigned supreme, attracting the bulk of middle-spending consumers and families. Here, Whitbread's Beefeater chain led the way. Introduced in 1974, by 1981 there were 50 outlets. Now the company has coverage throughout the UK and also operates in Germany.

Beefeater's success historically was attributed mainly to its staff training, its ability to target specific groups of customers and to update its trading concept to keep a fresh appeal to its well-honed target market. The company realised that such success was not guaranteed and placed a great deal of emphasis on staff training and customer care – the Beefeater care programme – with the aim of establishing a caring culture within the whole of the company. As Beefeater enters the 1990s its promotional activity –

Table 12.1 Catering outlets and eating out* in the UK, 1991

Profit sector	No. premises	%	No. meals†	%
Hotels	58,700	18.4	510m	5.8
Restaurants	16,050	5.0	330m	3.7
Pubs	72,800	22.8	1,380m	15.6
Fast food (chains only)	1,090	0.3	440m	5.0
Travel	1,170	0.4	381m	4.3
Cafés	15,900	5.0 ⎫	1,510m	17.1
Take-aways	18,800	5.9 ⎬		
Clubs and entertainment	52,930	16.5	928m	10.5
Total	237,440	74.3	5,479m	62.0
Cost sector	No. premises	%	No. meals	
Staff catering	23,750	7.4	1,470m	16.7
Health care	21,780	6.8	790m	9.0
Education	33,650	10.5	950m	10.8
Public services	3,050	1.0	135m	1.5
Total	82,230	25.7	3,345m	38.0
Total of both sectors	319,670	100.0	8,824m	100.0

Source: Marketpower estimates
Notes: *Eating out = Number of meals eaten away from home in the UK
    †A meal = Food served on a plate

mainly direct mail and sales promotions – is working hard to shed the staid steakhouse image. The chain now has a softer 'look' with informal, friendly interiors, less focus on red meat dishes and full scope for vegetarians.

AND THEN CAME FRIDAY'S

In the mid-1980s, the UK restaurant scene was altered beyond recognition when Whitbread followed up its strong presence in the restaurant market with the introduction of the American-originated TGI Friday's restaurant concept. Operators within this sector, customers and media had experienced nothing to equal or compare with the sheer vitality and enthusiasm, supported with quality control and excellent standards, of TGI Friday's.

US IN ORIGIN

The first TGI Friday's was opened on New York's First Avenue and 63rd Street in 1965. The restaurant boasted the same red and white striped awnings, wooden flooring, Tiffany lamp shades, bent-wood chairs and striped tablecloths retained in today's restaurants. An immediate success with sales of over one million dollars in the first year, TGI Friday's was an instant hit with young New Yorkers, quickly becoming *the* place to meet. By the early 1970s, the concept was being franchised and extended into Dallas. With this opening, the 'elegant clutter' which remains one of Friday's most famous features first appeared. The Dallas restaurant in its first year achieved sales of over 2 million dollars. By 1975 there were 10 restaurants in eight States, at which point the company was acquired by the Carlson Hospitality Group. Following the takeover, Friday's success was comprehensively analysed and a number of key philosophies were crystal-ised to form the basic principles by which Friday's operates today. Central to Friday's success was its ability to *care* for its guests, anticipating and supplying their needs more effectively, offering more enjoyment than competitors could match.

TGI Friday's is an American diner operating from 3,500 square metre sites (including parking), offering a full cocktail bar and restaurant service. Whether it is a simple coffee, an unpronounceable cocktail, a bowl of chips or a five-course meal, TGI Friday's will provide every customer or 'guest' with a truly memorable experience. In the UK, food accounts for 60 per cent of turnover and beverages 40 per cent.

From its original New York origins in 1965, the concept has become one of America's most famous eating places. There are now close to 150 TGI Friday's restaurants in 34 States. Whitbread brought it, unaltered, to Britain in 1986. TGI Friday's continues to reign the undisputed UK market leader of themed restaurants, despite a host of subsequent imitations. Friday's London Covent Garden restaurant is the busiest Friday's in the world with average weekly sales of over £100,000.

CONCEPT

The Friday's concept centres on a simple layout: a raised bar in the centre with dining area around the periphery of the one-storey building. All the artefacts/atmospherics are genuinely American, shipped from the Ameri-can host company to European franchisees. In the UK, the brewer Whitbread now operates 10 sites with a target of 25.

The restaurants' red and white striped awnings herald a theme which continues inside with striped tablecloths and the staff's striped shirts. The focal point in every Friday's is a large ornate wooden bar with brass rails, which complements the polished wood floors, bent-wood chairs and Tiffany lamps. But perhaps the most striking feature of the restaurants is what Friday's terms 'elegant clutter'. Half an eight-man rowing skull, an antique wooden aeroplane propeller, a pair of old skating boots and a rocking horse are all at home at Friday's; as is the rest of the clutter of items, each with a story to tell.

Staff are encouraged to express their personalities through wearing their own hats, braces and badges. They are trained to help guests relax and every member of staff provides the willing, professional service which is a key note of the successful American restaurants. Whitbread's stated ethical policy is for staff and company to have a basis of honesty, integrity and fair dealing. This is more than echoed within Friday's. At TGI's, guest satisfaction is of ultimate importance. The menu is culturally diverse offering more than 70 American, Tex-Mex, Cajun and Italian dishes, plus over 500 cocktails. To help recruit approximately 100 staff (150 in the larger branches) for each new restaurant, Friday's holds two days of auditions which act as an applicant screening process. Candidates tackle challenging tasks which test their manual dexterity, communications skills, determination and ability to deal with unusual situations and people.

TRAINING

Staff training and selection are a fundamental priority, with staff being selected for personality and dedication to looking after guests. The company has its own full-time training function, but for new store openings brings over experienced US trainers. With their experience of 20 or 30 new store openings, these US trainers are able to set the urgency and pace needed to get the job done. At the same time, the UK trainers learn the tricks of the trade from their US counterparts. The importance of the US tradition of service to TGIs is explained by Patti Hoban-Simpson, the UK's training manager: 'In the US there is not the tradition that service equals servile. In the UK we have actively to teach the American attitude to service and focus on the employer and the guests.' Having the US team working closely with the UK trainers also adds to the fun and cultural experience of the whole TGI's phenomenon.

'We may all speak English,' says US trainer Cheryl Domitrovic from Pittsburgh, 'but the words mean different things. It's been really amusing working out what means what – you have to be quite careful or you can cause hilarity without knowing why. It's suspenders and braces that really confuse me. In the US, suspenders hold your pants (trousers) up and braces run metal tracks around your teeth. In the UK, suspenders hold your panty hose (stockings) up and braces hold your trousers up. It's confusing!' The US training team has had to do more than adjust to the UK English language, having to develop new methods to get the best out of the UK trainees. 'We have to adjust our training methods to the British personality. In the UK we have to teach Friday's staff to make people feel comfortable and to treat customers as real guests – as real people. We also have to encourage new staff to show their personalities at work – this does not come spontaneously to the more reticent British. But once we show how, employees quickly catch on – suddenly work can be tremendous fun, rewarding and enjoyable! In a way, training in the UK is more rewarding than in the US because a transformation is so much greater.'

ATTENTION TO DETAIL

The focus on all facets of staff training is echoed by the management's control and expertise in running the successful US concept within the UK. Restaurant menus are carefully thought through to offer variety and 'mix and match' dining. Despite the elegant clutter and artefacts, hygiene and cleanliness standards are high. Rigorous cleaning and maintenance programmes, and tight management controls result in few problems for customers to worry about.

The attention to detail goes far. Once recruited, before working in a TGI's restaurant, staff members learn in the classroom and from numerous manuals how to look after all parts of the business. Although the button-badged adorned striped shirts and trousers with braces may look haphazard, there is a uniform and dress guide stringently enforced which specifies everything from the suitability of button badges, to length of hair and finger nails, use of plasters for cuts and grazes etc. Once selected to work in the restaurant, new recruits must pass step-by-step tests, immediately leaving the payroll if they fail to progress satisfactorily. For a new restaurant opening, the whole team comes together several weeks before the first paying guest visits the premises, working flat out for several days on volunteer customers and friends of the company so that the first paying customers are not the guinea pigs. This level of training, financial commitment, and attention to detail are all somewhat unusual in what is often a cost-focused industry.

THE 'FEEL'

'If all the world's a stage, then Friday's must compare to a first night on Broadway,' remarks Dave Donnelly, Friday's MD. In the UK, research shows that 25 per cent of customers return once a month. It is seen as a narcotic experience for customers: 'You will have a good time, but it won't be yours, it will be ours.' The vibrant buzz in the atmosphere is deliberate and well orchestrated. The buzz and vitality are the essence of the service product offered by Friday's.

The Friday's experience and atmosphere are difficult to communicate to non-users of the Friday's themed restaurants. Recently, the company embarked on a trend-setting campaign of three-dimensional advertisements. Friday's has proved that it is well ahead of the competition with an exciting communicative and totally 'off the wall' advertising campaign that didn't just aim to get people talking, but also hoped to make their mouths water and their hands reach out to pick a cocktail right off the page. 3D photos showing the fun and enjoyment for both guests and staff within the Covent Garden restaurant appeared, along with 3D glasses, in the up-market magazines *GQ, Tatler, Vanity Fair, Punch* and *Arena.* With just 10 restaurants, the use of television as a medium is prohibited by cost, but the written word and printed page of a normal press advertisement do little justice to the fun and excitement to be found in a Friday's restaurant. The 3D campaign went a long way to bringing into the homes of the magazine readers the TGI Friday's experience.

CUSTOMERS – THE GUESTS

The typical customer is in her thirties, intellectually secure, confident enough to dress down (be informally clothed) to go out in an evening; someone who can relax, sit, watch and enjoy the experience. However, the customer profile switches throughout the day: business lunches, families in the afternoon and early evening, couples and young adults in the later evening. Typical weekday guests are professional people between 25 and 49 years old. At weekends, Friday's is particularly popular among families with children. High chairs for babies, helium-filled balloons and a special kids' menu take the pain from eating out with young children.

Customer and staff loyalty is phenomenally high for the catering and restaurant industry. The whole themed concept is very much a carousel (a merry-go-round) which goes faster and faster as the night goes on, with both staff and customers living on adrenalin and the TGI brand of excitement. Regular visitors to Friday's talk about the Friday's experience – a mix of buzzing atmosphere, flamboyant décor and friendly staff, with a real will to please. Central to the Friday's concept is its emphasis on guest satisfaction. The staff treat guests as if they were valued visitors to their own homes. They are met at the door with a warm welcome and accompanied to their table in a true Friday's frenetic, good-humoured style.

The media has not been slow to recognise the unique proposition offered by Friday's. From Bruce Forsyth's *Generation Game* on BBC television and from the Dutch equivalent, to a BBC 2 *Business Matters* feature on staff training, to Children's TV *Motormouth* and to *Daytime UK*, most facets of the Friday's experience and company philosophy have been dissected, analysed, shown up to the public for inspection, and passed with flying colours. The expert bar staff were employed to train Tom Cruise for his exploits behind the bar in the film *Cocktail*. The company now sponsors a regular National Bar Tender of the Year competition, which featured prominently on BBC TV's *The Wogan Show*.

WHAT NEXT?

Friday's has its critics. Not everyone wants to eat in the middle of a circus. No matter how good the management and quality control, sometimes the guests may be disappointed. Success and popularity also bring the occasional queue and delay. However, the management philosophy is unbending, believing that there is an equal partnership at stake between the three components or elements of business success: the guest (the customer), the employee, and the company. This, Friday's coins the Triangle Theory – there must be an equal balance between guests, employees and the company, and if the balance and status quo are disturbed, the success of the company will be put in jeopardy. No single element must become dominant, nor must one component weaken.

The company is aware of the need to move forwards. New openings are planned in order to take the concept to new geographical markets. Whitbread holds the franchise for countries outside of the UK and is considering developing these options further. There is a regular programme of customer analysis and collection of customer thoughts and perceptions, all of which are fed into the on-going and evolving development of the TGI Friday's concept and business strategy. There will be change, but it will be carefully controlled and it will be 'Friday's change'.

BUT THEN CAME THE IMITATORS ...

As with any good product or service concept, in any market, if it is seen to be successful it will be copied. The financial investment in developing the brand, the product proposition, in attaining and developing sites, in training and motivating staff, in promoting and controlling the brand concept, is costly. Trade name and identity can be legally protected. There are, though, relatively no barriers to entry – except financial and human resources – for potential copycat competitors. In the UK there is already a host of direct rivals, ranging from the US-sourced Calendars and Old Orleans, to Mamma Bell's Mexican restaurants and various one-off locally focused rivals.

In many ways, Friday's has been a victim of its own success. Because of its commitments to training and authentically sourced artefacts for its restaurants, plus its desire for carefully selected sites, it has not been able to expand nationally perhaps as quickly as Whitbread may have desired. Where branches have opened, the impact on the local customer base has been dramatic with high footfall and terrific brand loyalty. However, this clear success has inspired many national and local rival restaurant operators to target this new market, which in many ways has been created by Friday's: a market which no longer is associated with the traditional steakhouse offering, pub grub, or fastfood snack.

So where does Friday's go from here? How can it maintain its quality, continue to motivate its staff, keep fresh its ideas both within its own organisation and with its exterior face as presented to its target audience? How can it successfully fend off the burgeoning number of direct rivals? Indeed, in a recession-hit UK economy in the early 1990s, with vastly reduced disposable income, less day-tripping, fewer holidays and vacations, and less money being spent on eating out, the restaurant sector in general is much more competitive and cut-throat than in the buoyant late 1980s when Friday's first entered the UK market. As a concept, Friday's has been highly successful. Financially, for Whitbread, the company has contributed significantly right from its first year of operation to the parent company's fortunes. There is little doubt that the first decade for Friday's in the UK will bring great success, but as with any service business it is difficult to expand and develop on success which is people and 'experience' based, while maintaining costs, controlling standards, and staying ahead of the competition.

Table 12.2 Restaurants – share by type

	%
Pubs (bars), clubs, wine bars	40
Hotel restaurants	17
Up-market eateries	6
Mid-market chains	19
Owner-run	15
Roadside	3

Source: Dibb, S., Simkin, L., Pride, W. and Ferrell, O.C. (1991) *Marketing: Concepts and Strategies*, Boston: Houghton Mifflin

Table 12.3 Frequency of visiting a restaurant, 1991

	Daytime	Evening
More than once a day	1.4	0.7
Once a week	2.8	1.7
2 or 3 times a month	6.1	6.4
Once a month	9.0	12.0
Less than once a month	22.1	33.8
Total (excluding 'Don't know')	41.4%	54.6%
Total visitors	47.6%	62.3%
Total non-visitors	52.4%	37.7%

Source: Target Group Index/BMRB, 1991

ISSUES

Services marketing is different partly because of the intangibility of the product and the extended marketing mix, particularly the role of personnel. These differences are well illustrated with TGI Friday's.

Intangibility of the product

For TGI Friday's what is the product: the drinks, the food, the atmosphere, the people or simply the overall experience? How difficult is it for Whitbread to create a differential advantage? Can this differential advantage be sustained?

Customer targets

TGI Friday's is a carefully honed concept, targeted at specific groups of customers. Who are they? What influences their choice of restaurant?

Promotional strategy

There are only 10 TGI Friday's in the UK. Promotional budgets are relatively limited. What is the promotional strategy adopted by management? Which are the main elements of the promotional mix? Should these priorities be any different? Against whom or what is Friday's competing?

THEORY NOTES

Chapter 29, Services marketing, pp. 231–4
Chapter 20, Consumer and organisational buyer behaviour, pp. 165–72
Chapter 28, Marketing communications, pp. 224–30

Chapter 13

Kodak Norge
The search for information

Kodak Norge AS (Kodak Norway Ltd) represents the face of the Eastman Kodak Company in Norway. More specifically, it is a wholly owned subsidiary of the large, US-based multi-national. Established in 1969, Kodak Norge splits its sales effort into three divisions: consumer products, industrial and commercial, and copy products. Through the divisions, the company offers many Kodak-branded lines including photographic film for slides, prints and films through to cameras, copy products, business-imaging services and film processing.

In consumer photoproducts, Kodak Norge is dominant with a 50 per cent share of the market. However, since the 1960s the company's market share has declined from an overwhelming 90 per cent, with Swedish companies taking more than 30 per cent of the processing market. During this period, key competitor Fuji was successful in entering the Norwegian film market. Today, Fuji is Kodak Norge's most aggressive competitor, accounting for around one-third of the film market. Management now believes that relatively sluggish reactions to changes in customer needs, particularly in the industrial and commercial sector, were partly to blame for this dramatic downturn in Kodak's fortunes.

As well as Fuji, Kodak Norge faces keen competition for graphic arts materials and professional films from Agfa. The Norwegian photo-processing market, attracting prices which currently are 15–20 per cent higher than the rest of Europe, is highly competitive, with local companies capitalising on the multi-nationals' premium prices by offering heavy discounts.

CUSTOMERS AND MARKET SEGMENTS

For Kodak Norge, the retailers of film and cheap cameras are key customers. The average consumer of photographic products, the 'snap-shooter', is seen as a relatively unsophisticated buyer, purchasing film products on impulse from petrol stations, hotel shops and a variety of leisure attractions. Kodak managers believe that the consumer does not differentiate much between different brands, buying the most readily available product. The key for Kodak Norge is to achieve as much shelf space as possible in these outlets.

In the photographic products market, segmentation has evolved at two levels: consumers and distributors. Perhaps most importantly, Eastman Kodak and its subsidiaries must understand thoroughly the requirements of consumers who use photographic products, enabling the company to consider the value of various segmentation schemes. For instance, Eastman Kodak currently groups consumers according to patterns of product usage: snapshooters, keen amateurs and professionals. These consumer groups are served by ranges of different quality and specification film products. In addition to segmentation at the consumer level, players in this market need to decide how best to segment and service the needs of distributors.

Managers at Kodak Norge have found that segmenting according to distribution channel has been an effective approach to follow in the Norwegian market. This involves servicing photodealer shops directly while supplying Kodak's distributors through wholesalers. In this respect Kodak Norge is in a stronger position than Fuji, which has only 20 employees in Norway and lacks distribution outside of the photodealers.

MARKETING RESEARCH

Each sales division is required to estimate its share of key markets and also highlight those areas where sales performance is weak. Management at Kodak Norge obtains market and customer information from both internal and external sources. Individuals within the company have responsibility for tracking aspects of the marketing environment, for example checking on the likely impact of any legislative changes. External information comes from government statistics, distributors and marketing research agencies, such as Nielsen. The focus for this external data is on market trends, such as ownership patterns of photographic equipment or consumer leisure activities, rather than individual consumer requirements.

Despite the existing research there is concern in the company (a concern echoed by most 'tuned in' companies) that efforts must be maintained to understand consumer needs and attitudes. For instance, how do consumers select their film products and what factors influence the choices which they make? How do consumers spend their leisure time and what role does photography play in it? What is the buying process like for company purchasers and what particular needs do they have? Quality information on these and a host of related issues is seen as vital to the development of effective marketing programmes. Competitor research must also be continually updated for Kodak Norge to make informed judgements about targeting and refine its product positioning so that a clear and sustainable competitive advantage can be ensured in its key markets. Kodak's position has been eroded, partly perhaps because insufficient information meant that management did not totally keep abreast of consumer and competitor activities and trends.

In order to plan future marketing research efforts, management at Kodak Norge must consider its information requirements and priorities. These priorities must then be satisfied using appropriate research techniques and data collection methods. Any survey – sample base, issues and material – must be carefully designed with specific targets in mind and the most suitable method for conducting the research selected. Analysis of resulting data and implementation of findings must also be planned in advance to ensure that the results are used to the maximum.

ISSUES

Kodak Norge, in common with many companies, believes it has an incomplete marketing information system and inadequate marketing intelligence. The company is highly successful but faces strong international and local competition. It is particularly important for Kodak Norge to understand its market segments and to control effectively its marketing channels.

Marketing research

What are Kodak Norge's marketing research needs? Which are the most appropriate research tools? Why?

Segmentation

What are the key market segments available to Kodak Norge? On what basis are these segments identified? Could a different approach to segmenting this market be adopted? How and why?

Channels

Kodak worldwide understands the importance of choosing effective marketing channels, and the need to control and assist its intermediaries. What are the main marketing channels in this market? How can Kodak Norge exert influence over them? Why is it important for such a major branded manufacturer to control its marketing channels?

THEORY NOTES

Chapter 21, Marketing research, pp. 173–80
Chapter 23, Market segmentation, targeting, positioning, pp. 189–96
Chapter 26, Distribution/marketing channels, pp. 214–18

Chapter 14

JCB

The backhoe digger – internationally into the dictionary

A small lock-up garage in rural Staffordshire producing farm vehicles from war-time scrap metal has grown into what is today a manufacturing and marketing success on a global scale. JCB's award-winning, fully landscaped modern production facilities continually set industry standards – as do the company's products. The company's founder is still at the forefront of product development and technical innovation, and the Bamford family controls one of the UK's main privately-owned companies. Continued growth is typified by the story of the backhoe digger and the reputation of a brand name now part of everyday language. As humorist Miles Kington of *The Independent* newspaper has written:

> I don't suppose the marketing managers of the Roman Empire ever sat down one day and worked out a snappy set of initials, then did some market research on it to see if it was going down well with the people they had just conquered. They just had SPQR on their plates and used it. A bit like JCB. If the man behind JCB had not been called Joseph Cyril Bamford, but something like Patrick James Walker, we would now be saying: 'Look at all those PJWs – they must be building a new road', or, 'Sorry I'm late – I was stuck behind a bloody PJW for five miles down a B road', or, 'Pardon, mais ma voiture fut attrapée derrière un sacré PJW pendant des heures'.

JCB, the UK construction and agricultural equipment manufacturer, breaks several rules. In the dictionary, 'JCB' is virtually defined as the generic term for the backhoe digger, irrespective of the manufacturer. As a middle-sized player in a highly competitive market dominated by US giants Caterpillar and Case, plus Japanese challengers Komatsu, the Staffordshire company bucked the economic recession of the early 1990s. Profits dipped from 1989's record £50 million on turnover of £460 million, but the company remained profitable in a period when US rivals reported losses ranging from $200 million to $800 million. With turnover close to £400 million, JCB is the market leader in Europe, and for several core products dominates markets from Israel to India, from North America to Nigeria.

According to management writer Robert Heller, 'JC Bamford, a very British company, is also devotedly international in two powerful senses. In the worldwide spread of its bright yellow machines to 140 different countries, and in its methods. Design-led, aggressively innovative, progressive in its manufacturing and European in its thinking. JCB has consistently raised its global market share in the teeth of world-class competition, while averaging high profitability over a sustained period.'

1945 – JCB founded by Joseph Cyril Bamford in a lock-up garage in Uttoxeter, producing farm machinery from war-time scrap metal.

1953 – First JCB Mark 1 backhoe loader launched onto the UK market.

1970 – First of seven Queen's Awards, five of which were for export achievement.

1973 – First of four Design Council Awards for technological design.

1977 – The trend-setting JCB 520 telescopic handler introduced.

1979 – Royal Society of Arts, Presidential Award for consistently distinguished design.

1980 – 3CX backhoe loader launched, taking JCB's world market share from 12% to 25%.

1985 – British Quality Award for product design and quality assurance.

1988 – JCB 801 mini-excavator launched, achieving 10% market share in its first year.

1990 – JCB 2CX compact backhoe loader launched, creating a significant new market.

1991 – JCB Fastrac/high mobility vehicle introduced, yet again setting new standards in performance and operator comport.

1991 – 4CX 4×4×4 high productivity backhoe loader launched, bringing innovative four-wheel steer to add to market supremacy.

1991 – 3CX 4×4 backhoe loader introduced, described by many as the formula for the 1990s.

1991 – The fruits of a joint venture with Japan's Sumitomo led to the 1992 successful launch of a new generation of crawler excavators, catapulting JCB into joint UK market leadership.

1993 – Further range extensions enabled JCB to more comprehensively enter the compact equipment market with a single-arm range of skid steers.

1993 – Europe's leading range of telescopic handlers extended and re-launched.

Figure 14.1 Milestones in the history of JCB

Source: *The JCB Experience*/JCB, 1992

HUGE MARKET

Worldwide the construction equipment industry is huge with sales close to $50 billion. The US giant Caterpillar tends to concentrate on the very large earthmoving and construction equipment. Similarly, the Japanese players such as Komatsu (number two worldwide to Caterpillar) and Hitachi compete for sales of the larger machines. JCB, however, dominates the middle ground, avoiding most small tools and heavy earthmoving equipment. The backhoe common to most construction sites, road works, many farms and traffic jams, is the company's staple product.

The company has over 20 per cent of the world's and close to 40 per cent of Europe's backhoe market, led by constant mechanical innovation and improved driver comfort: Case, Ford, Massey Ferguson all trail behind JCB. The JCB brand name is synonymous with this product, often being used as a generic term for the backhoe digger in the industry. Nevertheless, JCB is very much a growing company and the backhoe is only one of six core product areas. More are being added, based on thorough market opportunity analysis, comprehensive marketing planning and product innovation.

Articulated dump trucks	Asphalt finishers
Backhoe loaders[‡*]	Crawler dozers
Crawler excavators[†*]	Crawler loaders
Fork lifts	Mini-excavators[†*]
Motor graders	Motor scrapers
Rigid dump trucks	Rough terrain fork lift trucks[*]
Skid steer loaders[†*]	Tractors
Telescopic handlers[‡*]	Wheeled crawler excavators
Wheeled loading shovels[†*]	

* = JCB's product entries
† = UK leadership for JCB
‡ = World leadership for JCB

Figure 14.2 Major product groups – construction equipment

MARKETING ETHOS

The company has six bespoke dealers with 41 outlets in the UK, with an extensive array of franchised dealers throughout the world. In addition, core overseas markets have JCB-owned subsidiaries – locally formed companies which oversee local product enhancements, supervise dealers and run marketing programmes orientated to their markets' needs; all carefully orchestrated from the company's Staffordshire (UK) base. Here there are four core operations: JCB Sales handling marketing, planning, sales, dealer strategies; JCB Service orientated to product support and dealer control; Finance; and the various production units.

From once being product or technical innovation led, to becoming sales led, the company now benefits from a carefully integrated sales and marketing function which liaises closely with the production, finance and service functions. The air of 'entrepreneurial flair' still exists, but now is supported with a host of management skills which have together allowed a family-run business to more than adequately compete with the world's major construction and agricultural equipment manufacturers.

MARKETING PLANNING

Planning and analysis have enabled JCB's marketers to better understand their marketplace. The company has invested heavily in researching its core customer groups throughout Europe, utilising well the strengths of its subsidiaries' personnel in the field. Extensive evaluations of competitors' strengths and weaknesses, their competitive positions and likely strategies have led JCB to pre-empt successfully competitors' thrusts and to establish new product launches in target markets very quickly.

For backhoes, too, there have been lessons from this strategic marketing planning. For example, the indigenous Italian manufacturer FAI (partly owned by Japan's Komatsu) is strong only in its home market and poses a genuine threat in Italy, requiring a different set of tactics to those employed, for example, in the UK. The German construction industry has never really used backhoes, preferring instead larger excavators or smaller compact equipment. The opportunities presented by the united Germany and beckoning Eastern European markets, however, have led JCB to develop this market. For backhoes the Scandinavian market is small and sluggish, reflecting local cultural and competitive characteristics not common to the rest of Europe, but presenting a different set of marketing challenges.

VARIED CUSTOMERS IN A TURBULENT ENVIRONMENT

The market is highly competitive, and currently the victim of economic recession. Civil engineering projects are failing to find adequate financial backing, governments are suspending capital expenditure and halting infrastructure improvements, and housebuilding in the UK alone has declined to the extent that 50,000 construction workers lost their jobs in 1992. Lower numbers of new housing starts have a significant, harmful impact on the market. The purchase of equipment costing anything from £5,000 to £150,000 leads to prudent spending by purchasers, particularly in an economic recession. Product reliability, length of service, versatility in operation, residual operating values when re-sold/replaced, all become crucial issues to the operators of such equipment.

These customers range from owner-operator 'one-man' companies, to multi-depot plant/tool hirers, to large construction and extractive companies/contractors (ARC or Wimpey, for example) which own/hire and operate dozens of machines sourced typically from a variety of manufacturers and plant hirers/contractors.

Selling to the one-person owner-operator is not easy: a high retail price is a real obstacle; access is difficult as generally these customers are out on a job, rather than conveniently in an office; and their business acumen/sophistication is often limited. Potential profit rewards, though, are very good. The plant and tool hirers, on the other hand, do not use the equipment themselves, but their customers do. These renters/hirers often have little direct experience of the product or the different manufacturers' offerings: they are steered by the plant hire depot personnel's recommendations. At the other extreme, the large construction companies such as Tarmac or Wimpey both own and hire-in equipment. They purchase from various dealers and manufacturers. These companies may have well-defined purchasing routines and even specialist purchasing managers. The driver or operator is unlikely to be the purchase decision-maker or the budget holder in such organisations.

Plant hire	Tool hire
Extraction (mining/quarrying)	House building
Civil engineering	Agriculture
Contractors	Earthmoving
Landscaping	Waste disposal
Public utilities	Local authorities
Manufacturing	Industrial services

Figure 14.3 Key customer sectors – construction equipment

THE BACKHOE LOADER (DIGGER)

JCB's first backhoe was launched by Joe Bamford in 1953. Since the 1950s, most rivals in the manufacture of construction or agricultural equipment have produced copycat machines. Companies from Ford (5 per cent of the market) to Case, from Massey Ferguson (9 per cent) to Volvo have attempted to feed from a market created by JCB, now estimated to be worth £1,500 million worldwide, and £720 million within Europe. Despite this competition, JCB accounts for nearly 60 per cent of the near 2,500 annual backhoe sales in the UK, and for approximately 40 per cent of sales within Europe. Even the giant Caterpillar's share has declined, to 7 per cent. But the company now also competes in most sectors of the market: crawler excavators, wheeled loading shovels, telehandlers, tractors, mini-excavators, backhoe diggers, and from 1993 skid steers. Although successful in other product areas, the bulk of the company's success stems from its domination of the backhoe market.

JCB's key backhoe strengths are:

- the JCB brand name
- product awareness
- media domination within the category
- technology leadership
- product design and innovation
- coverage with distributor outlets/salesforce

Such market domination has not allowed the company to sit back. The 3CX (the traditional digger common to most building sites) had been the staple product. By the end of 1991, JCB had a range including the smaller, more manoeuvrable and versatile 2CX, supported by the larger and more powerful 4CX. The company had introduced the concept of four-wheel drive years earlier with great success. In 1991 it caught the competition napping by bringing on stream the 4×4×4 version of the 4CX model range: four equally sized wheels, four-wheel drive, plus four-wheel steering. With the promotional catchline of 'JCB. The formula for the 90s', the company had moved the backhoe into a new generation. One major competitor pulled out of backhoe production, while the others could only look on with resentful admiration.

Simultaneously, work continued to boost performance levels across the range, to enter unrealised markets, develop derivatives for specialist applications – particularly in the undeveloped German market – improve driver comfort and safety with air conditioning, greater sound proofing, and stronger, more durable cabs. JCB is highly aware of the growing concern for the environment. Biodegradable oils, lower noise levels, recyclable components (similar to BMW's actions in the car market), plus training literature and videos for operators are all integral to the overall product offering.

BACKHOE LAUNCHES IN THE 1990s

The backhoe loader is JCB's core product. The 3CX used to account for 60 per cent of the company's volume sales. As the *Financial Times* pointed out at the 1991 launch of the replacement 3CX, the event was in earth-moving circles as important as an innovative new product launch from a German or Japanese car manufacturer. As creator and brand leader of the world's backhoe market, the whole industry was primed with a sense of expectancy.

JCB had extended the versatility of its backhoe digger range with the introduction in 1990 of the smaller and more manoeuvrable 2CX. The competition thought that was the only newcomer for a while: after all, JCB had not introduced new backhoe models since 1980. In the summer of 1991, 300 dealers from around the world were flown into JCB's trend-setting headquarters. Along with representatives of the world's press, they were wowed first with the new, high-powered, technologically advanced 3CX. This was no model re-vamp: the new 3CX was a totally new design, extending the generic parameters for the whole industry. Audiences at the launch shows were visibly impressed. The revised 2CX then appeared, emphasising the newly extended range. To steal the show, and to truly dazzle the audiences, however, JCB had an ace still to play. On to the dry-iced and laser-decked stage came a third model: the 4CX. To complete the demolition of the competition, the company added 4×4×4 as its differential advantage – a technological breakthrough few other competitors had the resources to match for several years.

The launch was carefully planned. Catching competitors unawares because of 1990's 2CX launch, JCB's marketing director employed a well-orchestrated selection of promotional tools to gain maximum impact.

As indicated in Table 14.1, the trade press was used for an extensive advertising campaign, running over five months in the key titles. This UK campaign was replicated by JCB subsidiaries worldwide. Public relations, though, was the key tactic employed. The launch attracted terrific media attention, ranging from TV and radio interviews with Chairman Sir Anthony Bamford to in-depth features running over several pages in all of the specialist publications. National newspapers and local press were equally keen to give coverage to such a spectacular launch for such an important UK manufacturer. Press days were held at the Rocester head-quarters, main dealers, and at the main construction and agricultural trade shows such as England's SED construction fair, the Royal Agricultural Society of England's Royal Show, and Germany's massive Bauma festival.

The attention devoted to external target audiences did not detract from the effort intended to inform and encourage JCB's own personnel. Dealer training was fundamental given the technical enhancements to the backhoe product, but it became part of the morale-boosting fanfare surrounding the launch. Every few days for two weeks, international dealers and their personnel were flown in on chartered aircraft to London and East Midlands airports; over 1,000 visitors. They witnessed stage shows with simultaneous multi-lingual translation, lighting rigs and stage effects to shame many pop stars, plus fact-finding sessions and full product training. A huge investment, but anyone witnessing the buzz and excitement, the belief in the new models and JCB, would have found the expense difficult to fault. The show was also staged for the company's shop floor workers, creating equal excitement and commitment for the products and company.

The result was that in certain countries, JCB's market share doubled.

Table 14.1 Backhoe launch media schedule, UK, 1991

Journal	No. of insertions	Size	Position	August	September	October	November	December
							Insertion dates	
Construction News	1	5 × A4 teaser	Consecutive R.H. pages	29				
	2	6-page insert	Centre Spread		5, 12			
	9	Double page spread	Centre Spread		19	3, 17 31	7, 14 28	5, 19
Contract Journal	1	5 × A4 teaser	Consecutive R.H. pages	29				
	2	6-page insert	Early		5, 19			
	7	Double page spread	Early		26	3, 10 24	14, 21	19
Plant Managers' Journal	1	6-page insert	Early		•			
	3	Double page spread	Early			•	•	•

Source: JCB

The company more than dominates the bulk of its European markets, gaining the majority of sales in core markets in the UK and northern Europe. Sales of backhoes gained heavily, too, in North America, Africa, India, Israel and South East Asia. The new range had cost JCB £25 million in development and engineering costs, with nearly £5 million for new production lines, and £0.5 million on marketing launch expenses. With the company's overall market share in Europe climbing by close to 5 per cent and nearing the 40 per cent mark, the company's investment in backhoe developments and the introduction of other new ranges had paid off. There were short-term rewards, but also the creation of an enviable competitive positioning as market leader in Europe, posing a significant threat to the US and Japanese construction equipment giants.

1992's launch of the new crawler excavators, the result of a joint venture with Sumitomo of Japan, built on the success of 1991's backhoe launches. The venue for the equally slick and sensational launch this time around was Faro in southern Portugal, with dealers and press flying in from around the globe. Already, this new range – still far from complete – has increased JCB's crawler excavator market share by over 100 per cent, causing the market leaders Komatsu and Hitachi to take evasive action. In 1993 it was the turn of the more compact end of the construction equipment market. Joining JCB's mini-excavator range came the innovative range of single arm skid steers – the safest and most environmentally friendly on the market – to create JCB's new Compact Division.

WHAT NEXT?

JCB has been one of the UK's most successful privately owned companies. Despite its relatively limited resource base, the company has given its multi-national US and Japanese rivals severe problems. During the recession in the early 1990s, JCB is virtually alone in its industry in trading profitably. The marketing ethos has helped the company to stay ahead in its core markets: new product development which has innovated and grown markets, prudent target marketing to identify lucrative core customer sectors, and a commitment to dealer and customer service. The brand is in the dictionary. It and the famous yellow paintwork are synonymous with technical expertise, design and effective marketing. The company's success has, however, brought it increasingly to the attention of its global rivals, many of which dwarf JCB. The first half century has been an unqualified success. The future is a little more uncertain. JCB is a highly successful middle-sized player in a recession-hit market with brooding competing giants.

Table 14.2 Major European manufacturers of construction equipment

Caterpillar (parent USA), Belgium
Manufacturer of earthmoving machinery, excavators, diesel engines and wheeled loaders.

Sales (BF 000)	32,980,000 (1988)
Employees	5,100

Komatsu Europe (parent Japan), Belgium
Assembly, sale and marketing, importation of earthmoving equipment and related parts.

Sales (BF 000)	15,160,161 (1988)
	9,109,670 (1987)
Pre-tax profit (BF 000)	97,964 (1988)
	5,707 (1987)
After-tax profit (BF 000)	8,555 (1988)
	2,872 (1987)
Employees	160

Case Poclain (93% parent USA), France
Manufacture and assembly of construction equipment and agricultural machinery: hydraulic excavators and mobile cranes.

Sales (FF 000)	6,007,000 (1988)
	4,737,450 (1987)
Profit after tax (FF 000)	102,000 (1988)
	−128,744 (1987)
Employees	5,892

Liebherr, France (Swiss-based parent)
Manufacture of hydraulic excavators, re-sale of concrete mixers, earthmoving equipment and cranes.

Sales (FF 000)	2,026,000 (1988)
Profit after tax (FF 000)	37,000 (1988)
Employees	1,162

Atlas Weyhausen, Germany
Hydraulic excavators, loaders, truck-handling cranes.

Sales (DM 000)	420,000 (1989)
	370,000 (1988)
Employees	1,960

Case (USA parent), Germany
Manufacture of construction equipment.

Sales (DM 000)	560,000 (1989)
Employees	2,400

Hanomag Baumaschinen, Germany
Manufacture of construction equipment, including bulldozers and loaders.

Sales (DM 000)	280,000 (1989)
Employees	1,390

Fiat SPA, Italy
Automobiles, but also agricultural tractors and machinery, construction equipment. Associated with Japan's Hitachi in the production and marketing of construction equipment.

Net sales (L m)	44,308,000 (1988)
	NB: all products, incl. cars
Employees worldwide	227,000

Fiatallis (parent Fiat), Italy
Manufacture of earthmoving and agricultural equipment.

Sales (L m)	664,000 (1987)
Employees	3,070

Source: *Major Companies of Europe*

ISSUES

The JCB story is one of success for a large, privately owned UK engineering company. The case highlights reasons for this success on an international scale, featuring JCB's branding, positioning, marketing planning and promotional strategies. The difficulties of selling and marketing in industrial markets are more than evident.

Organisational/industrial buyer behaviour

Which are the main market segments? What are their buying characteristics, processes and influences? How can these be harnessed by JCB's sales and marketing activities?

Branding, product management and positioning

How important to JCB is the strength of its brand? How does the brand assist the company's marketing programmes? What is the positioning of the brand? How can this be maintained?

Promotional strategy

What are the principal promotional tools in industrial marketing? Which form the basis for JCB's work? What could be done additionally or differently?

Marketing planning

What is the main focus of effective marketing planning? How does JCB use the marketing planning process? What are likely to be the benefits of marketing planning to JCB? What problems in planning are to be encountered?

International marketing

How has JCB coped in its international markets? How has its growing presence outside of the UK altered its strategy and marketing programmes? What are the main considerations when adopting an international marketing strategy?

THEORY NOTES

Chapter 20, Consumer and organisational buyer behaviour, pp. 165–72
Chapter 25, Products and product management [branding], pp. 205–13
Chapter 28, Marketing communications, pp. 224–30
Chapter 31, Marketing planning, pp. 239–45
Chapter 32, International marketing, pp. 246–51

Chapter 15

ABN AMRO Bank
Global strengths, regional necessities

THE MERGER

On 22 September 1991 the merger between Algemene Bank Nederland NV (ABN) and Amsterdam-Rotterdam Bank NV (AMRO) was finalised, creating ABN AMRO Bank NV. The merger of these two largest Dutch banks created the dominant financial institution in the Netherlands, with a total market share of 50 per cent in the corporate sector and 33 per cent in the Dutch securities market. With assets of over Dfl 430 billion, the new bank is the seventh largest in Europe and the 18th in worldwide rankings. The leading financial magazine *Institutional Investor* believed each bank had core business strengths which complemented each other's. ABN was a solid, well-organised retail bank with a prestigious network of branches worldwide. AMRO had a smaller international presence but controlled 40 per cent of the Dutch corporate market, and was known to be a pre-eminent merchant bank with a strong marketing division. AMRO's bankers were described as aggressive, 'street fighters', whereas ABN was seen to be more of a 'gentlemen's club'.

Any merger of such large, established companies with differing management styles would lead to some resentment from the senior managers and employees. This merger was no different; many senior managers left the company as they jockeyed for positions in the new organisation. Theodorus Meys, a senior director, explained: 'Everyone expected the AMRO people to dominate but that hasn't happened. ABN got a lot more out of the deal, perhaps because ABN was more organised.' Nevertheless, despite early teething problems, the merger has been voted a success by the Dutch business press. The new bank has a unified front in a relatively short space of time. This easy transition has been helped by the two senior chairmen of the original banks; colleagues sharing a common goal.

Discussions about a possible merger started between Robertus Hazelhoff, ABN's chairman, and Roelof Nelissen, AMRO's chairman, shortly after AMRO's plans to merge with Generale de Banque failed in 1990. Talks between these two men were kept a tightly guarded secret, often taking place at each other's homes. 'In a couple of nights, we had decided everything – including who would be chairman for the first two years and who would take over for the next two years,' says Hazelhoff. Nelissen became the first chairman of ABN AMRO Bank, concentrating on the internal restructuring necessary with the merger, leaving Hazelhoff to consider the more strategic aspects of the new bank's position in its marketplace. Hazelhoff's priority was to show ABN AMRO to be a genuinely global concern, with a worldwide standing.

STRUCTURE OF THE NEW BANK

The two banks, now joined as ABN AMRO, had to consolidate their systems, customer databases, market segments, management and organisations. Figure 15.1 illustrates the newly devised management structure. The new structure principally has three core divisions: domestic, investment banking and global clients, and international.

	Chairman	*Vice Chairman*	
Domestic Division	*International Division*		*Investment Banking and Global Clients Division*

Wholesale banking
Electronic banking
Payment services
Domestic branch
  network
Consumer banking
	International branch
	  network
	– Europe
	– N. America, Central
	  and S. America,
	  Middle and Far East,
	  Africa
			Trading
			Sales
			New issues, corporate
			  finance and venture
			  capital
			Global clients
			Asset management and
			  trusts

Credit Division	*Personnel Division*	*Automation Division*	*Central Services and Policy Support Division*

Domestic credit
Foreign credit
			Application
			  systems
			Computers and
			  networks

Figure 15.1 Divisional structure of ABN AMRO
Source: ABN AMRO Bank Annual Report and Accounts, 1991

Domestic division

This core division which focuses on the home market in the Netherlands is organised on the basis of different key customer groups, enabling the bank's specialist staff to target each group separately with different products and services. Primarily there are seven core groups of customers, which are in two operating divisions:

1 *Wholesale banking*, focusing on small and medium-sized businesses, corporations, global clients and public authorities.
2 *Consumer banking*, concentrating on personal customers, affluent personal customers, and private banking.

Within these different categories, operational managers further segment each customer group, classifying for example personal customers as students, senior citizens, home-owners, or by affluence.

In the domestic division, ABN AMRO has market domination with a 50 per cent market share, due partly to its extensive branch network. However, other banks are targeting these customer groups. Rabobank, the number two bank in the Netherlands, has broken from its traditional agricultural basis and expanded into the very profitable wholesale banking market. Wouter Kolff, an ABN career banker who had left during the merger period, heads the newly restructured corporate finance division at Rabobank. His stated aims are to compete in the capital markets, mergers and acquisitions businesses and to be active all over Europe in the corporate sector, competing with ABN AMRO head-on.

ABN AMRO's share of personal customers (the retail market) lagged behind both Rabobank and NMB-Postbank which had extensive domestic networks, but lacked the international presence. ABN AMRO, therefore, has embarked on an extensive opening programme of new branches, introducing more ATMs (automated teller machines), with a newly developed corporate image making the bank seem more accessible to personal banking customers. Restructured marketing activity, with new databases, has given more attention to better targeting of specific groups, such as students, the medical sector, and the private affluent (very wealthy) customer segments.

Investment banking and global clients division

Prior to the merger AMRO had developed a *global clients* approach, which after the merger was adopted by the unified bank. This co-ordinates relationships with clients all over the world from ABN AMRO's central base at Amsterdam. A key function is to act as an intermediary between global clients and more specialist divisions within the bank. The organisation is structured on regional lines, with the exception of groups specialising in particular industries. The bank is aiming to foster these global relationships primarily by providing an extensive and superior range of products and services, such as project finance, export finance, aerospace finance and syndication departments.

Investment banking in ABN AMRO covers a wide range of customer groups and products, but the focus is to offer specific corporate finance facilities such as:

- New issues (shares, bonds)
- Trading (currencies)
- Corporate finance (mergers and acquisitions)
- Venture capital (equity and debt financing)
- Emerging capital markets (e.g. Far East, Eastern Europe)
- International private banking
- Global custody (dividends, safe-keeping of securities)
- Asset management

International division

The international arena is one of ABN AMRO's core areas of interest, with distinct advantages over many European rivals. There are 400 branches in 51 countries outside the Netherlands, allowing ABN AMRO to provide clients with a finely meshed banking network unrivalled by most competitors. The global network is of strategic importance to the bank, enabling it to provide the highest standard of service direct to local and international customers alike. The international service, though, is targeted mainly at business customers and affluent personal customers. The geographic spread of the network is directly related to the historical development of the bank, being strong in Europe and Asia. Recent acquisitions have been in North America, such as LaSalle National Corporation of Illinois. As Table 15.1 reveals, though, Western Europe still provides the major business of the international division.

With the view to EC deregulation in 1992, every effort was made to simplify and hasten cross-border payments within the Community; to give advice on business practices in neighbouring countries and advice to clients on the establishment of foreign subsidiaries. ABN AMRO combined has a strong presence in Eire and the UK. ABN Deutschland and AMRO Handelsbank have been merged to form one operation in Germany, but in France the existing trading entities have been kept separate because of strong customer loyalty: Banque NSM and ABN AMRO. The unified ABN AMRO has retained its market leadership in diamond financing with a market share (worldwide) of 30 per cent, focused principally on its Antwerp operation. The new group is one of the largest foreign banks in Switzerland, specialising in asset management. A sub-

Table 15.1 Geographical analysis of lending, for the international division, ABN AMRO Bank

| | Dfl bn | | |
	1991	*1990*	*% change*
Europe	38.8	35.4	10
N. America	29.7	28.1	6
Middle East & Africa	0.7	0.6	17
Asia & Australia	13.9	13.3	5
Central & S. America	2.4	2.1	14
Total	85.5	79.5	Av. 8%

Source: ABN AMRO Bank annual report, 1991

sidiary based in Vienna concentrates on the newly emerging markets in Eastern Europe, offering advice on financing for the privatisation of state operations and joint venture activities.

Operations in South America have continued under the name Banco Holandes Unido, mainly in Brazil and Argentina. Activities in the Middle East were severely hit by the Gulf War, although, with the end of the war, the Middle East is seen as an area for expansion, along with the Far East and Australia.

THE NEW STRATEGY

By 1992 the integration process was over, with branches, administration and systems consolidated. The bank's senior managers genuinely believe they are part of a global bank, simply enhanced by the merger. They do not see themselves as a Dutch-based bank, or even a multinational bank, but feel they operate on a truly global scale with no single ties to one nation or region. English had been established as the corporate language in the bank so that management in all countries can share information opportunities. The style of the bank is to the fore: a strong sense of direction coming from the corporate headquarters in Amsterdam, with each division and each national network having a strong degree of autonomy, led primarily by 'home-grown' senior managers who have progressed through the ranks. This has created a strong corporate culture and sense of belonging, but with little resentment of head office directives.

Although the chairman and senior directors feel the bank is a global player, some analysts and investors still believe ABN AMRO to be a large bank based in the Netherlands rather than a world bank. ABN AMRO will need to change perceptions held by certain sectors of the business community and journalists.

The bank has not entered new financial centres or areas of operation without a clear expectation of long-term benefit. Short termism is not part of the bank's philosophy. There is a stated belief that there has to be the opportunity to utilise its international strengths with a strong local understanding for ABN AMRO to build a presence in a particular country or industrial sector, taking into account the specific cultural needs and operations of the market. This is in direct contrast to the majority of international banks whose aim seems to be to 'cherry-pick' markets and customers, providing unlimited services to limited numbers of key, highly profitable customers. ABN AMRO's commitment to the long term is perhaps unusual. It necessitates the establishment of strong local banking capabilities and networks, and heavy capital outlay.

Within this semi-autonomous system is *global relationship management*, designed to identify 'global' customers – servicing their needs from head office, but linking various networks and branches as relevant. At a local level, though, branches are given autonomy to try to identify those market segments for which their history and capabilities are best suited. In Switzerland, for instance, the bank's private banking customers are of key importance to the branch; whereas in Germany the corporate customer base takes priority. This, by necessity, means that each country's branch network develops its own ranges of tailored products and services designed for its own local market needs.

MARKETING STRATEGY – THE DIRECTION

ABN AMRO offers clients a range of quite varied services in many different locations across the world. Its strategy has been one of cautious expansion using the tried and tested formula of a strong local network, international capabilities, with a loose senior management structure and a great deal of autonomy for local managers – with the ultimate belief that the bank is a global operation. This has been a successful strategy, with profits of Dfl 1.5 billion in 1991. Table 15.2 sums up the financial performance for the bank.

The fundamental feature of the bank's business is its understanding that it is a service provider. As such, successful marketing strategy has to take account of the very different nature of a service organisation. *Internal marketing* and *interactive marketing* are central themes. Internal marketing describes the work done by the company to motivate its staff to deliver a consistent and superior service. The bank believes it is only as good as its people – those individuals who, to many customers, represent the service being provided. Interactive marketing highlights the employees' skill in handling this customer contact.

There is the belief that the bank is international, but the provision of local autonomy helps to motivate staff and enable them to perform and feel rewarded for their work. Managers, tending to be home-grown, see career

Table 15.2 Financial data for ABN AMRO Bank

Consolidated balance sheet of ABN AMRO Bank NV (Dfl billion), year end 31 December

	1991	1990	% change	% International 1991
Assets				
Liquid assets and investments	57.1	49.8	14.7	43
Banks	106.9	106.1	0.8	24
Public sector lending	33.4	32.4	3.1	12
Private sector lending	210.3	197.9	6.3	42
Total lending	243.7	230.3	5.8	22
Other assets	7.4	7.1	4.2	
Total assets	415.1	393.3	5.5	
Liabilities				
Group equity and subordinated loans	24.9	23.1	7.8	
Debt securities and non-subordinated loans	53.2	51.6	3.1	
Funds entrusted	218.1	209.9	3.9	
Banks and other liabilities	118.9	108.7	9.4	
Total liabilities	415.1	393.3	5.5	

Consolidated profit and loss account, ABN AMRO Bank NV (Dfl million) year end 31 December

	1991	1990	% change
Income			
Interest	7,348	6,329	16.1
Commission	2,778	2,609	6.5
Other income	1,193	1,072	11.3
Total income	11,319	10,010	13.1
Expenses			
Salaries, pension and social insurance	4,584	4,194	9.3
Other expenses	2,490	2,206	12.9
Depreciation of fixed assets	591	529	11.7
Total expenses	7,655	6,929	10.6
Gross profit	3,654	3,081	18.6
Provisions	1,320	1,200	10.0
Profit before tax	2,344	1,881	24.1
Taxation	774	489	58.3
Group profit	1,560	1,392	12.1
Third party interests			
Net profit	1,536	1,325	15.9

Sources: ABN AMRO Bank annual reports and accounts

opportunities and reasons for performing well. Head office control is kept to a minimum; only 60 staff handle 16,000 employees in the international division, keeping demotivating and irritating corporate rigidity to a minimum. At times, however, this means there is a lack of information and knowledge at head office of specific local operating characteristics and market trends.

ABN AMRO Bank – with its incremental, cautious development, long-term aims, federal structure and marketing strategy centred on service provision – has succeeded in fulfilling fundamental services marketing prerequisites. The bank has established itself in most international markets and emerged as one of the major financial organisations of the 1990s.

Much has happened in a short space of time. Two already large, successful organisations have merged. Within the strong international corporate identity and ethos, a great deal of attention has been given to allowing local managers discretion to focus on key market opportunities and customer segments. This brings its own problems, but is proving very successful in terms of profit generation for ABN AMRO. The bank has not lost sight of the importance of its people: they must be motivated to succeed and do well; similarly they must impart a professional and caring impression to their customers, be they local, private account holders, or international corporations. Whether or not this focus of thinking internationally but acting locally can be the basis for a longer-term competitive advantage remains to be seen.

ISSUES

ABN AMRO recognises, with its *internal* and *interactive marketing*, the importance of personnel and the interaction with customers in a service business. The bank has global ambitions, but has not lost sight of local needs and the importance of establishing an operating hierarchy which enables national managers to fully understand their markets.

Services marketing

What are the core aspects of ABN AMRO's marketing mix? How do these reflect the bank's provision of customer service and financial services?

International marketing and branding

ABN AMRO's federal structure is intended to encourage national managers to target local customers and their requirements more successfully than most global banking operations. Is this approach to international marketing likely to succeed? What are the advantages and possible pitfalls?

Market targeting and segmentation

The bank is prudent in its selection of customer groups to target. Which are the core market segments targeted by ABN AMRO? What are the segmentation bases used? How effective is this categorisation? How adaptive is this approach to local needs?

THEORY NOTES

Chapter 29, Services marketing, pp. 231–4
Chapter 32, International marketing, pp. 246–51
Chapter 23, Market segmentation, targeting, positioning, pp. 189–96
Chapter 18, Introduction to marketing, pp. 155–60

Chapter 16

EuroDisney
Disney into Europe

DISNEY CORPORATION

After the death of its founder, Walt Disney, in 1966, the Walt Disney Company seemed to lose its creative edge. As other studios diversified into television and video, Disney seemed content with its library of feature films and animated classics. The company was producing only three or four new movies a year, most of which failed at the box office. Disney also pulled out of television after 29 years of network programming. By the mid-1980s, Disney was dependent on theme parks and real estate development for about 75 per cent of its revenues.

Today, however, Disney executives are intent on recapturing – and building on – the old Disney magic. Company executives say the Disney name, culture, movies and library are the company's biggest resources, and Disney's plan is to simultaneously rejuvenate old assets and develop new ones. While continuing its traditional appeal to the family segment of the movie market, Disney, through its Touchstone Pictures division, is turning out films for adult audiences as well. The company is releasing both old and new programmes for television syndication and testing new promotional and licensing projects. In addition, the Disney theme park has been exported. The Tokyo Disneyland is attracting millions of people a year, and hopes are high for the $2 billion EuroDisneyland which opened near Paris in 1992. Disney's overall strategy is to channel the company's revived creativity into improved theme parks, to use the parks to generate interest in Disney films, and to promote both parks and merchandise through Disney television shows.

NEW BEGINNING

Disney received its new lease of life a few years ago when threats of a corporate takeover prompted the company to replace its top executives. The new management moved quickly to tap the resources of the Disney television and film library. About 200 Disney films and cartoon packages were made available on videocassette, and other classic films, such as *Snow*

White, will be released on homevideo every five years instead of every seven. The studio plans to release into cinemas one new animated movie – such as the award-winning *Beauty and the Beast* – for children every 18 months and about a dozen adult films a year.

Disney is back on network television as well, with the return of the Disney Sunday Movie. The company also produces the comedy show *The Golden Girls*, along with two top-rated Saturday morning cartoon shows. Following the lead of other studios, Disney has moved into television syndication by marketing packages of feature films, old cartoons, and *Wonderful World of Disney* programmes. The company is syndicating *The Disney Afternoon*, a block of children's cartoons that will run from 3:00 to 5:00 p.m. New shows are also being produced for syndication. They include the popular game show *Win, Lose or Draw*, a business news programme, and film reviews by Gene Siskel and Roger Ebert. In America, in an otherwise flat cable television market, the number of subscribers to the family-orientated Disney Channel has jumped dramatically – to four million. The channel now offers 24-hour features and more original programming than any other pay service. Disney has even signed an agreement with the Chinese government to broadcast a weekly television series starring Mickey Mouse and Donald Duck. The company may license the Chinese to produce Disney merchandise as well.

In the United States, too, marketing of Disney characters is receiving considerable emphasis. Recently, Mickey, Donald and others visited hospital wards and marched in parades in a 120-city tour. Snow White and all seven dwarfs made a special appearance on the floor of the New York Stock Exchange to promote the celebration of Snow White's 50th birthday. Minnie Mouse now has a trendy new look and appears on clothing and watches and in a fashion doll line. Disney is also working with toy companies to develop new characters, such as Fluppy Dogs and Wuzzles, both of which will be sold in stores and featured in television shows. In addition, the company has opened non-tourist retail outlets. Located primarily in shopping malls in the United States, Europe and South East Asia, Disney stores carry both licensed products and exclusive theme park merchandise.

THEME PARKS

Disney's revitalised market presence has been credited with increasing attendance at the US Disney theme parks to more than 50 million people. In Florida, Disney has recently completed new hotels and a movie studio/tour attraction. Moreover, Disney is constructing a 50-acre water park and adding $1.4 billion worth of new attractions to Walt Disney World. The company is also considering regional centres that would combine restaurants and shopping with evening entertainment.

Disney intends eventually to reduce the company's financial dependence on parks and hotels. The strategy is to triple the proportion of company profits from movies and television and to acquire such distribution outlets as movie theatres, television stations, and record companies. Recent business deals with Procter and Gamble Co., McDonald's Corp., Coca-Cola Co., Time Inc., M&M/Mars, and Sears, Roebuck and Co. will help increase Disney's profits and market presence still further. The move away from such a dependence on theme parks and hotels will be difficult in the current recession. The less than successful first season of EuroDisneyland makes this an important strategy, however.

EURODISNEY

EuroDisney opened in time for the 1992 summer season to a fanfare, with pop and movie stars encouraging a media blitz. Located close to Paris, though, French 'cultural snobs' rejected the US-themed concept, and French farmers, unhappy that good farming land had been taken for the US corporation's desires, blockaded access routes. Visitor levels by July had dropped to only 35,000 per day, way short of the targeted summer levels of 45,000. In August, Disney closed ('temporarily') one of its six resort hotels and laid off 5,000 staff. Tour operators, too, cancelled long-term block bookings. Although the company claims its European site is successful, there are clearly problems at the French EuroDisneyland.

UNFAVOURABLE ENVIRONMENT

Since its April 1992 opening EuroDisney has been subjected to a wave of negative publicity. French politicians and cultural leaders objected to the imposition of such a visible symbol of US culture. Disney's famous characters may have gained French names, local employment opportunities may have grown beyond belief, and French may have joined English as the joint official language for the new theme park, but to many French people EuroDisney was seen as an inconvenience rather than an asset.

The climate in Europe is not as kind as that enjoyed year round by visitors to Disney's US sites. The company depends on the three key summer months of June, July and August. The weather in 1992 was poor: cool and wet. Furthermore, much of Europe's economy was in recession with reduced day tripping and less disposable income for consumers to spend on holidaying. Problems with the ERM – the EC's exchange rate mechanism – squeezed British and French economies in the autumn of 1992, additionally reducing visitor levels. Rival leisure attractions in, for example, the UK had to aggressively compete for visitors with numbers declining in the UK's recession (cf. Table 16.1), which further hit Euro-Disney's visitor targets.

Table 16.1 Leisure day visits* – number of visits and expenditure, 1988–9

Great Britain	Visits (ms)		Millions and £ million Expenditure (£ m)	
	20 miles and over	40 miles and over	20 miles and over	40 miles and over
Attractions				
Park, garden, common	14	8	154	130
Temporary show or carnival	16	12	87	72
Zoo, aquarium, bird sanctuary, safari park	13	10	83	62
Theme park	9	7	58	43
Museum or art gallery	9	6	68	50
Castle, ancient monument	8	5	57	43
Stately home	6	5	49	39
Cathedral or church	4	2	21	15
Historic ship or steam railway	3	2	21	17
Outdoor activities				
Taking part in outdoor sport	23	13	384	325
General tour, sightseeing	66	52	245	211
Walking, hiking, rambling, climbing	22	12	130	85
Swimming, sunbathing	20	11	69	47
Watching outdoor sport	21	16	74	60
Fishing	7	5	41	35
Picnicking	8	6	6	4
Horse riding or pony-trekking	1	1	19	18
Canoeing, rowing, sailing, windsurfing	3	3	22	18
Power or motor-boating, water skiing	3	1	11	8
Other activities				
Party, celebration, anniversary	27	12	248	96
Dance or disco	13	5	132	56
Visits or meetings with friends or relatives	144	92	582	422
Theatre, opera, cinema, ballet, concert	25	13	296	166
Bingo or casino	1	0	12	1
Public house or wine bar	18	5	141	44
Restaurant or café	27	11	400	157
Taking part in indoor sport	14	5	73	32
Watching indoor sport	1	1	6	4
Shopping trip (not routine)	64	37	1,458	880
Other	36	24	266	218
Total[†]	630	379	5,212	3,358

Source: Leisure Day Visits Survey, Employment Department, English Tourist Board in *Social Trends* 22, © Crown copyright 1992

Notes: *Round trips from home of 3 hours or more, excluding work-related trips and routine shopping trips
   [†]Includes 4 million visits where purpose was not given

Towards the end of its first summer season, Disney acknowledged its worries about the impending winter season. The company needs a steady flow of visitors year round; it cannot survive only with a summer peak in visitor levels.

By the end of 1992's summer the company found itself talking to its major tour operators. The UK's second largest tour operator, Airtours, warned it may close its EuroDisney programme for 1993. Sunworld confirmed it was pulling the plug on its Disney operation because Euro-Disney had priced itself out of the market. It had hoped to sell 10,000 packages in the summer of 1992, but sold less than 5,000.

Disney realised it needed to act and to re-establish itself in the market. In a new spirit of co-operation – previously Disney had a reputation for being aloof and inflexible in negotiations – Disney renegotiated its terms with its select club of privileged suppliers. The company slashed prices for its winter hotel rates to boost visitor levels in the low season. It also shortened its high season, originally set from April to October, to allow more discounting and dealing either side of the three peak summer months. The company embarked on a major promotional campaign: joint deals with leading travel operators such as American Express, competitions in the regional and national press, discount schemes for 'frequent' visitors, plus television, radio and press advertising.

DISNEY'S PROGRESSION

Disney was faced, though, with a dilemma. EuroDisney was still far from finished: there were plans for additional attractions and facilities. The investment before the 1992 launch was hefty and required a good return and payback. The park had its detractors, but also hundreds of thousands of happy, satisfied visitors, many of whom had visited more than once in EuroDisney's first season alone. Disney needed to build on its brand image and strong marketing assets. The company had to convince its various suppliers, customers and the influential media pundits that the EuroDisney theme park would develop, establish a successful presence for Disney in Europe, and increase its popularity. For many Disney executives and tour operators, however, the less than auspicious launch season had been a surprising blow to the corporation's reputation and fortunes.

ISSUES

Assets do not necessarily travel! Disney assumed its brand reputation and success in America would automatically transfer to Europe. The company didn't take account of cultural differences or the marketing environment in Europe.

Marketing assets/marketing environment

What were Disney's US core marketing assets? How applicable were they to its French base in Europe? What aspects of the marketing environment did Disney ignore? How could it have researched these?

International marketing/global branding

The Disney brand is famous worldwide. Did the brand identity and corporate image need altering for the launch of EuroDisney?

PR and promotional activity

The launch of EuroDisney was subject to great media attention, due largely to Disney's launch promotional strategy. The set-backs in 1992 necessitated different tactics and aims. How important was PR in Disney's handling of the negative comments received during 1992? What other elements of the promotional mix were employed?

THEORY NOTES

Chapter 31, Marketing planning [assets], pp. 239–45
Chapter 19, The marketing environment, pp. 161–4
Chapter 28, Marketing communications, pp. 224–30
Chapter 25, Products and product management [branding], pp. 205–13
Chapter 32, International marketing, pp. 246–51

Chapter 17

Chester Zoo
Conservation cannot wait

In June 1931 Chester Zoological Gardens were opened to the public for the first time. An earlier site in Shavington near Crewe was initially run as a small market garden by the Zoo's founder, George Saul Mottershead and his family. George Mottershead had, as a child, been concerned about conditions in zoos he visited. His concern, which led to the development of a spacious environment in which animals could roam with minimal restraint, was to be instrumental in changing the way animals in captivity were kept. Initially he concentrated his efforts on developing a small animal collection which later was to form the basis of the Zoological Gardens outside Chester.

The North of England Zoological Society was founded in 1934 to manage the Zoo and Gardens. Following a split with a business partner, George Mottershead had to find a new and larger site for the Zoo. After several months of consideration, in 1931 he purchased Oakfield, a Victorian mansion in seven acres of grounds located in the village of Upton, two and a half miles from Chester city centre. The purchase price of £3,500 necessitated taking out a large mortgage. However, the well-maintained grounds and collection of large outbuildings meant the property was ideal for his zoological aspirations. In the Zoo's early days it was Mottershead's family who undertook the day-to-day running. Mottershead's daughter recalls the division of labour:

> My mother, who was a farmer's daughter, loved animals. All her life she kept a sharp eye on their well-being in the zoo. However, it had been decided that to add to our income my mother would run a café in the reception rooms of the Oakfield. Morning coffee, cold lunches and afternoon teas were served. The free roaming peacocks and pheasants would beg titbits from the customers. My most vivid memory of those days is of the piles of washing-up that had to be done each evening.
>
> My 75-year-old grandfather took over the garden. In the kitchen garden he grew vegetables and fruit for use in the café and as food for the animals. The main gardens consisted of rose beds in front of the

house and herbaceous flower beds at the rear. The rest of the gardens were made up of lawns, Victorian shrubberies with clipped holly and yew trees. Amongst these, my father had built pens and enclosures. He also put up a wooden pay-box near to the black and white lodge where my grandparents lived. It was my grandmother's job to collect the entrance fee of one shilling (5p) adults and six (old) pence children!

(June Williams, *Chester Zoo Life*, Summer 1991)

Throughout the 1930s Mottershead continued to buy land around the Zoo site. The Zoo's success was cemented during World War II, as it remained open and vibrant throughout the war years proving popular with locally based servicemen and Merseyside families. Today, covering 110 acres, with the Zoological Society owning an additional 350 acres of land, Chester Zoo is the largest wildlife leisure attraction in the UK.

CHESTER ZOO IN THE 1990s

In 1991 the North of England Zoological Society looked after more than 4,800 animals from 512 different species. These comprised 732 mammals, 867 birds, 360 reptiles, 125 amphibians, 2,116 fishes and 635 invertebrates. During this year the costs of maintaining the animal collection, which ate its way through 795 tons of food, reached £1.2 million, approximately 25 per cent of the total running costs. This represented an increase of more than 13 per cent on the previous year.

Site facilities include catering ranging from the formal Oakfield restaurant, to the relaxed Jubilee café, Oasis snack bar and kiosks selling a variety of ice-creams, confectionery, crisps and drinks. The souvenir hunter is also well catered for with a number of large and small shops and kiosks which cater for every pocket, selling postcards, books, pens and a range of gifts and toys. The keen rose gardener can even purchase a bag of 'Zoo Poo' (courtesy of the elephants) with which to adorn his/her own garden. To maximise the visitor's enjoyment the Friends of the Educational Department Services (FEDS) run a variety of services from free guided tours and mobile displays to activity centres for the children.

The gardens, always a feature of the Zoo, for many visitors form the focus of their visit rather than an additional benefit. Consistently successful in the Britain in Bloom and Chester in Bloom competitions, the gardens find popularity with young and old visitors alike. The staff of 22 gardeners are responsible for the raising and planting of 80,000 spring flowers and another 80,000 summer flowers. They tend everything from 15,000 roses in the gardens to banana plants, palms and rubber trees in the tropical house and buddleias, azaleas, honeysuckle and viburnum in the butterfly garden.

As in any service organisation the staff are an important feature of Zoo life. Training is seen as an essential part of the Zoo's activity. More than 50 keepers, 15 maintenance staff, 13 groundstaff, eight education specialists, 12 marketing personnel and 17 in finance and administration, not to mention the many individuals involved in retail activities and a host of others, work together to ensure the enjoyment of the Zoo visitor. During the summer months numbers of retail, catering, gate cashier and ground staff more than double.

LEISURE TRENDS

Surveys of leisure trends generally indicate a rise in the attendance at both free and paid-for popular leisure attractions (see Table 17.1). This is not particularly surprising given that overall time for leisure is on the increase

Table 17.1 Attendances at tourist attractions
(A) Attractions with free admission

| | Millions | |
	1986	1990
Blackpool Pleasure Beach	6.5	6.5
Albert Dock, Liverpool	2.0	6.0
British Museum	3.6	4.8
Strathclyde Country Park	–	4.2
National Gallery	3.2	3.7
Palace Pier, Brighton	–	3.5
Tate Gallery	1.1	1.6
Pleasureland, Southport	–	1.5
Bradgate Park	1.2	1.3

(B) Attractions charging admission

| | Millions | |
	1986	1990
Madame Tussaud's	2.4	2.5
Tower of London	2.0	2.3
Alton Towers*	2.2	2.1
Natural History Museum	2.7[†]	1.5
Chessington World of Adventure	0.8	1.5
Blackpool Tower	1.4	1.4
Royal Academy, London	0.6	1.3
Science Museum	3.0[‡]	1.3
London Zoo	1.2	1.3
Kew Gardens	1.1	1.2

Source: British Tourist Authority
Notes: *1990 figure not comparable with previous years
         [†]Admission charges introduced in 1987
         [‡]Admission charges introduced in 1989

Table 17.2 Leisure hours per week by sex and employment status

	Full-time* M	F	Part-time F	Retired M	F
Employment and travel[†]	48.2	43.7	21.8	0.3	0.7
Essential activities[‡]	25.9	44.2	57.7	28.5	41.7
Sleep[§]	49.0	49.0	49.0	49.0	49.0
Free time	44.9	31.1	39.5	90.2	76.6

Source: Leisure Futures Time Use Survey, Henley Centre
Notes: *Excludes the self-employed
[†]Travel to and from place of employment
[‡]Essential domestic work and personal care. This includes cooking, essential shopping, attending to household chores, personal hygiene and essential child care
[§]Seven hours sleep per night for all persons is assumed

taking up between 31 per cent and 90 per cent of total hours per week for the average adult (see Table 17.2).

This upward trend in leisure activity (see Figure 17.1) is reflected in Chester Zoo attendance figures for the last 10 years. Despite the slight fall in 1991 annual attendance to just under 900,000, Chester Zoo comes close to hitting the top ten UK leisure attractions. The economic recession and inclement summer reduced 1992 attendances, but the Zoo is still within the top paid-for attractions listings in the UK.

Management at the Zoo makes every effort to understand the customer base as fully as possible. There have been series of focus groups conducted both at the Zoo and within major target conurbations, such as Greater Manchester. These aimed to properly understand visitors' views of the Zoo, but also rival attractions and consumer choice criteria.

In addition, the Zoo's marketing personnel regularly interview visitors regarding demographic information, plus the scope and impressions of their visit. Of particular interest to the marketing department is the information this survey yields on visitor home locations (see Figure 17.2). This information gives crucial information about drive times and likely competitors. The competitive insight provided is especially helpful to the marketing department, which is at pains to point out that the Zoo does not only compete with other wild life attractions. Alton Towers, Blackpool Pleasure Beach, Trentham Gardens, historic Chester or even a picnic in the park are just a few of the numerous alternative days out in which the leisure seeker can indulge.

The market surveys also provide an important indicator for television and press advertising spend. An understanding of where the visitors travel from and how long they are prepared to spend in transit highlights where advertising, publicity and promotional spend should be focused. With 3.3 per cent of expenditure, a relatively small £167,000, allocated to advertising

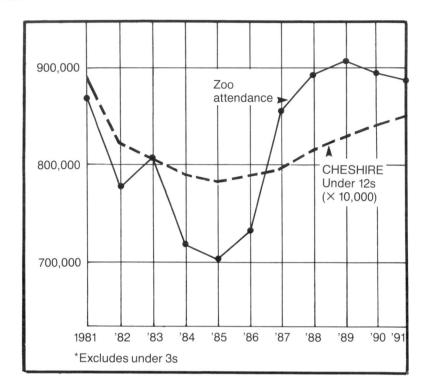

Figure 17.1 Chester Zoo attendances
Source: Chester Zoo annual report, 1991

and promotions, it is essential to minimise waste and make every £ spent work as hard as possible. Membership of the North West Tourist Board, the Yorkshire and Humberside Tourist Board, the North Wales Tourism Association, the Cheshire Tourist Attractions Consortium and the Association of Leading Visitor Attractions, all helps to spread awareness at minimum cost. Through these links, member attractions actively promote the visiting of neighbouring sites. For instance, in the current issue of the *Chester Zoo Guide* (obtained only once visitors are within the Zoo) visitors are encouraged to take trips to the following members of the Federation of Zoological Gardens of Great Britain and Ireland:

- Welsh Mountain Zoo, Colwyn Bay, Clwyd
- Knowsley Safari Park, Prescot, Merseyside
- The Wildfowl and Wetlands Trust, Martin Mere, Lancashire
- Blackpool Zoological Gardens, Blackpool
- Southport Zoo, Southport, Merseyside

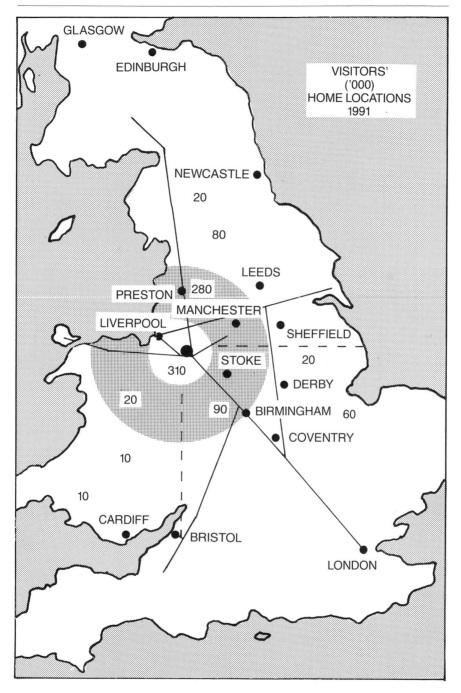

Figure 17.2 Where the visitors to Chester Zoo originate from
Source: Chester Zoo, annual report, 1991

EDUCATION AND THE NORTH OF ENGLAND ZOOLOGICAL SOCIETY

In 1950 the scope of the North of England Zoological Society was broadened to become an educational and scientific trust. These themes, together with an emphasis on the need for conservation, remain today with membership now exceeding 4,200, over 1,300 of which are in the junior category. On the scientific side the Society aims to continue to expand its programme of breeding endangered and vulnerable species – in co-operation with other zoos in the UK, Europe and further afield – and has already participated in several re-introduction programmes. The establishing of Zoo breeding programmes is seen as an important route to ensure the conservation of threatened species. Even the Zoo's advertising strap line 'Conservation Cannot Wait!' follows the theme. The success of the breeding programmes is obvious with nearly all the Zoo's mammals and over 90 per cent of the birds and reptiles being Zoo bred. In addition the Society seeks involvement in joint ventures with other wildlife establishments through its membership of the Federation of Zoological Gardens of Great Britain and Ireland and IUCN, the World Conservation Union.

Through its links with the World Conservation Union, the Zoo has enjoyed considerable success in its breeding programme and conservation efforts. In 1983 the Rodrigues Fruit Bat (*Pteropus Rodricensis*) was the focus of attention as the Zoo co-operated with a rescue bid fronted by the Jersey Wildlife Preservation Trust, acting on behalf of the Government of Mauritius. This involved setting up a carefully controlled breeding programme, initially with 10 bats. In 1992 the colony had more than quadrupled to 41. A similar scheme involving the Polynesian Partula snail has resulted in a colony of well over 600 (and still counting) snails.

Education activities at the Zoo are diverse. The education division, staffed by qualified teachers, works in conjunction with teachers from middle, secondary and tertiary establishments. Booklets aimed at Pre-School, Primary, Middle and Secondary levels cover a full range of practical and written activities, information and work sheets, fully tied into National Curriculum requirements (the UK's Department for Education guidelines for school exam syllabuses). In addition, a wide variety of information sheets about the Zoo inhabitants is available. These are detailed in the 40-page ZEST (Zoo Education Services for Teachers) booklets updated each year for teachers. With its volunteer element of over 100 active FEDS (Friends of the Education Division), the division offers free tours, two children's activity centres, puppet theatres, a storytime service, and organises Christmas journeys around the Zoo in December.

The success of the Education Division is marked by the 1991 increase in numbers of teachers seeking information about the Zoo. For example, one of the Education Officers reported dealing with 182 different teachers, a

50 per cent annual increase. This rise in contact with teachers was coupled with an increase in the number of pupils attending the Zoo for educational visits to 68,013, up 7.4 per cent on the previous year. All at a time when other leisure attractions report falling numbers of school visits.

MARKETING ACTIVITIES AT THE ZOO

From photographic competitions, animal adoption schemes and sponsorship, through to birthday parties, children's menus and the junior members' club for youngsters, the diversity of the marketing activity is obvious. Activity for 1991 involved publication of the first full colour Functions and Party Planner; the colour printing of *Zoo Life*; extensive advertising and publicity; newspaper and television coverage, including a feature on BBC Radio 4's *Punters* programme (about elephant manure!).

The annual photographic competition has proved especially popular with the visitors. With prizes of a safari holiday, a Canon camcorder, BA tickets to Europe, and family visits to the Lego 'n' Lions Model Safari in Scandinavia, competition for the best 'Favourite memory of Chester Zoo' is intense. The Zoo's photo points, selected in conjunction with Kodak and detailed in the Zoo guide, help highlight the best views.

The Zoo's animal adoption scheme continues to be a success bringing in more than £80,000 (see Figure 17.3). This enables individuals, families and companies to contribute towards the upkeep of their favourite animal in exchange for a certificate of adoption, free tickets, and their name on a plaque in the relevant enclosure.

Seventy-five per cent of all advertising is now spent on TV. Newspaper advertisements often focus on special offers timed to coincide with key bank holidays. Budgets mean that television advertising is concentrated in Granada, Central, Yorkshire and Harlech (HTV) regions with 30- and 10-second commercials. Slots are booked for immediately prior to and during peak visiting periods, supported by regional and local press adverts, with some radio slots and PR activity. In 1991 these concentrated on the recently opened Zoofari Monorail and the Zoo's current celebrity, a baby black rhino called Emma.

Chester Zoo marketing staff believe to be credible on television, advertising must exceed 600 TVRs in the target area. Television advertising was originally concentrated on Granada and HTV ITV regions. As the Zoo's marketing has become more sophisticated and its target catchment has grown as motorways have improved, clever use of the ITV companies' different transmitters has meant an expansion into the Yorkshire Television and Central regions. The focus is still on the Granada (North West England) area, but now includes South and West Yorkshire, the north Midlands and some spots on HTV (Wales).

Adopt an Animal at Chester Zoo

Adopt a mammal, bird or reptile

Could you feel maternal to mongooses? Take a clutch of wigeon under your wing? Do you have a soft spot for leopards? All the animals at the zoo can be adopted and, while we can't let you take them home, we hope that you will feel a close involvement with your chosen animals.

The zoo opened in 1931 and has gained a worldwide reputation for keeping and breeding animals. We are most concerned with the plight of many animals in the wild, as the loss of habitat is proceeding at a truly alarming rate, particularly in many of the underdeveloped countries. We believe that in the future the situation will become so desperate that zoos will have to become a lifeboat for many of the world's species - at least until the problems in the wild can be sorted out.

It costs over £180,000 each year just to feed all our animals and another £100,000 to keep them warm.

Company Adoptions

A company adoption is a unique and exciting way of promoting your business. An individual colour plaque is designed by our talented wild-life artist, and includes your company logo and advert sing slogan. This is mounted on the enclosure of your choice, to be seen by over 900,000 visitors. Choose one of our many endangered species, to show your concern for the world's rapidly disappearing wild life. Further details from Company Adoption Scheme, Chester Zoo, Chester CH2 1LH.

How adoption works

The scheme is devised for private individuals, school classes, youth groups, etc. An adoption makes a unique birthday or Christmas gift. It is based on units of £30. One or more units make up the whole cost of feeding a particular animal for a year. For example: one unit would pay the entire cost of feeding some of the smaller animals but a lion, which costs around £600, would take 20 units. There are £15 units for some of the very tiny creatures. There is no limit to the number of units you may buy and obviously we would be delighted if you took on the whole cost of feeding one of our larger animals!

At Chester Zoo, we concentrate on breeding endangered animals, and the adoption helps to finance this vital work. For this reason, we need as many adoptions as possible, so there is no limit to the number of adopters for each species. If we reach the happy state where one group of animals is fully adopted, any extra money donated through the scheme, helps the overall feeding bill.

The total sum raised in the adoption scheme is used solely for our animal feeding costs and is paid into a special Trust Fund, which is identified separately in our annual accounts.

Because zoos are co-operating with each other to manage the breeding of many animals, we ask you to adopt one of a group of animals, rather than an individual. Like all living things, the animals are subject to change and they could be moved to another collection, or become sick or old and die. If we should totally go out of one species, you will be offered the option of transferring your adoption to another species. All adoptions run for a full calendar year and a renewal reminder will be sent on the appropriate date. If you wish to buy an adoption as a gift we will make sure it arrives on the correct date.

What do you get in return?

For each £30 donated, the adopter will receive two complimentary entrance tickets; an adoption certificate; their name on the adoption plaque on the appropriate enclosure and a car sticker. There are annual adopter days at the zoo.

How to become an adopter

Choose the type of animal you would like to adopt from the list on the back of this leaflet. Fill in the attached form and post to:

Animal Adoptions, Chester Zoo,
Chester CH2 1LH

If you have any queries, please telephone:
Chester (0244) 380280

Adopt a Bird, Mammal or Reptile

Figure 17.3 Zoo animal adoption leaflet
Source: Chester Zoo

MAKING THE MOST OF PUBLICITY

Emma, the first second-generation black rhino to be born and reared in a British zoo, was born on 28 February 1991. She joined just 16 other black rhinos in British collections. Unfortunately Esther, her mother, did not produce sufficient milk for the underweight youngster, so Emma was keeper reared. With companionship provided by Jessica, a Vietnamese pot-bellied pig, bottle rearing proved an entertaining business, for keepers and crowds alike.

In addition to its contribution to the conservation aims of the Zoo, Emma's birth provided the publicity department with an important PR opportunity. During the first year of her life Emma was the subject of numerous press releases (see Figure 17.4), helped pull in sponsorship from the Dunlop Footwear Company, and starred in her own 10-second television commercial, one of three produced during the year. Emma's celebrity status was enhanced by the use of signage which helped direct the hoards of enthusiastic visitors to her house. There was a most memorable birthday party, featured by Granada TV, complete with cake and 25 other Emmas from all parts of the North West who shared rhino Emma's birth date.

The romance of Emma's parents, Esther (Rantzen) and Michael (Parkinson), was used by various publications including the *Guardian* and *Daily Mirror* newspapers to spoof an affair between the famous television personalities. This was all helpful publicity for the Zoo.

KEEPING THE CUSTOMERS HAPPY

At Chester Zoo, careful focusing on customer needs and close attention to detail allow management to maintain high service standards. These standards are essential if the visitors are to be encouraged to return. (Most of the Zoo's visitors have been at least once before.) Persuading new customers to visit and existing ones to return must be achieved without the assistance of the large advertising and promotions budgets on which organisations in other sectors are able to rely. Communications with the customer base, which is spread widely through the Midlands, North West, Wales and Yorkshire, must be conducted prudently, maximising the use of limited resources.

As recession bites, with rising unemployment and less spare money available, the difficulties of maintaining visitor levels are likely to increase. These problems look set to continue well into the mid-1990s with increasingly gloomy economic forecasts. Even the competitive stakes have changed, with basic necessities such as food and rent competing with money spent on leisure activities. Now, more than ever, Zoo management will need to pursue initiatives which persuade the hard-pressed consumer of the benefits of a visit to the Zoo.

LITTLE EMMA WEIGHS IN – AT 60lbs

☐ Little and large – Emma and Esther take their first photo call   Picture: CHRIS VERE

Rapture over rhino's birth

CHAMPAGNE corks have been popping at Chester Zoo to celebrate the birth of a black rhino.

Emma is, of course, unaware that she is one of only 17 of her species in British zoos and one of about only 3,000 left in the world.

Emma, who weighs 60lbs, is the first calf born to Esther, whose pregnancy lasted about 14 months, and her mate, Cecil.

In Africa, the black rhino population has fallen by 90pc over the last 20 years, mainly because of the killing of rhinos for their horns, in powdered form much sought after in South East Asia for its alleged aphrodisiac properties.

Figure 17.4 Using publicity to attract customers

Sources: *Liverpool Daily Post*, 2 March 1991; *Daily Mirror*, 5 March 1992

A new Zoo entrance, new parking facilities adjacent to Chester's 'park and ride' service, plus the extension of paddocks to accommodate increases in the rhino and elephant stocks, provide extra stimulus for the Zoo to move successfully into the next century. With the junior Asian elephant in the Zoo's herd pregnant, the breeding programme is well on target – and the opportunities for media exposure and publicity.

Table 17.3 Financial data for the North of England Zoological Society

Income and expenditure account for the year ended 31 December 1991

	1991 £	1991 £	1990 £	1990 £
Turnover		5,147,358		4,697,351
less direct costs of:				
Catering	1,026,717		1,014,183	
Souvenir shops	495,433		474,812	
Animal welfare	972,729		857,691	
Garden upkeep	264,241		227,476	
Monorail system	174,754		–	
		2,933,874		2,574,162
		2,213,484		2,123,189
Indirect costs (including £506,945 Maintenance (1990 £447,927)		2,215,008		1,981,682
Operating (deficiency)/surplus		(1,524)		141,507
Other income		28,678		30,827
		27,154		172,334
Interest receivable	1,364		4,700	
Interest payable				
– Monorail system	(87,004)		–	
– Other	(99,712)		(73,100)	
		(185,352)		(68,400)
(Deficiency)/surplus on ordinary activities		(158,198)		103,934
Transfer from capital expenditure grants		6,375		16,375
		(151,823)		120,309
Accumulated surplus brought forward		1,711,443		1,591,134
Accumulated surplus carried forward		1,559,620		1,711,443

Balance sheet at 31 December 1991

	1991 £	1991 £	1990 £	1990 £
Fixed assets				
Tangible assets				
Special buildings, enclosures and equipment	2,058,332		1,975,750	
Monorail system	1,315,395		13,451	
Freehold property	492,628		473,315	
Animals	1,000		1,000	
		3,867,355		2,463,516
Investment in subsidiary company		100		–
Current assets				
Stocks	240,196		199,008	
Debtors	55,275		55,920	
Balance at bank	4,743		4,641	
Cash in hand	40,522		28,248	
Trust fund bank account	121,156		103,584	
	461,892		391,401	
Current liabilities				
Creditors: amounts falling due within one year				
Finance leases				
– Monorail system	184,556		–	
– Other	1,165		7,488	
Bank overdraft (secured)	1,285,321		774,497	
Trade creditors	182,695		168,623	
Taxes and social security costs	67,931		50,098	
Other creditors	55,586		23,586	
Accruals	32,873		14,434	
	1,810,127		1,038,726	
Net current liabilities		(1,348,235)		(647,325)
Total assets less current liabilities		2,519,220		1,816,191
Creditors: amounts falling due after more than one year				
Finance leases				
– Monorail system		838,444		–
– Other		–		1,165
Net assets		1,680,776		1,815,026
Reserves				
Income and expenditure account		1,559,620		1,711,442
Trust fund		121,156		103,584
		1,680,776		1,815,026

Cash flow statement for the year ended 31 December 1991

	1991		1990	
	£	£	£	£
Operating activities				
Operating (loss)/surplus	(1,524)		141,507	
Depreciation charges	390,929		233,090	
Loss on sale of tangible fixed assets	1,096		3,429	
Decrease/(increase) in stocks	(41,188)		(62,311)	
Decrease/(increase) in debtors	645		(10,690)	
Increase/(decrease) in creditors (excl. finance leases)	82,344		62,414	
Net cash flow from operating activities		432,302		367,439
Returns on investments and servicing of finance				
Rents received	28,678		30,827	
Interest received	1,364		4,700	
Interest payable	(186,716)		(73,100)	
Net cash outflow from returns on investments and servicing of funds		(156,674)		(37,573)
Taxation – not applicable				
Net cash outflow from taxation		–		–
Investing activities				
Receipts of capital expenditure grants	6,375		16,375	
Receipts from disposal of tangible fixed assets	2,086		18,650	
Payments to acquire tangible fixed assets				
– Monorail system	(1,448,099)		(13,451)	
– Other	(349,850)		(451,831)	
Payments to acquire investments in subsidiary	(100)		–	
Net cash outflow from investing activities		(1,789,588)		(430,257)
Net cash outflow before financing		(1,513,960)		(100,391)
Financing				
Receipts of sponsorship, donations, legacies etc.	17,572		13,942	
Receipts from financial leases				
– Monorail system	1,023,000		–	
– Other	(7,488)		8,316	

Increase in bank overdraft	510,824		102,069
Repayment of loans	–		(11,091)
Net cash inflow from financing		1,543,908		113,236
Cash and cash equivalents			
Increase of cash at bank and in hand	12,376		(1,097)
Increase in trust fund bank account	17,572		13,942
Net increase in cash and cash equivalents		29,948		12,845

Source: The North of England Zoological Society

ISSUES

Persuading consumers to value a service, here a leisure attraction, is the main theme for this case. Services marketing and the promotional mix are well illustrated, along with aspects of marketing research and competition.

Services marketing

The leisure industry is one sector of the services industry. It is, though, not essential to the health and well-being of consumers, being a leisure time activity. Value for money and enjoyment must be part of the product offered. What are the principal elements of Chester Zoo's marketing mix? On which aspects must the Zoo's marketers concentrate their attention?

Promotional mix

With relatively limited budgets, Chester Zoo aims to attract close to a million visitors annually. Where is the focus for the Zoo's promotional mix? What could be attempted to enhance this promotional activity? Why?

Marketing research

Research is expensive, but the Zoo mixes informal, ad hoc research with more formal techniques such as focus groups. What are the main issues requiring examination and on-going monitoring? Design a suitable programme of marketing research.

THEORY NOTES

Chapter 29, Services marketing, pp. 231–4
Chapter 28, Marketing communications, pp. 224–30
Chapter 21, Marketing research, pp. 173–80

Part III

Theory notes

Chapter 18

Introduction to marketing
What is marketing?

1 DEFINITIONS

Peter Drucker, one of the great gurus of modern business thinking, defined marketing thus:

> The aim of marketing is to make selling superfluous. The aim is to know and understand the customer so well that the product or service fits him/her and sells itself.

This is perhaps one of the most famous definitions in marketing. If a company researches its market and its customers so well that it understands exactly the product attributes required by its customers, the desired point of purchase, pricing, promotional imagery and selling methods, then the product should be so much in line with the desired needs of the customers that it sells itself. The two key points of the definition are that marketing should therefore make selling superfluous, and the basic need of marketing management is the understanding of customers.

The Chartered Institute of Marketing defines marketing as:

> The management process responsible for identifying, anticipating and satisfying customer requirements profitably.

This definition takes Drucker's ideas a little further, adding the element of profitability. This is true for all organisations, not just those seeking high profitability, in that most utilities, public sector organisations and non-profit organisations (such as charities) are also intending to create the biggest surplus of revenue over costs.

Dibb, Simkin, Pride and Ferrell (1991) say:

> Marketing consists of individual and organisational activities that facilitate and expedite satisfying exchange relationships in a dynamic environment through the creation, distribution, promotion and pricing of goods, services and ideas.

Marketing is, indeed, dynamic. The solution proved successful one week may not be adequate to tackle a similar situation a few weeks later. Marketing, by its very nature, is taking place in a changing environment. Consumer needs change, competitors alter their products and strategies, and the general economic environment can change dramatically resulting in the need for different marketing strategies and programmes. The latter part of the Dibb *et al.* definition introduces two important concepts: the creation of the right *product*, the channel of *distribution*, *promotion* and *pricing* – these are the elements of what is termed the *marketing mix*. The basic marketing mix is often nicknamed 'the 4Ps' (product, place/distribution, pricing, promotion); these elements being the basic weapons in the marketer's armoury – aspects that can be manipulated to keep ahead of the competition. The final point of the definition makes the important distinction between goods, services and ideas. It is easy when reading many marketing texts to think of marketing as only applicable in the FMCG sector (fast-moving consumer goods). There is more to marketing than the selling of Heinz Baked Beans, Persil washing power or Kodak film. Marketing is prevalent in most areas of commercial and industrial activity, and also for many of us in daily life – even in education!

Clearly each of these three definitions is different, focusing on various angles. To some extent this also sums up the nature of marketing. There is an element of science in certain techniques of marketing, but not in the true sense. Marketing is more subjective and is open to wide-ranging interpretation. Marketing *is* about understanding the needs of customers, anticipating what they require, and offering them the correct marketing mix in a way that is different to competitors' marketing strategies and programmes.

2 THE BIRTH OF MARKETING

It is a widely held belief that marketing has evolved, growing up in the 1950s in America.

Production era: 1850s–1920s
   The industrial revolution occurred
   Mass production
   Rigidly structured jobs

Sales era: 1920–50s
   Focus on personal selling and advertising
   Sales viewed as major means of increasing profits

Marketing era: 1950s–present
   Customer orientation
   Companies determine needs and wants of customers

At the turn of the century, products were developed by inventors, and then sold into the marketplace. As more companies entered emerging/growing markets, the level of competition forced a greater focus on aggressive selling. As customers have become more sophisticated, and competition more convoluted, there has been more of an emphasis over the past few decades on genuinely identifying and anticipating customer needs, gearing up production accordingly – the birth of marketing.

3 SELLING VERSUS MARKETING

Figure 18.1 illustrates the distinction between selling and marketing. Under selling, the product is first produced, then sold, and the consumer is only involved in the process in terms of being the final element in the chain (the purchaser/consumer). Under the marketing philosophy, customers are consulted at every stage of the process, the marketing mix being varied accordingly.

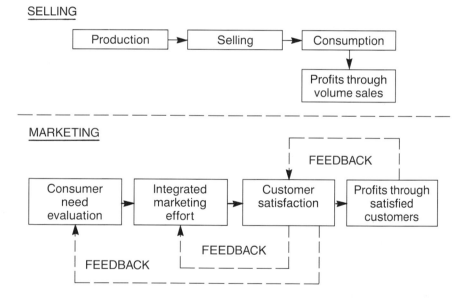

Figure 18.1 Selling and marketing

Marketing philosophy
Key characteristics:

- Consumer orientated
- Two-way process (interactive)
- Appropriate adaptation to marketing environment

- Broad view of consumer needs
- Emphasis on groups of consumers
- Marketing research determining output
- Longer-run goals
- Profit and market share orientated
- Integrated planning and feedback

Sales philosophy
Key characteristics:

- Sales orientated
- One-way process
- Little adaptation to environment
- Narrow view of consumer needs
- Emphasis on single customers
- Output 'sold' to customers
- Short-run goals
- Volume orientated
- Informal planning and feedback

4 MODERN MARKETING

There are two key stages in modern marketing: the development of a marketing strategy and the construction and implementation of a marketing programme. Marketing strategy is the identification of consumers to target and the positioning of a product or service, against competitors in the marketplace. The implementation of a marketing programme is facilitated through the development of a marketing mix, the core elements of which are:

product
place (distribution)
price
promotion

In addition, for most marketing situations there is a fifth important element to the *marketing mix* [cf. Chapter 29]:

personnel/people

However, as the schematic to marketing in Figure 18.2 indicates, neither marketing strategy nor a marketing mix can adequately be developed unless there is a thorough understanding of customers, or competitors, and of the marketing environment. This very often requires 'marketing intelligence' collected through *marketing research* [cf. Chapter 21].

Figure 18.2 Marketing and strategy

Once a company has analysed its market and targeted a specific group of customers – its target segment (or segments) – the goal is a marketing mix which matches the wants of these targeted customers, but a mix which is superior (either in real terms or as perceived by these consumers) to competitors' marketing mixes. If successful, the company has developed a *differential advantage* – i.e. there is a reason for customers to prefer its products rather than those offered by competitors.

The 'nuts and bolts' of marketing are the elements of the marketing mix – product, price, place, promotion and people – supported by marketing research and marketing intelligence. Without careful analysis of the market and development of a clear marketing strategy, the marketing mix is likely to be flawed: not correctly positioning the product or service in the targeted market segment; no differential advantage; and probably not achieving the company's corporate goals. Marketing as a philosophy is increasingly essential if a company or organisation is to successfully meet customer requirements and beat competitors. Marketing, though, must be part of a carefully thought-through strategy which satisfies corporate objectives.

5 USEFUL REFERENCES

Baker, M.J. (1991) *Marketing, An Introductory Text*, London: Macmillan – UK.

Dibb, S., Simkin, L., Pride, W., and Ferrell, O.C. (1991) *Marketing: Concepts and Strategies,* **Boston: Houghton Mifflin – UK/Europe.**

Doust, P. (1986) *Marketing Q & A: Fundamentals of Marketing*, London: Financial Training Publications – UK.

Kotler, P. (1991) *Marketing Management,* **Englewood Cliffs: Prentice-Hall – USA.**

McCarthy, E.J. and Perreault, W.D. (1990) *Basic Marketing*, Homewood, Illinois: Irwin – USA.

6 WEEKLY TRADE MAGAZINES

Marketing, Haymarket Publishing, London.
Marketing Week, Centaur Communications, London.
Campaign, Haymarket Publishing, London.

Each of these magazines presents an up-to-date summary of the latest product launches, communications strategies, research techniques, and thinking in the subject (*Campaign* focusing primarily on the world of marketing communications/advertising). They are readily available on news stands in London and major conurbations, and to order on subscription or through any newsagent/CTN. Major 'breaking' stories are similarly covered in all three, so there is no need to take all of these titles.

Chapter 19

The marketing environment

1 DEFINITION

The marketing environment is defined as those external forces that directly or indirectly influence an organisation's acquisitions of inputs and generation of outputs.

In other words, they are aspects of the trading environment over which the company has very little direct control, but they are elements which will tangibly affect the way in which the company can do business and will perform.

To monitor changes in the marketing environment, marketers must scan and analyse continuously. Many companies have individual marketing managers or committees whose function is to collect and collate data related to trends in the market and aspects of the marketing environment. *Environmental scanning* is the process of tracking information from observation, secondary sources (particularly the trade press and government reports), and marketing research.

The marketing environment generally is broken into two key sections, termed the *macro* marketing environment and the *micro* marketing environment.

2 MACRO ENVIRONMENT

The main elements are:

Legal forces

Many laws influence marketing activities; for example: procompetitive legislation and consumer protection legislation.

Regulatory forces

Interpretation of laws is important, but so is an understanding of the enforcement by the various government and non-government regulatory bodies; for example: government ministries, local authorities, trade and professional associations.

Political forces

Many marketers view the actions of government as beyond influence, while others successfully lobby and influence the policy-making and legislating bodies of central and local governments.

Societal forces (culture)

These are the dynamics and workings of society: groups and individuals often ignore the activities of companies and marketers until they infringe – usually negatively – on their lifestyles and choices. Perhaps the most significant example currently is consumer pressure on companies to produce products which are less harmful to the earth's environment, with less waste, and which are produced in a more ecologically sensitive manner.

Technological forces

This refers to the technological expertise with which to accomplish tasks and goals. Technology is quickly evolving and changing, affecting how people satisfy their needs and lead their lives. It also affects what products marketers can bring to the marketplace, and how they are presented to the consumer.

Economic conditions

General economic conditions – recession or boom – will impact on any market, as will consumer demand and spending behaviour. These are important considerations for any marketer, particularly as such conditions are prone to dramatic changes, patterns and fashions.

3 MICRO ENVIRONMENT

The elements of the micro marketing environment are aspects which are peculiar to the individual company/organisation concerned, rather than market specific, over which the company has little control. The key items to consider here are:

- direct competition, including that from substitute products [cf. Chapter 24];
- supplier influence/power;
- the company's resource base [cf. Chapter 31];
- customers' specific requirements and perceptions [cf. Chapter 20].

4 THE INFLUENCE OF THE MARKETING ENVIRONMENT

No matter what the company or market, there are always elements of the marketing environment which directly impact on the competence of a company's performance.

For example, until 1992 EC deregulation, the UK car market was quite rigidly controlled by the manufacturers. The franchised dealers were prohibited by their suppliers (the manufacturers) from retailing vehicles produced by rival manufacturers. Dealers, therefore, were unable to build showrooms containing model ranges of rival manufacturers, even though consumers might prefer to be able to visit one site to look at all relevant models on offer at a similar price point. Dealers were also restricted from building separate showrooms for the retailing of different manufacturer marques adjacent to each other.

With the deregulation and the EC directive prohibiting 'block exemption' and manufacturers' anti-competitive practices, dealers will now be free to negotiate with much more freedom with rival manufacturers. Indeed, new retail outlets may choose to open which deliberately do not tie in with a particular manufacturer, choosing to source from a selection of rival manufacturers in order to put together a portfolio of vehicles relevant to a particular target market. This changed situation was not brought about by either the dealers or the manufacturers, but as a result largely of bureaucratic intervention and the changing of rules and regulations.

Even for a product such as margarine, the marketing environment can have significant impact on the fortunes and activities of the companies producing and selling this everyday product.

Margarine was invented in 1869. Vitamins were added in 1924, but the first significant branded launch was in 1964 with the regional test of Flora, positioned as light and delicate. In 1968 Flora was repositioned as the first brand high in polyunsaturated fat, two years ahead of Outline's launch as the UK's first low fat spread. In 1976 Flora received support with the Royal College of Physicians recommending saturated fats be replaced with unsaturated fats. This was bad news for brands high in saturated fats, but a boost for margarine's claims of being healthier than traditional butter. These claims were helped with the 1984 Government COMA Report demanding a 17 per cent reduction in the fat consumption of UK residents.

Flora, along with other leading brands, had to alter its marketing in 1984 when the Food Labelling Act banned brands from overtly linking polyunsaturated fat with a reduction in heart disease (despite earlier medical evidence supporting these claims). In 1987 Unilever's Van den Berghs launched Lätta as the first low fat spread also high in polyunsaturates. St Ivel responded in 1989 with Gold Lowest, with only 25 per cent fat content, creating the very low fat spread sector. Lätta was dropped, re-appearing as Flora Extra Light to capitalise on the Flora name. As a response to social changes and health worries, in 1991 Van den Berghs developed Olivio, Europe's first oil-based monounsaturated fat spread, creating yet a new sector in the highly competitive margarine market.

This brief case history shows the importance of many elements of the marketing environment, both *macro* and *micro*. Influential bodies – the Royal College of Physicians – government reports, legislation, all altered the 'rules' of combat for the food manufacturers competing in this dynamic market. Changing social behaviour and consumer patterns forced St Ivel and Van den Berghs continually to modify existing products and launch new brands [cf. Chapter 25]. Competitors used changing production processes, consumer needs and aspirations, the welcome or damaging publication of health and food reports, or the introduction of new legislation to develop an edge over each other.

5 USEFUL REFERENCES

Bennett, P.D. (1988) *Marketing*, New York: McGraw-Hill.
Dibb, S., Simkin, L., Pride, W. and Ferrell, O.C. (1991) *Marketing Concepts and Strategies,* **Boston: Houghton Mifflin.**
Drucker, P. (1981) *Management in Turbulent Times,* London: Heinemann/Pan.
Kotler, P. (1991) *Marketing Management,* **Englewood Cliffs: Prentice-Hall.**

Chapter 20

Consumer and organisational buyer behaviour
The characteristics and contrasts

1 DEFINITIONS

Consumer buyer behaviour equals the decision processes and acts of individuals (you and me) involved in buying and using products.

Organisational buyer behaviour is the purchase behaviour of producers, re-sellers, government units, and institutions.

(Dibb *et al.*, 1991)

2 THE IMPORTANCE OF UNDERSTANDING

It is important that selling organisations properly understand how and why people and organisations buy. This understanding gives an insight into how best to influence the buying activities and can result in the development of a more suitable marketing mix (product, price, promotion, distribution, people) for the customers targeted.

3 CONSUMER BUYER BEHAVIOUR

3.1 Consumer buying decision process

There have been many attempts to model the way that people buy. Figure 20.1 illustrates a typical model.

(i)   *Problem Recognition*
      This is the point where the consumer realises that a purchase is required. For example, a household appliance (such as a washing machine) that is broken beyond repair must be replaced.

(ii) *Information Search*
      At this stage, the consumer begins searching for information to help with the required purchase. During this stage a list of criteria is implicitly drawn up together with a number of alternative products/ services.

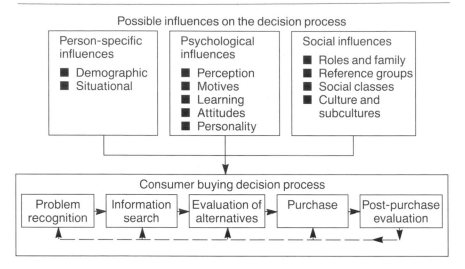

Figure 20.1 Consumer buying decision process and possible influences on the process
Source: Dibb, S., Simkin, L., Pride, W. and Ferrell, O.C. (1991) *Marketing: Concepts and Strategies*, Boston: Houghton Mifflin, Figure 4.1

(iii) *Evaluation of Alternatives*

This is where the consumer must choose between the alternatives (sometimes referred to as the *evoked set*) by measuring the different product/service options against the criteria selected. In some cases, insufficient information will have been collected, causing the consumer to return to the information search stage.

(iv) *Purchase*

The complexity of purchase varies according to the type of product being bought. Compare for instance the simple act of buying a newspaper with the complexity of a house purchase.

(v) *Post-Purchase Evaluation*

After any purchase, particularly one which is expensive, there will be a period of post-purchase evaluation. This is where the consumer tries to judge the success of the purchase made. The result will have an impact on what the consumer buys in the future, as the evaluation feeds back into subsequent decision-making.

3.2 Influences

There are a number of factors which influence the way in which people buy. These can be grouped:

- *Person Specific Influences*
  These relate to demographic issues (age/sex/occupation) and situational factors (external conditions which exist when a purchase is made).

- *Psychological Influences*
  Different consumers have different perceptions, motives and attitudes towards what and how they purchase. Other factors, such as the level of knowledge about a particular item and personality, have an impact, too.

- *Social Influences*
  All consumers are influenced by social factors when they buy. For example, tastes tend to be influenced by social class and culture and behaviour is radically affected by family roles and reference groups (friends/colleagues).

Models of buyer behaviour are beneficial to marketers, bringing an understanding of the factors which impact on people's buying decisions. In addition, by appreciating the processes which consumers go through, marketers can decide what kind of marketing effort to target at consumers as they pass through the different stages. For instance, some of the car advertisements appearing on television are aimed to stimulate brand awareness so that when consumers recognise they need to buy a new car (early in the process), they may consider a particular brand as advertised. Later on in the buying process, the companies must be prepared to provide detailed information about product offerings together with test drives.

As with all 'models' which represent reality, buyer behaviour models are subject to criticisms. A number of difficulties are readily apparent:

- Different products are bought in different ways.
- The length of the buying process varies according to the type of buying decision (routine response, limited decision-making, or extended decision-making).
- For some products, stages are omitted altogether. (Eg. buying a newspaper is a routine activity with little information search).

How appropriate the model is also depends on whether a product has been purchased before. That is, is the product a routine re-buy, modified re-buy or completely new buy?

4 ORGANISATIONAL BUYER BEHAVIOUR

4.1 Different company types

Organisational markets can be classified into:

- *Industrial or producer markets*: these companies buy products for use in

the manufacture of other products or to support that manufacture. For example, Nestle buys glucose syrup/cocoa powder/sugar etc.
- *Re-seller markets*: companies in this category buy goods for re-sale to customers. Generally they do not alter the physical nature of those goods. For example wholesalers or retailers, such as Marks and Spencer's, W.H. Smith's, Esso.

These companies deal in physical goods.

- *Institutional markets*: companies in this category include charities, libraries, hospitals, educational establishments etc.
- *Government markets*: this category includes both local and national government.

These companies are generally involved with the handling of services.

This distinction into company type is important: it may affect the characteristics of the buying process. For instance, government markets are known for their bureaucratic buying processes – often operating through a series of committees seeking tenders, taking many months.

4.2 Contrasts with consumer buyer behaviour

The marketing concept applies to both consumer and organisational markets: that is, it is an organisation's aim to define the needs of target markets and adapt products/services to satisfy those needs in a more effective way than the competition. There are, however, a number of obvious contrasts between consumer buying behaviour and the behaviour exhibited by organisations. These can be shown by highlighting the particular characteristics of organisational buyer behaviour.

Group Activity   Generally more people are involved in organisational buying behaviour than in consumer buying behaviour. Those involved in buying in an organisational situation are collectively referred to as the *Buying Centre*. The roles within the Buying Centre include those of buyers, users, influencers, technologists, gatekeepers, policy makers and deciders. The number of people carrying out these roles varies by organisation, and also within the same organisation according to the type of purchase being made. Other factors which impact on how many people are involved in buying include perceived risk, time pressure, company size, and degree of centralisation of decision-making/ordering.

High Risk   As a general rule, buying for organisations tends to be more high risk than consumer purchase. This is not to say that some consumer purchasers are not high risk. Risk in organisational purchases can come from high product value, the possible consequence of purchase, lack of knowledge about the product or service being bought, and uncertainty about the buying process or how to deal with suppliers. This risk can be handled in a number of ways (see Figure 20.2). These include involving other people in the buying process, seeking more information, engaging in trial orders, deferring the decision, remaining loyal to suppliers who are known and trusted ('no one was ever fired for ordering IBM'), using multiple suppliers (the BCCI scandal has highlighted the importance of this in the financial service sector).

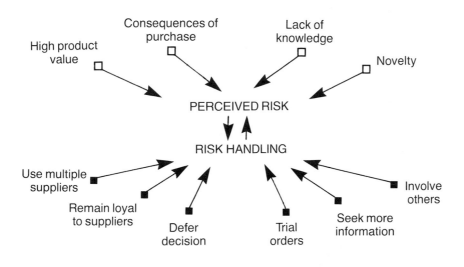

Figure 20.2 Ways to handle risk

Fewer and Larger Buyers   FMCG companies tend to aim their products at mass markets. By contrast many companies in organisational markets are reliant on relatively few customers. This has two impacts: (a) there is a tendency for long-term relationships to be developed. The benefits of these can be measured in terms of reduced risk, trust, mutual adaptation, time saving and the definition of clear roles and tasks; (b) there is more use of personal selling (face-to-face contact) especially in high risk situations.

Figure 20.3 illustrates the exchange which takes place in personal contact between buying and selling companies. The length of time taken to swop information, products, finance and to interact socially will be dependent on the nature of purchase.

Formal Buying Process   In organisations, buyers are often restricted by certain company rules/procedures. They therefore have a fairly limited say in the purchase which is made. Some organisations are particularly

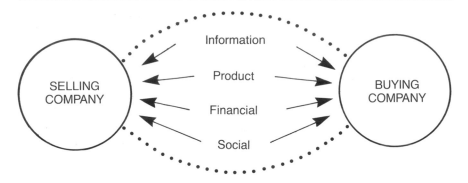

Figure 20.3 Personal contact and buyer/seller exchange

bureaucratic. Generally, there is extensive use of formal quotes and tenders.

Nature of Demand   Demand in organisational markets is derived from demand for products or services in consumer markets. This means it tends to fluctuate according to the level of demand for consumer goods. (E.g. the demand for glucose syrup is affected by the demand for confectionary.) A characteristic of derived demand is that it also leads to elastic demand in organisational markets. This is because a reduction in price of components or raw materials is unlikely to lead to a radical change in primary demand.

Geographic Concentration of Buyers   There is a tendency for concentration of certain industries to occur in different areas. For example, in the UK, shipbuilding was concentrated in the North East while the textile industry grew up around Manchester; information technology (IT) is now centred on the M4 corridor.

4.3 The organisational buying process

Various attempts have been made to model the organisational buying decision process. Figure 20.4 illustrates a typical example of this model. It consists of the following process:

(i) *Recognise Problem*
     This is the stimulus for the purchase of a new product. It can come from inside the organisation (such as when an existing piece of equipment breaks down) or from outside (perhaps as a result of technological advance).
(ii) *Establish Product Specification to Solve Problem*
     Here the organisation must decide exactly what attributes it is looking

for from the products/services sought. The length of time taken to do this will depend on whether the item is a routine re-buy, modified re-buy or new buy.

(iii) *Search for Products and Suppliers*
Buyers may choose to patronise existing suppliers or search for new information from trade shows, journals and personal contacts.

(iv) *Evaluate Products Relative to Specifications*
The process of evaluation also concerns the supplier. Offerings are compared with the specification drawn up. Comparisons are also made between the various offerings.

(v) *Select and Order Most Appropriate Product*
Sometimes this follows on naturally from the evaluation of products relative to specifications and sometimes further information is required before a decision can be made.

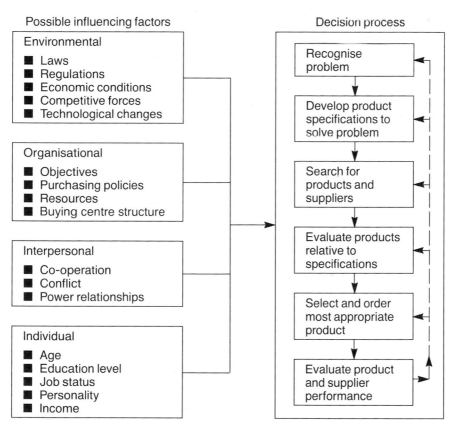

Figure 20.4 Model of the organisational buying process
Source: Dibb, S., Simkin, L., Pride, W. and Ferrell, O.C. (1991) *Marketing: Concepts and Strategies*, Boston: Houghton Mifflin, Figure 5.3

(vi) *Evaluate Product and Supplier Performance*
This is an important stage of the process because it will impact on the decisions which are made in the future.

There is a range of factors which impact on the nature of buying and how that buying takes place. These include:

- *Environmental*: such as laws, regulations, economic conditions, competitive forces and technological change. For example, the impact of 1992 EC deregulation and more freedom to buy will have a strong effect on how the process takes place.
- *Organisational*: including company objectives (which may be short or long term), purchasing policies (such as 'Buy British'), resources, and the structure of the buying centre.
- *Interpersonal*: anyone involved in buying for an organisation will understand the power of relationships, conflict and co-operation which can impact on the decisions made.
- *Individual*: as in consumer buying, individual factors such as age, education level and job status will have an impact on the choices which are made.

5 USEFUL REFERENCES

Assael, H. (1991) *Consumer Behaviour and Marketing Action,* **Boston: Kent.**
Engel, J.F., Blackwell, R.D. and Miniard, P.W. (1992) *Consumer Behaviour,* Chicago: Dryden Press.
Gross, A.C., Banting, P.M., Meredith, L.N. and Ford, D. (1993) *Business Marketing,* **Boston: Houghton Mifflin.**
Hutt, M.D. and Speh, T.W. (1992) *Business Marketing Management: Strategic View of Industrial and Organisational Markets,* **Forth Worth, Dryden Press.**
Peter, J.P. and Olson, J.C. (1987) *Consumer Behaviour,* Homewood, Illinois: Irwin.
Powers, T.L. (1991) *Modern Business Marketing,* St Paul, Minnesota: West.

Chapter 21

Marketing research

1 DEFINITION

A formalised means of obtaining/collecting information to be used to make sound marketing decisions.

(Tull and Hawkins, 1990)

From the basic definitions of marketing, it is clear marketers must understand their customers. Information on customers, their needs, preferences, product choices etc. often comes from marketing research. However, marketers – in order to develop strategies and implement marketing programmes – require information pertaining to many aspects, not just customers. Marketing research is used to examine market trends and company factors:

customers
competitors
distributors
marketing environment

2 MARKETING INTELLIGENCE/RESEARCH/MIS

2.1 Marketing research

This is the collection of data/information (often in an ad hoc fashion) to solve specific problems. In other words, a situation arises where the marketing department feels uncomfortable at making a decision with the available marketing intelligence/understanding, and instigates the collection of additional information with the purpose of assisting in the specific decision-making in question.

According to Mintel, within the UK, only 2 per cent of spending on marketing services in 1990 went on marketing research. The vast majority (90 per cent) was spent on marketing communications/promotional activity.

2.2 Marketing intelligence

Marketing intelligence is all of the data and ideas available within a system (such as a company or marketing department). This may be stored formally, for example being documented or computerised; or held informally, for example ideas/experiences in the heads of key managers.

2.3 Marketing information systems (MIS)

These are *frameworks* for managing and accessing internal and external data. The Marketing Information System can be as simple as a directive from a board of directors to each of its key departments to share information. At the other extreme, it could be in the form of an IT solution using state of the art data processing, retrieval, transmission technology. Both marketing intelligence and marketing research form the key elements of a marketing information system (see Figure 21.1).

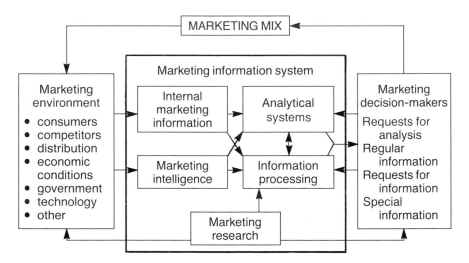

Figure 21.1 Marketing research/marketing intelligence within an MIS
Source: *Q&A Marketing* (1986) London: Financial Training Publications

3 RESEARCH VERSUS INTUITION IN MARKETING DECISION-MAKING

If every decision made by a marketer were to be based purely on formal marketing research, very few decisions would ever be made. Marketing by its very nature is in a dynamic, ever-changing environment. Daily, marketers have to make decisions about changes in product attributes, pricing, promotional activity, distribution, sales support etc. Usually, such decisions are made using any information to hand plus the general experience/ intuition of the managers in question. Where the risk of making the wrong decision is large and there may be severe ramifications for the company's well-being (and the marketer's job), marketing research will often form the basis for a more rigorous appraisal and decision-making process.

Marketing research is by nature more formally planned than judgements based on intuition, with clear goals and research methodology. Marketing research tends to be used to confirm hypotheses or to carry out systematic surveys and classifications.

Intuition, on the other hand, is preference based depending on personal feelings and experience. Such intuitively based decisions can be shown to have been correct or wrong within a very short space of time. By demonstration, if experience is shown not to be adequate, the marketer can simply change his/her mind. Therefore, more minor problems solved quickly, through consideration of experience and with obvious practical consequences, are tackled using intuition.

4 THE MARKETING RESEARCH PROCESS

Figure 21.2 shows the five stages of the marketing research process.

- Define and locate problems to be researched
- Develop research hypotheses
- Collect relevant data
- Analyse and interpret research findings
- Report research findings

Figure 21.2 The five stages of the marketing research process

The overall problem may be a sudden drop in market share or profitability, or the impending launch of a competitor's innovative product. However, to instigate marketing research on such a vague, widely defined, basis would be costly and resource wasteful. In order to focus the efforts of the researchers, so reducing time and budgets, it is necessary for the marketer to hypothesise the more specific aspects which need to be examined (for example: Is the product simply obsolete?; Is it over-priced?; Is the competitor's new channel of distribution superior?; and so on).

It is important to consider the final two steps in the process before actually collecting the data. A great deal of time and money are wasted when data are collected without a thorough understanding of how they will be interpreted. Costly recoding and convoluted statistical analyses can easily result. Similarly, it is important to know how a particular programme of research will be reported and to whom, so that the level of information can be fine-tuned to suit the understanding of the target audience (marketing colleagues or board of directors).

5 DATA AND DATA COLLECTION TECHNIQUES

Marketing researchers work with quantitative or qualitative data. Research findings which can be analysed and expressed numerically are quantitative; information based on value judgements and difficult to quantify is qualitative [cf: Glossary].

Data collection techniques fall into two categories: *primary data* collection and *secondary data* collection. Despite its name, primary data collection should not be the initial concern. Secondary data ('second-hand' information) is, as the name suggests, already available.

5.1 Secondary data

There are two types of secondary information.

– Internal Sources
  This is information already available within the organisation or company, such as accounting records, marketing information, R&D reports, sales force returns etc.

– External Sources
  These can be census information, DTI libraries, embassies, periodicals, trade reports etc.

Secondary information has already been collected for another purpose but, by definition, therefore already exists on a shelf collecting dust, on a computer file or in a library. As such, it should be sifted first to ascertain whether or not it contains enough information for the decision to be made. Frequently, because this information has been collected for another purpose, it will not meet the exact needs of the marketer in the new situation. The marketer must then make a decision as to whether or not the additional secondary-sourced information, coupled with his/her experience and intuition, will be an adequate base on which to make a decision. If it is all deemed insufficient, then there is the need to instigate primary data collection – the collection of bespoke/customised information to tackle the specific solution at hand.

5.2 Primary data collection

There are two key types of primary data collection:

- Observation: Personal or Mechanical
  For example, supermarket managers watching the behaviour of queues, patterns of trolley pushing, and manipulating store layout accordingly; video cameras in fast food restaurants monitoring customer behaviour.
- Surveys: Mail/Postal, Telephone or Personal

5.2.1 Mail surveys

The two key advantages of mail surveys are their economy and lack of interviewer bias. Potentially, the lowest cost per response. Costs include typing, photocopying/printing and postage. Because there is no face-to-face contact, there can be no bias from the interviewer to the respondent. However, there are significant deficiencies with the technique. It is a particularly inflexible research tool. The questionnaire must be short, easy for respondents to complete, with no probing questions which may cause offence/non-response. In addition, there is often a long lead time in terms of mailing out, following up, and receiving responses. Respondent rates can be quite disappointing. In the UK, obtaining up-to-date mailing lists is notoriously difficult, even from the professional mailing houses, and many questionnaires tend to end up in the waste bin. Researchers work on the basis that 25 per cent of addresses on a mailing list become obsolete every 12 months.

A response rate in consumer marketing of 30 per cent is believed to be very favourable, but typically in business-to-business situations response rates can be as low as 1–2 per cent. A great deal of research has been undertaken to find out whether or not response rates can be improved by adding incentives such as a 20p piece for coffee from a vending machine, a free pen, or whether coloured paper may improve response rates. The additional cost incurred in amending the questionnaire along these lines has not been deemed worthy of their further consideration. However, in certain situations incentives such as prize draws (bottles of champagne/whisky, holidays) have been seen to significantly improve response rates. Personalising the questionnaire is also known to significantly improve the chances of gaining a response: it is important to find out the name of the person to whom the questionnaire should be sent rather than just the job function title. If in doubt, the Managing Director should be the choice. Questionnaires sent to a 'junior' will rarely be passed upwards to a more senior member of staff.

5.2.2 Telephone surveys

These avoid interviewers' travel expenses, but – typically because outside agencies need to be sub-contracted – are more expensive than postal questionnaires. Telephone surveys are more flexible than mail shots because interviewers can ask certain probing questions and can build a rapport thus encouraging respondents to answer. However, because most research agencies pay their telephonists on a piece rate, telephonists are often reluctant to extend interviews with unnecessary explanation and discussion. There is some anonymity, but it may be hard for interviewers to develop trust over the phone with respondents, particularly with the growing trend of teleselling. With the increasing ownership of telephones, sample bias is less of a problem than in the past, although for business-to-business marketing research there is a significant problem in terms of gatekeeping: if the target for the telephone interviewer is a manager, it is highly likely that the call will not get through the secretary.

5.2.3 Personal interviews

There are four types of personal interviews:

- The in-home interview (extremely detailed, good response rates), paid for, honest answers (on home territory) but expensive.
- Quali-depth interviews: a relatively new innovation, whereby 25-minute interviews are conducted in hired halls/meeting rooms, for example close to the high street, for a minimal incentive.
- Shopping mall intercept: the person with the clipboard, with three or four minutes' worth of questions, with some chance to build rapport, explain questions, follow up answers, but relatively limited scope to get a detailed understanding of the issues.
- The focus group. These are two- or three-hour discussion groups, typically with eight respondents, generally one sex, held in a hotel room, studio, or relevant retail outlet. Such discussions, led by a moderator from a marketing research agency, tend to start with a general free-flow discussion, before focusing on the product, market, advertising concept in question (hence the term focus). Focus groups are one of the most useful and commonly used market research techniques.

Of all the survey techniques, personal interview surveys are the most expensive, and of the personal interviews, in-home interviewing is the most costly (mainly because of the interviewer's time, with an average of one interview per evening). Interviewing is the most flexible technique in that respondents can react to visual material, researchers can assist in filling out questionnaires, follow up responses, and interrogate in more detail. One of the drawbacks to the technique can be interviewer bias, although there is the potential advantage of the interviewer building up a rapport with respondents. The personal attributes of the interviewers may, though, bias respondents' answers and responses.

Respondents' cooperation is not generally a problem, particularly as for certain types of in-home interviewing and/or focus group interviewing there is usually a cash incentive. For shopping mall intercepts, many people may refuse to participate, but generally interviewers are in busy thorough-fares and there are many potential targets to seek. Because the numbers of respondents are generally much lower in the survey design than for tele-phone or mail surveys, sampling is a potential pitfall and must be carefully orchestrated. For example, in the marketing research industry it is a widely held belief that eight focus groups well structured around the country, mixing different social classes, can represent the whole of the country's population. In other words, 64 people's opinions may form the basis for a product launch or promotional strategy.

6 SAMPLING

There are three types of *probability* sampling:

- Random (everyone in the population has an equal chance of being included in the sample).
- Stratified (each separate group identified in the population gets propor-tionate representation in the sample).
- Area (typically geographic units; sampling of people or units in the specified area).

The main type of *judgemental* sampling is *quota*. Based on specified criteria (typically age, sex, education, race – simple demographics), inter-view targets are preselected by interviewers, typically based on appcarancc. For example, a researcher may be told to interview 50 ladies aged between 40 and 55, all of whom are from 'a good background'. The interviewer cannot ask his/her targets their age/social status, but must make a judge-ment based on the person's appearance and manner. There is significant room for error in this approach, particularly as often such researchers are part-time, sub-contractors paid on piece rates, and the sooner their quota is met the sooner they can go home!

7 MARKETING RESEARCH PREREQUISITES

Marketing research must match the following key criteria:

- Reliability. Were the research to be repeated with a similar sample frame and survey design soon after the original survey, the results should be similar.
- Validity. The survey findings must be in line with the research problems and hypotheses.
- Robustness. The research programme and statistical analysis techniques should not crash through poor design.
- Communication. The research findings must be capable of communi-cation to the client and client audiences.

8 WORTH REMEMBERING

- Information is always needed in marketing, but circumstances may mean formal marketing research is not possible or completely necessary.
- It is often possible to reach a compromise between intuition and formal research.
- Secondary sources of information should be scanned prior to conducting primary research.
- There is a sliding scale of accuracy in survey techniques from face-to-face interviewing, through telephone interviewing, to mail surveys.
- In most marketing situations a mix of research techniques is used in the research programme, rather than just one approach.
- Despite the emphasis in textbooks on consumer marketing, marketing research is not just orientated to consumer research. Trade marketing research (particularly examining competitors and distributors) is very important.

9 USEFUL REFERENCES

Birn, R. (1990) *The Effective Use of Market Research*, London: Kogan Page.
Breen, G. and Blankenship, A.B. (1982) *Do It Yourself Marketing Research*, New York: McGraw-Hill.
Chisnall, P.M. (1992) *Marketing Research*, London: McGraw-Hill.
Parasuraman, A. (1991) *Marketing Research*, Reading, Massachusetts: Addison-Wesley.
Tull, D.S. and Hawkins, D.I. (1990) *Marketing Research*, New York: Macmillan.

Chapter 22

Forecasting

1 FORECASTING IN MARKETING

In marketing, forecasts of market size and market share are required to enable marketers to:

- estimate market attractiveness;
- monitor performance;
- allocate resources effectively;
- gear up production to meet demand:
    excess stocks cost money/use resources;
    too low production leads to missed sales/
    customer and distributor unease.

2 FORECASTING MODELS

The following types of models are available to marketers seeking to achieve a better understanding of market size and share:

- Product Class Sales Model (or Industry Sales Model)
  This type estimates the total number of units of a product category purchased by the population of all spending units.
- Brand Sales Model
  Here, the total number of units is estimated of a particular brand bought by the population of all spending units.
- Market Share Model
  This model assesses the relative number of units of a particular brand purchased by the total population, i.e. relative to the total number of units of the product class.

3 METHODS OF FORECASTING

Other than astrology and other methods of the occult, there are basically three categories of forecasting models for sales/marketing issues:

> – Judgemental
> – Time series and projection
> – Causal

3.1 Judgemental

3.1.1 Sales force composite

This is simply where sales representatives/field managers are asked to estimate their sales. The overall forecast is then arrived at by summing up their forecasts. The advantages of this approach are that it is:

- widely used;
- relatively accurate over the short term (one or two quarters);
- inexpensive;
- gives customer by customer records of expected sales per field representative in industrial markets. This is particularly useful for monitoring and evaluating the sales force.

Problems with this method:

- It is difficult to motivate sales representatives/field managers to take the time to be conscientious in forecasting.
- Individual pessimistic/optimistic biases come to the fore.
- Group/company biases are not ruled out. It is therefore necessary to make allowances for biases.

The sales force/field managers tend to be highly aware of changes in likely customer purchases in the short term (the next few months), but often are unaware of broad economic trends or movements which are likely to affect customers' industries or clients. Therefore, this judgemental technique is weak in the longer term and in identifying turning points in underlying market trends.

3.1.2 Expert consensus

This is a jury of experts who offer opinions. Experts include marketers, marketing researchers, company executives, consultants, trade association officials, trade journal editors, and in some cases government agency officials. This is a very widely used technique.

There are basically three types of expert consensus: point forecasts, interval forecasts, probability distribution forecasts.

Point.   Sales forecasts are for a specific amount of sales (i.e. an absolute amount with no room for mistakes or margin of error). Taken in isolation, particular point forecasts – for example, a particular group of managers stating categorically that in one particular territory sales of a particular product will be 80,000 units over the next three months – can be prone to bias and error. It is therefore better to have several different points forecast by different groups of managers and to aggregate their predictions.

Interval forecasts.   This is where a particular measure of confidence in the forecast is given. In other words, the managers above could be 80 per cent confident that 80,000 units will be sold in the three-month period.

Probability forecasts.   In this case, different forecasts for the same product in the same market are given with different percentage accuracies attached. For example, the managers above could be 80 per cent confident that sales of 80,000 units could be achieved, only 50 per cent confident that sales of 100,000 could be achieved, and only 10 per cent confident that 110,000 units could be achieved. This option allows the 'best' and 'most pessimistic' forecasts to be clearly identified.

The problem with using a jury of expert opinion is that there is a need to 'weight' the value of each expert's forecast. There are four methods for '*weighting*':

- Use of equal weights (the simple averaging of all experts' forecasts, giving each expert equal prominence).
- Assigning weights proportional to an assessment of each expert's level of expertise/knowledge/common sense.
- Assigning weights proportional to a self-assessment of expertise (allowing each expert to give a measure of his/her expertise).
- Use weights proportional to the relative accuracy of past forecasts (i.e. looking at how accurate each expert's forecasts have been in the past and make allowances for the new forecasts accordingly).

There is no evidence that any one of these four methods of weighting is better than the others.

3.1.3 Delphi

This is a commonly used approach and one recommended by many marketing researchers and consultants. The simple steps are:

(i)   participants (e.g. field managers) make separate, individual forecasts;
(ii)   central analyst (e.g. at head office) independently aggregates these forecasts;
(iii) a revised forecast is returned to each separate participant in the field;
(iv)   participants then make revised forecasts in the context of the new 'picture';

(v)   the analyst at head office then centrally pulls the forecast together to produce the final overall forecast.

The Delphi technique avoids the weighting problems discussed above. The median of the group's overall response will tend to move towards a truer answer. This technique is useful for short-, medium- and long-term forecasts, and also for new product developments where there is no historical information on which to base a forecast.

3.2 Time series models

Time series models involve a set of observations being evaluated to identify trends. In many cases this involves the use of simple graphs, e.g. sales in units against time – typically then, sales per month or per quarter or per year over a particular period of time. The assumption is that past patterns/ changes can be used to predict the future. Figure 22.1 gives an example of a time series graph.

It is important to identify the underlying trend, *standardised* for cyclical, seasonal and random variation (statistical noise). It is therefore common to use data which have been averaged-out over time.

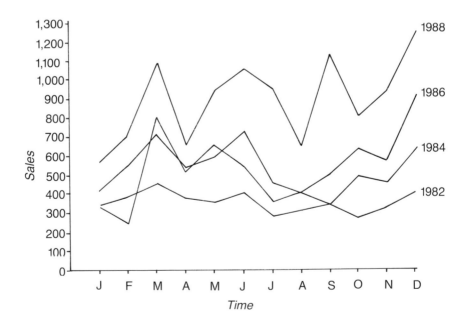

Figure 22.1 Example of a time series graph

3.2.1 Naive

This approach is characterised by a reliance on the last period's sales as a basis for forecasts for the next period's sales. It is only useful if the underlying trend of sales is flat rather than at a particular peak or trough (in which case, a particularly good or bad period of sales would be used to forecast the next period's sales, even though the underlying trend may show that there is in reality no relationship between the two neighbouring periods). Typical use is for forecasting monthly or quarterly sales.

3.2.2 Moving averages

This is where the average of the values for the last X periods is taken into account and updated – 'moved' – each period. In other words, were sales figures available for eight periods, the newest sales figures would be added to make nine periods in total. The average would be then taken for the most recent eight periods, dropping the initial period (period number 1). Typically, eight periods ('the recent past') are used.

> 'Sales for the next period would be equal to the average sales for the average last X [say eight] periods'

Forecasts generated using this method would probably need adjusting by a seasonal index figure (e.g. c. −5 per cent for a known trough, or c. +8 per cent for a known high point in the seasonal pattern).

It is important to remember that this is a forecast suitable for predicting only one sales period in advance (one month or one quarter). Its main use, therefore, is for inventory control.

3.2.3 Exponential smoothing

This method uses a 'weighted' moving average. The more recent the period, the heavier the weight given; in other words the more recent the period the greater the importance re the prediction. This assumes that more recent sales are a better indication of future sales. This approach tends to be computer based, using complicated algorithms and statistical packages. There are various derivatives of this technique, such as Double Exponential Smoothing, Adaptive Smoothing, Winter's Extended Exponential Smoothing.

3.2.4 Statistical trend analysis

This is the determination of the underlying trend or pattern of growth, stability or decline in a series of data. It is typically based on simple regression analysis of Time versus Sales. The approach is orientated towards statistical computer packages, although some graphics packages can also undertake this task.

3.2.5 Box-Jenkins

Major economic cycles are inherent in sales patterns. With such cycles, most of the above techniques have been proved to be unhelpful (they do not pick up the cycles). There is a need, therefore, for a Box-Jenkins routine: a specially designed statistical routine requiring computer support. A major drawback is that there needs to be a minimum of 45 sales periods of information, although the routine can consider underlying cycles inherent in trends.

Note:

– Clearly, there is a need to have managers' knowledge of expected market changes in any forecasting.
– Before choosing a particular forecasting technique, it is important first to examine a plot of sales data and to visually eyeball the *pattern/trends* before deciding how far back in the data set to proceed and which technique to use.
– Typically, it is better to use a combination of forecasting techniques and to aggregate the various forecasts to come up with one overall prediction of sales.

3.3 Causal forecasting

These forecasting approaches look at changes in sales due to fluctuations in one or more market variables (e.g. competitor activity, price etc.) other than simply time.

3.3.1 Barometric

This method relies on changes in one variable predicting a rise or fall in another. For example, marketers of baby food may argue that sales depend on levels of births. In construction, sales of backhoe diggers depend on the number of housing starts. Therefore it is important to attain data on sectors/industries relevant to a particular product's sales, and correlate this information with product sales. The problem is mainly one of false messages and of using several different indicators at once. Still, this is a useful technique for helping to explain some of the trends and patterns, or even helping to validate predictions resulting from some of the above time series or judgemental techniques.

3.3.2 Buyer intentions – surveys

Here, surveys obtained through marketing research of buyer intentions are used. If these surveys are undertaken at regular points in time, a plot can be made of the customer survey expectations of purchase intent against real sales occurring during similar periods. Over time, through graphs and simple correlation, the overall pattern can be identified and therefore the value/error of the predictions made from marketing research surveys can be quantified. These surveys can then be used on a regular basis knowing the expected margin of error to put on the claim for customer expectations of purchases. In other words, the evaluation of past surveys' results against real sales, gives a weighting to future surveys' findings and their accuracy.

3.3.3 Causal regression

This is the most widely used causal model of forecasting. A multivariable regression equation relates sales to various predictor variables such as disposable income, price relative to competitors, levels of advertising, numbers of products on the market, etc.

The Multiple Regression Process:

(i)   Identify the dependent variable; what is to be predicted – e.g. sales.
(ii)   Identify (through discussions with management, previous research studies, etc) the relevant predictor (independent) variables.
(iii) Collect time series or cross-sectional data (time series data give the same information collected for various points in time; an historical record/trend. Cross-sectional data give a snapshot in time – in other words 'a one-off hit').
(iv)   Identify whether the relationship between sales and predictor variables is linear (a straight line), or curvilinear (with various peaks and troughs).
(v)   Use regression on a standard computer package (e.g. SPSS or Minitab) to attain the coefficients (each individual independent variable's weighting or relative impact) and percentage of accuracy. In other words, each of the predictor variables such as disposable income, price etc. will have a different impact on sales and until all of the relevant predictor/independent variables have been identified there will not be a high percentage level of accuracy for predictions (known as the R^2). In other words, if key market characteristics which determine sales are omitted, the level of accuracy will be low.

(vi) Repeat steps 1 to 4 adding in additional predictor variables until the overall R^2 – the level of predictive ability usually measured as a percentage – is 'good' (over 70 per cent).

3.3.4 Econometric models

These models apply mathematical analogues and equations using multi-variate statistical techniques similar to regression but more complicated (AID, factor analysis etc.).

4 BUT WHICH TECHNIQUE?

Overall, experts believe that the causal techniques are more effective than judgemental.

Within the judgemental category, no one technique has been proved to be better than the others, although the *Delphi* technique is extremely popular and widely used.

Within the causal approach, it is again hard to prove that one technique is better than others. The barometric approach and buyer intention survey are both widely used and can be extremely useful in explaining/describing forecasts made using the more statistical techniques or time series graphs. Of the statistical techniques, *causal regression* (taking into account many marketing variables) has been shown to be a very useful technique.

The overall conclusion is that it is better to use a mixture of forecasting techniques rather than just one. The *Delphi* technique is an extremely useful one to consider, supported in the first place by simple *time series graphs* and the moving averages approach. In order to explain some of these trends, it is useful then to look at the *barometric* approach (specifically looking at how sales of products compare with customers' sales, e.g. housing starts if supplying construction equipment). Often in the slightly longer term (owing to resources), it is a beneficial exercise to develop a simple *multiple regression* model which ultimately, once developed, will typically run on a very straightforward spreadsheet (e.g. Lotus 1,2,3).

5 USEFUL REFERENCES

Harvard Business Review (1991) *Accurate Business Forecasting,* **Boston: Harvard Business Review Paperbacks.**

Lilien, G.L. and Kotler, P. (1983) *Marketing Decision Making,* New York: Harper and Row.

Naert, P. and Leeflang, P. (1978 *Building Implementable Marketing Models,* Leiden: Martinus Nijhoff.

Tull, D.S. and Hawkins, D.I. (1990) *Marketing Research,* **New York: Macmillan.**

Chapter 23

Market segmentation, targeting, positioning

1 SEGMENTATION

1.1 Market segmentation

High-growth companies succeed by identifying and meeting the needs of certain kinds of customer, not all customers, for special kinds of products and service, not all products or all services. Business academics call this market segmentation. Entrepreneurs call it common sense.

(Clifford and Cavanagh, 1985)

Customers have different product needs and wants yet it is usually unrealistic for companies to customise their products for each individual. For this reason companies are increasingly moving away from mass marketing towards a target marketing strategy where the focus is on a particular group (or groups) of customers. This identification of target customer groups is *market segmentation*. Market segmentation allows companies to go some of the way towards satisfying the diversity of needs while maintaining certain scale economies. Customers are aggregated into groups with similar requirements and buying characteristics. The organisation selects which group or groups on which to target its sales and marketing. The marketing mix is constructed around the specific requirements of the targeted group(s) or segment(s) of customers. The product or service is then positioned directly only at the targeted consumers. This positioning takes into consideration the offerings of competing organisations within the same segment.

1.2 The segmentation process

The market segmentation process consists of three distinct stages. These stages are illustrated below.

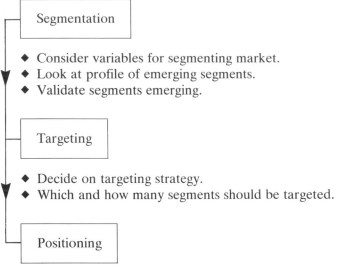

- Consider variables for segmenting market.
- Look at profile of emerging segments.
- Validate segments emerging.

- Decide on targeting strategy.
- Which and how many segments should be targeted.

- Understand consumer perceptions.
- Position products in the mind of the consumer.
- Design appropriate marketing mix.

The principle of the three stages is that 'similar' consumers can be grouped. For example, were an audience of 100 students asked which would be their favourite car model to purchase, there might be 100 separate responses. However, several of those responses would be on the lines of students desiring a sports car, several would be for a four-wheel drive off-road vehicle, several may be centred on an executive car, etc. Where such 'similar' consumers could be grouped into large enough groups, such *segments* could be profitably targeted by companies.

The benefits of a market segmentation approach to companies are many:

- Better understanding of customer needs and wants. This can result in a more carefully tuned and effective marketing programme being devised.
- Improved understanding of the competitive situation. Such additional insight can help companies develop and maintain a differential advantage.
  More effective resource allocation. To target 100 per cent of a market is not usually realistic. Focusing on certain segments allows organisations to make the best of their resources.

1.3 Carrying out segmentation

There are two fundamental steps:

(i) Segmentation variables (also called *base variables*) are used to divide markets up into groups of customers with similar product needs. Many different segmentation bases can be used (see Figure 23.1), but the key is to select bases which effectively distinguish between different product requirements.

In industrial or organisational markets, the list of potential base variables includes some which are the same as in consumer markets and some which are different:

Geographic location
Type of organisation
Customer size/characteristics
Use of product

(ii) Once segments have been identified using one or a combination of the base variables above, as much as possible must be done to understand the characteristics of the customers in those segments. This understanding will make it easier for the marketer to design a marketing programme which will appeal to the segment targeted. Building up a fuller picture of the segments is called *profiling* and uses *descriptor variables*. Descriptors can include variables relating to customer characteristics or product-related behavioural variables. In fact, the more extensive the picture, the better.

1.4 Uses of effective segmentation

Careful market segmentation can help companies to take advantage of marketing opportunities which might otherwise be missed:

– *Market penetration*: increasing percentage of sales in present markets by taking sales from competitors.
– *Product development*: offering newer, improved products to current markets, through the expansion of the product range.
– *Market development*: selling existing products to new markets by finding new applications.
– *Diversification*: moving into new markets by offering new products.

1.5 Essential qualities for effective segments

Whatever choices are made it is essential that segments which are to be implemented satisfy a number of key criteria:

– *Measurable*: the segments must be able to be delimited and measured/assessed for market potential.
– *Substantial*: in order to warrant marketing activity, the identified segment must be large enough to be viable and therefore worthwhile targeting with products/services.

BASIC CUSTOMER CHARACTERISTICS

Because of the ease with which information concerning basic customer characteristics can be obtained and measured, the use of these variables is widespread.

DEMOGRAPHICS
Age
Sex
Family
Race
Religion
The family life-cycle concept is an imaginative way of combining demographic variables.

SOCIO-ECONOMICS
Income
Occupation
Education
Social class
Different income groups have different aspirations in terms of cars, housing, education etc.

GEOGRAPHIC LOCATION
Country
Region
Type of urban area (conurbation/village)
Type of housing (affluent suburbs/inner city)

PERSONALITY, MOTIVES AND LIFESTYLE
Holiday companies often use lifestyle to segment the market. Club Med, for example, concentrates on young singles while other tour operators cater especially for senior citizens or young families.

PRODUCT-RELATED BEHAVIOURAL CHARACTERISTICS

PURCHASE BEHAVIOUR
Customers for tinned foods, like baked beans, may be highly brand loyal to Heinz or HP or may shop purely on the basis of price.

PURCHASE OCCASION
A motorist making an emergency purchase of a replacement tyre, while on a trip far from home, is less likely to haggle about price than the customer who has a chance to 'shop around'.

BENEFITS SOUGHT
When customers buy toothpaste they seek different benefits. For some, fresh breath and taste are essential while for others fluoride protection is the key. Macleans Sensitive caters for a minority group which requires treatment for sensitive teeth.

CONSUMPTION BEHAVIOUR AND USER STATUS
Examining consumption patterns can indicate where companies should be concentrating their efforts. Light or non-users are often neglected. The important question to ask is why consumption in these groups is low.

ATTITUDE TO PRODUCT
Different customers have different perceptions and preferences of products offered. Car manufacturers from Skoda to Porsche are in the business of designing cars to match customer preferences, changing perceptions as necessary.

Figure 23.1 Variables for segmenting consumer markets
Source: Dibb, S., Simkin, L., Pride, W. and Ferrell, O.C. (1991) *Marketing: Concepts and Strategies*, Boston: Houghton Mifflin, Table 3.1

- *Accessible*: having identified a market segment, and checking on its potential viability, the marketer must be able to action a marketing programme with a finely developed marketing mix to targeted consumers. Occasionally, although there are sufficient consumer similarities for consumers to have been grouped together in an identified market segment, the similarities are not sufficient to enable a marketer to implement full marketing programmes.
- *Stable*: there must be an assessment of a segment's short-, medium-, and long-term viability, particularly in the light of competition and marketing environmental changes.

2 TARGETING

Once segments have been identified decisions about how many and which customer groups to target must be made. The options include:

- *Mass marketing strategy*: offering one product/retail concept to most of the market, across many market segments. Although scale economies can be achieved, there is the risk that few customers will be adequately satisfied.
- *Single segment strategy*: concentrating on a single segment with one product/retail concept. This is relatively cheap in resources, but there is a risk of putting all the eggs in one basket – if the segment fails the company's financial strength will rapidly decline.
- *Multi-segment strategy*: targeting a different product/retail concept at each of a number of segments. Although this approach can spread the risk of being over-committed in one area, it can be extremely resource hungry.

Which target segment strategy a company adopts will be dependent on a wide range of market, product and competitive factors. Each of these must be carefully considered before a decision is made about segments to be targeted:

- a company's existing market share/market homogeneity (a company's knowledge of an existing market).
- product homogeneity: a company's expertise, on which to build, in an existing product field.
- level of competition.
- customer needs.
- segment size and structure.
- company resources.

3 POSITIONING

3.1 Perceptions in consumers' minds

Product Positioning refers to the decisions and activities intended to create and maintain a firm's product concept in customers' minds.

Market Positioning is arranging for a product to occupy a clear, distinctive and desirable place – relative to competing products – in the minds of target customers.

The product must be perceived by the selected target customers to have a distinct image, vis-à-vis competitors, in line with their own desires/ expectations. The position of a product is related to the attributes ascribed to it by consumers, such as its standing, its quality and type of people who use it, its strengths and weaknesses, and any other unusual and memorable characteristics it may possess, its price and the value it represents to the consumers. The whole of the marketing mix is important in developing an effective positioning, as the product attributes must be closely in line with the targeted customers' expectations and needs, as must the associated price points and channels of distribution. However, promotional activity is one of the fundamental elements of creating an effective positioning as it is through promotion that the positioning is communicated to the target audience.

3.2 Steps in determining a positioning plan

(i)   Define the segments in a particular market.
(ii)   Decide which segment (segments) to target.
(iii)   Understand what the target consumers expect and believe to be most important when deciding on a purchase.
(iv)   Develop a product or retail brand which caters specifically for these needs and expectations.
(v)   Evaluate the positioning and images, as perceived by the target customers, of competing products/retail concepts in the selected market segment (or segments).
(vi)   With knowledge of a product/brand, the needs and expectations of target customers, their perception of competing brands' positioning, select an image which sets the product or brand apart from the competing brands – ensuring the chosen image matches the aspirations of the target customers. The selected positioning and imagery must be credible.
(vii)   The marketer must communicate with the targeted consumers about the product – the promotional element of the marketing mix – as well as making the product readily available at the right price, with the associated development of the full marketing mix.

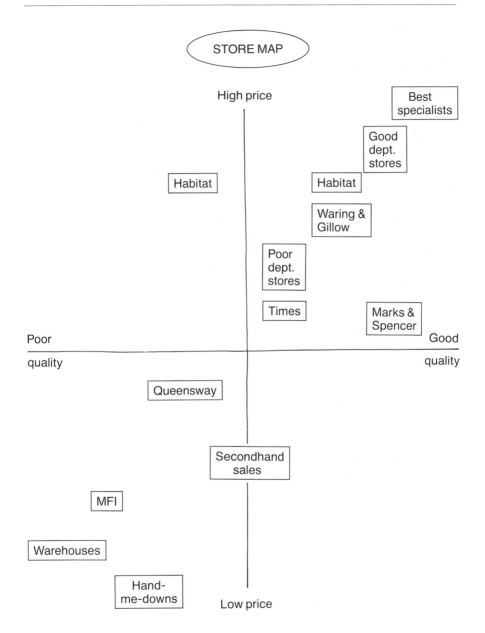

Figure 23.2 A perceptual map for the UK furniture industry

3.3 Perceptual Maps

Perceptual mapping is based on a variety of mathematical and subjective approaches designed to place or describe consumers' perceptions of brands or products on one or a series of 'spatial maps'. It is a means of visually depicting consumers' perceptions, showing the relative positionings of different brands or companies. The core attributes must be identified through consumer research, with follow-up confirmatory research identifying the relative positionings of the brands or companies to be plotted. For example, the perceptual map of the UK furniture market, as produced in the late 1980s, identified 'value for money' as the key attribute (see Figure 23.2). Research showed that consumers were in reality more concerned with price and product quality. It is important for all marketers to understand the positioning of their products on such a spatial map, vis-à-vis competitors, particularly in order to develop realistic and effective marketing programmes.

4 USEFUL REFERENCES

Davies, G.J. and Brooks, J.M. (1989) *Positioning Strategy in Retailing*, London: Paul Chapman.
Dibb, S., Simkin, L., Pride, W. and Ferrell, O.C. (1991) *Marketing: Concepts and Strategies,* **Boston: Houghton Mifflin.**
Frank, R. and Wind, Y. (1971) *Market Segmentation*, Englewood Cliffs N.J.: Prentice-Hall.
Ries, A. and Trout, J. (1981) *Positioning: The Battle for Your Mind,* **New York: McGraw-Hill.**

Chapter 24

Competition

1 DEFINITION

Competitors are generally viewed by a business as those firms that market products similar to, or substitutable for, its products aimed at the same target market.

(Dibb *et al.*, 1991)

2 THE NEED FOR COMPETITOR ORIENTATION

Decisions about marketing strategy must take into consideration the competitive situation in which companies operate. It is often argued that success is dependent upon becoming 'competitor orientated'. Understanding competitors' relative strengths and weaknesses, market shares and positionings is essential. Taken in conjunction with an appreciation of key customer needs, companies should have an indication where to position their product offerings, now and in the future.

Various approaches have been proposed for analysing the competitive environment. One of the most widely quoted is that of Porter. Other writers discuss competitiveness in terms of warfare strategies: offensive and defensive.

3 PORTER'S VIEW OF COMPETITIVE STRATEGY

3.1 The competitive arena

Porter considers the competitive arena to consist of competing organisations jockeying for position in an environment determined by a number of outside forces (see Figure 24.1).

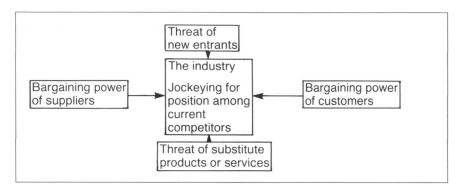

Figure 24.1 Industry forces in the competitive arena
Source: Porter, M.E. (1979) 'How competitive forces shape strategy', *Harvard Business Review* 47 (March–April): 137–45

Bargaining Power of Suppliers

The impact of the supplier depends on the availability of alternative suppliers and product substitutes. In monopoly situations the bargaining power of the supplier is particularly high. This can result in high prices and inflexible, poor quality, product offerings. At the other extreme, industries with many suppliers and much substitution frequently lead to relatively low bargaining power for supplying companies.

Bargaining Power of Buyers

High buyer bargaining power usually occurs in industries where suppliers' power is low. Where buyers purchase large volumes of standardised items which can readily be sourced elsewhere if necessary. Often these items form only a part of the final product.

Threat of Substitute Products or Services

A proliferation of substitute products within an industry can significantly limit the growth potential and long-term profits. Competing companies have less control over price and can even face problems of over-capacity.

Threat of New Entrants

New entrants in a market lead to increased capacity which can limit the market share of profits of existing competitors. The likely impact of new entrants is determined in part by the barriers to entry which prevail. Some typical barriers to entry include the presence of strongly branded competitors, economies of scale, control of distribution and high capital requirements. In markets where barriers are high, the number of new entrants will be limited.

3.2 The generic strategies

Porter identifies three generic strategies which, he claims, can result in success for companies competing for position in any particular market. These are *cost leadership, differentiation* and *focus* (see Figure 24.2). The dangers of trying to adopt a mix of these strategies can result in companies becoming 'stuck in the middle'.

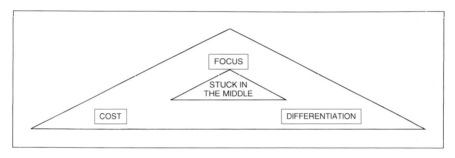

Figure 24.2 Porter's three generic strategies
Source: Porter, M.E. (1980) *Competitive Strategy: Techniques for Analysing Industries and Competitors*, New York: Free Press/Macmillan

Cost Leadership

Involves developing a low cost base, often through economies of scale associated with high market share, to give high contribution. This can then be used to further develop the low cost base. Very tight cost controls are essential to the success of this strategy.

Differentiation

Companies adopting a differentiation strategy strive to offer a product/marketing effort which has a distinct advantage or is different to that offered by competitors. Differentiation can be achieved on a number of fronts. Creative and innovative product or brand design are possibilities, as are novel distribution channel and pricing policies.

Focus

Focused companies must maintain close links with the market so that product and marketing effort can be designed with a particular target group in mind. Often of small size, unable to achieve cost leadership or maintain significant differentiation, such companies succeed by effectively meeting customer needs which may be being missed by larger players in the market.

4 WARFARE STRATEGIES

The analysis of competition and the development of competitive strategies have been linked to military principles. Under this scenario, competing companies represent the enemy to be defeated. The principles are based upon the concept that in any market there are four different types of competitive position which companies can occupy.

4.1 Competitive positions

Market Leader

This is the highest market share company which retains its position by trying to expand the total market (market development), perhaps by finding new uses for a product, or increase market share (market penetration), for example through an aggressive advertising campaign. The aggressive measures are balanced by a desire to protect current market share.

Market Challenger

One or more non-market leaders which *aggressively* attack for additional market share.

Market Follower

These are low share competitors without the resources/ market position/ R&D/commitment to challenge or seriously contend for market leadership.

Market Nicher

Companies which specialise in terms of market/product/customers by finding a safe, profitable market segment. As markets mature, increasing competitiveness tends to mean large companies become more interested in such segments which then for a niche-only company are more difficult to retain.

Different marketing strategies are appropriate for companies which occupy different competitive positions within markets, including aspects of attack and defence.

4.2 Strategies for competitive positions

4.2.1 Principles of defensive warfare

The skill to adopt a defensive position is important if companies are to protect their existing market share. However, defence should not be regarded solely as a negative activity. Strong defence involves striking a balance between waiting to be attacked and parrying that attack. In general, the following basic rules apply:

- Only the market leader should consider adopting a defensive role. Even in these circumstances it is necessary to combine defensive with offensive strategies.
- Don't sleep behind high walls – they won't be high enough. Companies adopting a myopic view of their market position are readily open to attack from aggressive market challengers.
- The best defensive strategy is the courage to attack.
- It is essential that strong competitive moves are blocked.

Adopting a defensive position does not necessarily mean remaining static. Companies should be ready to move and respond to aggressive marketing effort from competitors (see Figure 24.3).

- Build walls around strong positions. This requires companies to fully understand their true strengths (for example brand name), and to be proactive in their attempts to retain that strength.
- Protect weak areas. Attention on weak areas can sometimes be diverted by marketing tactics which focus on other aspects of the product/marketing offering.
- Be mobile and ready to move. Companies should be quick to exploit new markets, products and opportunities.
- Withdrawal from market/product if absolutely necessary. It can be sensible to consolidate in areas which are strong, thus focusing resources. Such action should not leave weak areas which might allow competitors access to key markets.

4.2.2 Principles of offensive warfare

These principles apply particularly to companies in a non-market leading position, which are challenging aggressively for additional market share. It

| HOW TO DEFEND! |

1. Build walls around strong positions.
2. Protect weak areas.
3. Be mobile. Ready to move.
   New markets/products/opportunities.
4. Run away! Withdraw from market/product.

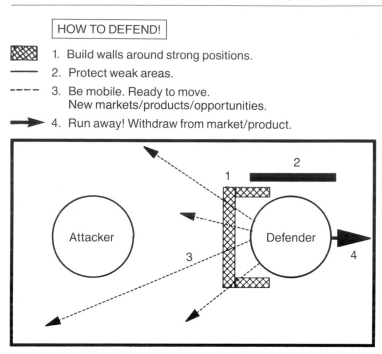

Figure 24.3 How to defend

is often regarded as low risk to attack market followers and market nichers rather than the market leading organisation.

- The main consideration is the strength of the leader's position. It is essential to be aware of the dangers of antagonising the powerful, resource-rich market leader.
- Find a weakness in the leader's strength and attack at that point. When a decision is made to attack the leader, this should always be in an area which the challenger feels able to sustain (and the decision should consider the challenger's cost structure and resources).
- Launch the attack on as narrow a front as possible. Being focused in challenging is important because it ensures that resources are not spread too thinly.

Figure 24.4 shows how to attack.

- Head-to-head. This full frontal method of attack is in many ways the most difficult to sustain. The challenger tries to match the market leader blow by blow on some aspect of the marketing programme (for example price). Challengers which attempt this approach often fail!

HOW TO ATTACK!

━━━ 1. Head-to-head.
─── 2. Attack weak points.
──── 3. Adopt a multi-pronged strategy.
─── 4. Guerilla attack.

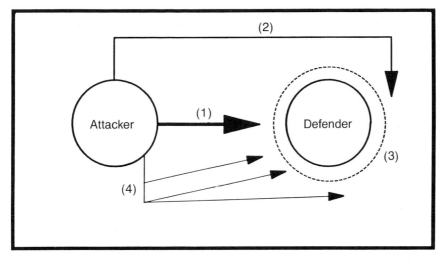

Figure 24.4 How to attack

- Attack weak points.
- Adopt a multi-pronged strategy. It can be appropriate to overwhelm competitors, thus diluting their ability to respond.
- Guerrilla attack. This type of challenging is not large scale and prolonged. The intention is to annoy competitors with unpredictable and periodic attacks.

4.2.3 Strategies for market followers

Although there are opportunities for followers in markets, companies occupying these positions are often vulnerable to attack from their larger competitors. Companies adopting this position should therefore consider the following suggestions:

- Use market segmentation carefully. Concentrate only on areas where the company can cope.
- Specialise rather than diversify so that resources are not spread too thinly. The emphasis should be on profitability rather than sales growth.
- Use R&D as efficiently as possible. If there are only resources to compete in certain areas they must be matched with the R&D effort.

4.2.4 Strategies for market nichers

In many markets nichers are the most vulnerable competitors. They must avoid competition with other organisations in order to ensure their success. This can be done by:

- Finding safe market segments. These should be areas where big companies do not believe it is worth competing. Unfortunately, as markets mature, such segments become more difficult to defend.
- Securing a niche by specialising on a particular market, customer or marketing mix.
- Being strong in more than one niche. If there is an aggressive attack on one niche segment, this means that there may be opportunities to switch resources to another.

5 APPLYING THE MARKETING MIX

As they develop the marketing programmes, companies in different competitive positions have at their disposal the full range of the extended (7Ps) marketing mix [cf. Chapter 29].

- Price can be used through discounting or offering other payment methods.
- Product can be varied through product innovation, proliferation or repositioning.
- Promotion can be used on many fronts. Advertising, sales promotion, personal selling and publicity are all at the disposal of competing organisations with different requirements, targets and promotional budgets.
- Distribution can be improved by seeking out innovative ways in which the customer can be reached.
- People, Process and Physical Evidence, sometimes regarded as the elements of the services marketing mix, are an important consideration for companies wishing to improve or differentiate these aspects of their marketing efforts.

6 USEFUL REFERENCES

Davidson, J.H. (1972) *Offensive Marketing*, New York: Penguin.
Lehmann, D.R. and Winner, R.S. (1988) *Analysis for Marketing Planning*, Plano: Business Publications.
Porter, M.E. (1979) 'How competitive forces shape strategy', *Harvard Business Review*, 47 (March–April): 137–45.
—— **(1980) *Competitive Strategy: Techniques for Analysing Industries and Competitors*, New York: Free Press/Macmillan.**
Saunders, J. (1987) 'Marketing and competitive success', in M. Baker (ed.) *The Marketing Book*, London: Heinemann/CIM.
Weitz, B.A. and Wensley, R. (1988) *Readings in Strategic Marketing*, Chicago: Dryden Press.

Chapter 25

Products and product management

1 DEFINITIONS

Product
Everything (both favourable and unfavourable) received in an exchange: a product is a complexity of tangible and intangible attributes, including functional, social and psychological utilities or benefits. A product may be a good, a service, or an idea.

Product Management
A form of marketing management where the marketing function and department are orientated around individual products/brands or product portfolios. Product management tends to have a more strategic view of the role of marketing. It is proactive rather than marketing as a service function within a company or organisation.

Key product management tasks include:

- branding decisions
- portfolio management
- modifying/deleting/developing products
- product positioning
- the development of marketing programmes (marketing mixes)
- marketing research/MIS

2 PRODUCTS

2.1 Products in marketing

Product is one of the basic elements of the marketing mix (the 4Ps). In many ways, it is the foundation stone for a marketing programme: a true marketing philosophy would dictate that consumer needs have been adequately identified so that the products are developed in line with such requirements. Without first having a product defined it is difficult to develop the rest of the marketing mix – pricing, place/distribution, promotion.

According to Kotler (1991), a product is broadly defined as:

Anything that can be offered to a market for attention, acquisition, use or consumption that might satisfy a want or need. This includes physical objects, services, persons, places, organisations, and ideas.

2.2 Classification of products

2.2.1 Consumer products

Convenience goods: products bought quickly, frequently, typically with little shopping around; such as soap powder, cigarettes, newspapers, some food items.

Shopping goods: consumers tend to shop around comparing quality and price; clothing, furniture, electrical appliances.

Speciality goods: usually pre-selected by brand, with consumers searching for suitable outlets stocking the chosen brand; Porsche car, B&O hi-fi, Gucci designer fashions.

Unsought goods: goods which initially the customer is unaware of, not recognising a need for such a product, often until stimulated by promotional activity; smoke detectors, CD in its early days, life insurance.

2.2.2 Service products

As discussed under services marketing [cf. Chapter 29], service products tend to be more intangible in their make-up, often requiring the active participation of the consumer in the production process. Services include:

Tourism/Catering
Travel
Health
Leisure/Entertainment
Education
Financial
Some Retail
Government/Administration
Non-Profit/Voluntary/Charitable
Business/consultancy

2.2.3 Industrial products

– Raw materials: cotton, crude oil, iron ore etc.
– Component parts: manufactured materials and parts used as components in subsequently produced products.

- Capital items: installations such as factories, offices, heavy machinery, plant.
- Accessory equipment: PCs, desks.
- Consumable supplies: paint, cleaning fluids, pencils, photocopying paper, etc.
- Services: maintenance, repair, legal or consultancy.

3 BRANDING DECISIONS

For nearly all products, there is now an associated brand (the obvious exception being pharmaceutical generics). Many marketers believe that product differentiation is the name of the game. *Product Differentiation* is the use of the marketing mix to differentiate a company's products from its competitors' products, with the hope of establishing the superiority and preferability of its products relative to competing brands. A brand, therefore, is essential to the effective marketing of many products in order to create a unique identity for a particular product: a *brand* is a name, term, symbol, design, or combination of these that identifies a seller's products and differentiates them from competitors' products.

For any product, service or idea there is a need to determine whether or not to have a brand. In most cases, the answer is affirmative and therefore there are key branding decisions for the marketer.

3.1 The need for brands

The brand should 'say' something about the product – make it more distinctive; brands make shoppers more efficient – many shoppers go out with specific brands on their 'shopping list' so reducing time spent in distributors/retail outlets; brands facilitate product differentiation – the real key to marketing.

3.2 Types of brands

Manufacturer: Heinz, Ford, IBM, JCB, Abbey National launched brands;

Private/own label: retailers' own labels, such as St Michael in Marks and Spencer, Saisho in Dixons, No. 7 in Boots; or simply the retailer's name as the branding foundation: Sainsbury's, Tesco, Debenhams own label products;

Generic: currently very few examples as there is little scope for product differentiation, but many pharmaceutical products are not associated with a specific manufacturer overtly, being known by their pharmacy description.

3.3 Quality

All products have an in-built life-cycle/quality threshold often determined by the R&D researchers. Frequently consumer research is fed by marketers into the development of products and their associated quality levels.

3.4 Family branding

Here there are three choices for a company:

- Individual brand names for each separate product (e.g. Procter and Gamble – P&G – separately brands Tide and Bold; Mars separately brands Snickers, Mars Bar, Bounty).
- Blanket family name. Here the company attaches its own name and identity to every product in its portfolio (the Del Monte approach).
- The company name combined with individual brand name. A very popular approach in marketing whereby individual products are given their own identity, but the company name is also attached to create the overall brand name and identity (Kellogg's Rice Krispies or Kellogg's Raisin Splitz; Ford Granada or Ford Mondeo).

3.5 Brand extension and multi-branding

Marketers must decide between *brand extension* and *multi-branding*. Under *brand extension*, a product is launched and given the identity of an existing product which will also carry on in production. The new product must have similar attributes and psychological values to the existing product. For example, when Fairy Liquid – previously only a washing-up detergent – was chosen to name Procter and Gamble's new attack on Unilever's washing powder (clothes) Persil, it was deemed that both washing-up detergent and washing powder/liquid were bought by the same member of the household, from the same part of the same type of retail outlet, and used in the same room of the house, the kitchen. Hence, the new washing powder/washing liquid was named Fairy. In retaliation, Unilever launched a washing-up detergent named Persil. For brand extension, it is essential that the attributes of the products in question are similar.

Or, the company can opt for *multi-branding*. Here, every product is given its own identity. For example, most toothpastes, washing powders, cleaning detergents are in tact produced by only a handful of companies. Each company has a whole host of separate brands and most consumers would not know that they were all produced by only two or three different companies. Similarly, in confectionery and petfood, two or three companies dominate the market. However, these companies go to great lengths to create separate identities for their products, often giving them separate production bases, distribution channels, and marketing teams.

Although there is an element of cannibalisation within a company's portfolio with several competing products all vying for consumers' attention, the companies that practise this technique believe that it overall gains them market share and shelf space. If they launch a new product they appreciate it will cut the market shares of their existing brands, but they hope to steal shares from competitors' brands so that overall the company has a net gain. In addition to gaining overall shelf space, the companies therefore hope to gain brand loyalty for each separate brand, and indeed create in-company competition keeping their teams on their toes. It also facilitates product differentiation, one of the key bases of modern marketing.

3.6 Naming of the product

Some companies have poorly chosen names and make them part of their marketing tactics – 'great unpronounceables of our time' introduces the press advertising for Bunnahabhain: 'unspeakably good malt'. However, most companies wish to be more circumspect in their selection of brand name. The choosing of the brand name is essential to effective marketing, and the name should:

- say something about the product
- be easy to say/reproduce
- be distinctive
- translate into languages
- be suitable for legal protection in home and overseas markets

However, as the once successful and market leader slimming aid chocolate brand will testify, despite all the careful research and plans of marketing managers, occasionally the broader marketing environment [cf. Chapter 19] plays a role: Aydes was the victim of the increasing awareness of HIV AIDS.

3.7 Packaging/labelling

Packaging and labelling are very much part of the marketing process, not just the *primary* packaging (the immediate container), but also the secondary packaging (the shipping packaging). The packaging and labelling must reflect the brand image, identity, and intended attributes of the product within.

3.8 Customer service

Be it after sales, warranty provisions, ease of communication channels between consumers and customer service personnel, or follow-up tracking consumer attitude research, conscious decisions must be made by the marketing team responsible for a product in terms of the provision of customer service: too little will alienate customers and leave opportunities open to competitors; the provision of 'too much' customer service will be wasteful for the company's resources.

3.9 Product mix decisions

In Europe, Mars (trading in the UK as Pedigree Petfoods) has eight of the 10 leading pet food brands: Whiskas, Pedigree, Cesar, Sheba, Brekkies, Frolic, Kitekat, Pal. Most companies have a portfolio of products, and whether each product has a separate marketing team or one marketing team is handling the whole portfolio, it is necessary to be aware of the ramifications for the strategy and marketing programme of one product in a company's portfolio on the remaining products.

The *product portfolio approach* to marketing attempts to manage the *product mix* (the composite of products an organisation makes available to consumers) in an attempt to create specific marketing strategies to achieve a balanced mix of products aimed at producing maximum long-run profits. There are various product portfolio management techniques available, the most famous being the BCG Box and the DPM Models [cf. Glossary]. It is important for marketing managers to evaluate on a regular basis the relative strengths and weaknesses of the products in their portfolio, so knowing to which products to devote additional resources, which products to identify for phasing out, and which products to depend on in terms of cash generation.

3.10 Positioning

Finally, one of the key tenets of marketing is effective positioning. As discussed in Chapter 23 product positioning results from decision activities directed towards trying to create and maintain the firm's intended product concept in customers' minds. It is the creation of a product's perceived image. Branding is often instrumental as the identifier for such imagery/positioning.

4 THE PRODUCT LIFE CYCLE (PLC)

Figure 25.1 illustrates the typical stages of the product life cycle: *introduction, growth, maturity* and *decline.* All products and markets pass through such a cycle, although an individual product may be at a different point in the life cycle than the overall market (for example, a company entering late into a market may have its brand or products at the introduction or growth stage, when in fact the overall market is in maturity or even decline).

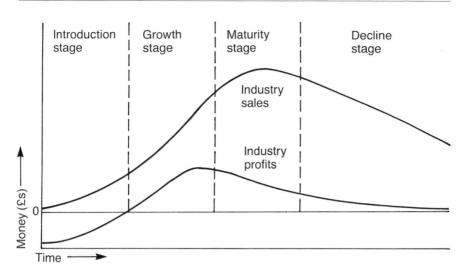

Figure 25.1 The PLC
Source: Dib, S., Simkin, L., Pride, W. and Ferrell, O.C. (1991) *Marketing: Concepts and Strategies*, Boston: Houghton Mifflin, Figure 7.5

Industry profits peak ahead of industry sales, as earlier on in the life cycle there tends to be a lower level of competition and higher pricing. As a product moves through these stages, the strategies relating to competition, product development, pricing, promotion, distribution and market information must be evaluated and probably changed.

5 MANAGING THE PRODUCT MIX

A host of techniques (e.g. Boston Consultancy Group's Growth-Share Matrix, or the Directional Policy Matrix) assists in identifying products which have a great deal of potential/growth/future sales; those with only relatively little potential; and products where there are severe problems and for which possibly no obvious future. As such, three of the key facets of product management are:

- modifying existing products
- deleting products
- developing new products

5.1 Modifying existing products

Quite often marketing managers become aware through feedback from the salesforce/dealers, or consumer research, that a drop in fortunes of a particular product is not because the product is fundamentally flawed but because it needs updating/revising. As such, with perhaps only relatively minor changes in the quality, function or style aspects of the product, or pricing, there can be a prolonged life and viability for the product.

5.2 Deleting products

One of the hardest tasks in marketing is to delete a product. Products that are patently at the end of their life cycle may once have been the star performers in a company and certain executives may harbour desires to see such success re-kindled. For other products, potential has never been reached but executives may believe there is still the chance. All companies and organisations have products in their portfolio that should have been deleted many years previously. There are three options for deleting products:

Phase out: long-term planning identifies a point in time when a particular product or brand will be deleted and replaced with a new product offer (very common in the car market, for example).

Run out: a decision is made to curtail production of the product and so cease ordering components and supplies. However, existing stocks will be worked out into finished products to be sold.

Immediate drop: the performance of a product is particularly catastrophic, often using up scarce resources, with no benefits to the company whatsoever. The decision is made to drop the product immediately, often with associated financial write-offs of inventory and marketing effort, and with the risk of alarming consumers and dealers. However, the financial burden of carrying on producing such a product outweighs the potential pitfalls.

5.3 Developing new products

Marketing depends on identifying consumers' needs and wants. These are forever changing [cf. Chapter 20], with the result that marketers must perpetually update their product portfolios. There are key stages in the development of new products:

(i)   Idea Generation
(ii)   Idea Screening
(iii) Business Analysis
        – Does the proposed product fit with the current product mix?
        – Is there demand for the new product and will it last?
        – Will its introduction harm/help the short-term company performance?
        – Are there future marketing environment/competitive changes

which will impact on this product's performance?
- Can the company's R&D, engineering, production cope?
- If new facilities are needed, how much and when?
- Is money available for the full product launch?

(iv) Product Development
- Is the product technically feasible?
- What marketing mix will be required?

(v) Test Marketing
The full-scale trial of a product in the marketplace: actually sold through selected distribution channels and supported as an existing product in a portfolio. Typically, in one television region where promotional effort can be constrained and made cost effective, and the merits of the marketing programme/sales can be adequately reviewed.

(vi) Commercialisation
If test marketing is successful, full-scale production is instigated, with a full market launch, and the development of a full marketing mix and support programme.

6 USEFUL REFERENCES

Baker, M.J. (1991) *The Marketing Book*, London: Heinemann/CIM.

Dibb, S., Simkin, L., Pride, W. and Ferrell, O.C. (1991) *Marketing: Concepts and Strategies*, Boston: Houghton Mifflin.

Handscombe, R. (1989) *The Product Management Handbook*, London: McGraw-Hill.

McCarthy, E.J. and Perreault, W.D. (1990) *Basic Marketing*, Homewood, Illinois: Irwin.

McDonald, M.H. (1989) *Marketing Plans*, Oxford: Butterworth-Heinemann.

Wind, Y. (1982) *Product Policy: Concepts, Methods and Strategy*, Reading, Massachusetts: Addison-Wesley.

Chapter 26

Distribution/marketing channels

1 DEFINITION

Distribution (the *place* element in the marketing mix) is the selection of a distribution or *marketing channel*.

A marketing channel is a channel of distribution, a group of interrelated intermediaries which direct products to consumers.

There are two major types of marketing intermediaries: merchants which take title to merchandise and resell it; or agents and brokers, which receive a fee or commission for expediting exchanges. For most products and services (with the exception of some factory shops and farm shops) intermediaries are used in order to simplify the producers' selling and marketing efforts, and the consumers' purchasing. For example, were five producers and five buyers in a market, all dealing separately and directly with each other, there would be 25 transactions for them all to communicate with each other. If in the same market there was a major middleman or intermediary – such as a wholesaler – there would only have to be five channels between the producers (one each) and the wholesaler, and five channels between the buyers and the wholesaler (one each), or ten transactions in total.

2 SELECTING DISTRIBUTION CHANNELS

When a company is selecting a distribution channel for a particular product or range of products, it has to take into account:

- its organisational objectives and resources
- market characteristics
- consumer behaviour
- product attributes
- environmental forces

In particular, it has to make a conscious decision on the desired *intensity of market coverage*. Here, there are three options:

intensive: many outlets with relatively small catchment areas and significant levels of competition (convenience items);

selective: for more expensive shopping goods, where the customer base and catchment area must be larger;

exclusive: where prestigious products are deliberately restricted in terms of the numbers of distributors (Chanel perfume or Riva sports boats), or where a company's resources limit the number of distribution outlets it can support (e.g. Saab cars).

3 MARKETING CHANNELS

Figure 26.1 illustrates the typical, conventional market channel, as well as a vertical marketing system, showing the functions handled at each stage.

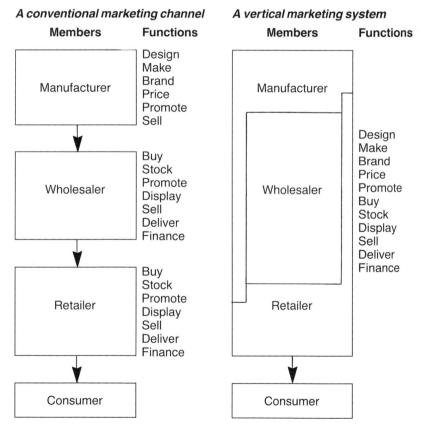

Figure 26.1 Examples of Channels
Source: Dibb, S., Simkin, L., Pride, W. and Ferrell, O.C. (1991) *Marketing: Concepts and Strategies*, Boston: Houghton Mifflin, Figure 9.7

Typical Marketing Channel for Consumer Products	*Typical Marketing Channel for Industrial/Organisational Products*
A Producer	A Producer
B Agents or Brokers	B Agents
C Wholesalers	C Industrial Distributors
D Retailers	D Industrial Buyers
E Consumers	

3.1 Consumers

Not all products pass through such a convoluted distribution channel involving all of these stages, although many items of fashion clothing and certain food items such as biscuits often do. Fruit and vegetables and most other clothing miss out stage B, passing directly from producers to wholesalers. Non-process foods, electricals, DIY goods, and furniture typically pass straight from producers to retailers, missing out stages B and C. There are relatively few examples of stages B, C and D being missed but, in farm shops and factory shops, produce and merchandise pass directly from producer to consumer.

3.2 Industrial

Cars/construction equipment exported often pass through all four stages of this marketing channel, with agents shipping vehicles and distributors selling them. Computer equipment often passes from agents to industrial buyers, with agents required to help sell, display and advise consumers, but there being no need for stage C. Where there is relatively little selling involved, but more repeat ordering, there is often no need for agents (items such as gears, components and parts, passing directly from producers to industrial distributors, missing out step B). For very large plant and equipment, such as turbines, there is no marketing channel with manufacturers dealing directly with industrial buyers.

4 KEY TASKS CONDUCTED BY INTERMEDIARIES

- *Sorting out*: classification of heterogeneous supplies to homogeneous groups.
- *Accumulation*: developing a bank or stock of homogeneous products to provide aggregate inventory (stock).
- *Allocation*: breaking down homogeneous stocks or inventories into smaller units.
- *Sorting*: combining products into collections or assortments that buyers want (e.g. ranges).

5 CLASSIFICATION OF CHANNEL PARTICIPANTS

There are two key groups of channel participants: those which actually participate in negotiations within the distribution process, and those which simply facilitate the distribution chain.

5.1 Facilitating agencies

These are bodies which enable the exchange to take place:

Transportation firms
Storage firms
Advertising agencies
Financial firms
Insurance firms
Marketing research firms

5.2 Member participants: contractual organisations

Producers and manufacturers
Intermediaries:
    Retailers
    Wholesalers
    Distributors
Final users:
    Organisations/Businesses

6 CHANNEL LEADERSHIP

Two of the key desires in marketing are control and power within marketing channels. Organisations at different levels in a particular channel are to some extent dependent upon cooperation and mutual understanding, but similarly will be vying for channel leadership so as to be able to dictate strategies and policies relating to their products and their product areas.

Determinants of channel leadership include:

economic sources of power:
    control of resources
    size of firm
non-economic sources of power:
    reward power
    expert power
    referent power/opinion leadership
    legitimate/genuine leader
    coercive power

These elements pull together to determine a particular overall level of power for each organisation or player within a marketing channel. The overall position of power for a company or organisation in the marketing channel depends on the roles and positions of the other channel members and willingness to lead.

7 USEFUL REFERENCES

Dibb, S., Simkin, L., Pride, W. and Ferrell, O.C. (1991) *Marketing: Concepts and Strategies,* **Boston: Houghton Mifflin.**
Fernie, J. (ed.) (1990) *Retail Distribution Management: Strategic Guide to Developments and Trends,* London: Kogan Page.
Gattorna, J. (ed.) (1983) *The Physical Distribution Handbook,* Aldershot: Gower.
Powers, T.L. (1991) *Modern Business Marketing,* **St Paul, Minnesota: West.**
Shipley, D. (ed.) (1989) 'Industrial distribution channel management', special edition, *European Journal of Marketing* 23 (2) Bradford: MCB.

Chapter 27

Pricing

1 DEFINITION

Price is a value placed on that which is exchanged (the good, the idea or service).

2 THE IMPACT OF THE COMPETITIVE SITUATION

Companies must set prices which are consistent with the competitive situation operating in the particular market. There are several competitive situations:

- *Pure monopoly*: a single seller only.
- *Pure competition*: many sellers (and buyers) selling similar goods or services; each with only some influence on demand. Market conditions (market forces) set price.
- *Oligopolistic competition*: few sellers who are highly susceptible to each other's actions. Price fixing often in collusion.
- *Monopolistic competition*: despite the name given to such a situation, there are many sellers (and buyers) offering different products over a range of prices.

3 FACTORS AFFECTING PRICING DECISIONS

Companies do not have a completely free hand when determining pricing levels. There is a range of factors which warrant careful consideration before such decisions can be made:

Organisational and marketing objectives

Prices must be consistent with company objectives. Companies requiring a rapid increase in market share will have different pricing strategies (e.g. price cutting) than those requiring very high profitability in the short term (where margins need to be maintained).

Elements of the marketing mix

Price levels must not be determined in isolation of other marketing mix elements. Each element must be consistent with the others so that a cohesive mix is developed. A product with an 'up-market' image and promotional campaign requires an appropriately 'high' price rather than a discount price, as well as a select channel of distribution and selling programme!

Costs

Although in the short term companies may set prices which do not re-coup production, distribution and marketing costs, long-term survival depends on the costs being fully met of producing and selling an item.

Customer perceptions

Companies must understand the importance which customers place on price. This will vary according to the market and target segment under consideration.

Legal and regulatory issues

National and local governments sometimes impose controls which impact on prices. In addition, consumer legislation exists to protect customers from unreasonable or unfair pricing.

4 STAGES FOR ESTABLISHING PRICES

(i) Develop pricing objectives

A variety of both short- and long-run objectives shape the pricing decisions which are made. These include cash flow, survival, profit, ROI (Return On Investment), market share, maintaining status quo and product quality.

(ii) Assess target market's ability to purchase and evaluation of price

The sensitivity of different customers to price is variable. Companies must understand whether target markets will tolerate high prices and to what degree these customers will be prepared to shop around. Customer tolerance will relate to income, economic conditions and perception of value.

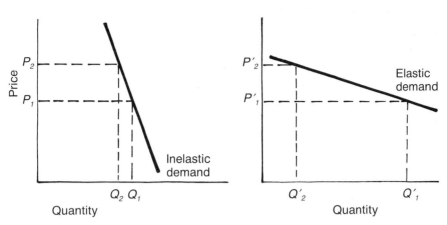

Figure 27.1 The elasticity of demand

Source: Adapted from Dibb, S., Simkin, L., Pride, W. and Ferrell, O.C. (1991) *Marketing: Concepts and Strategies*, Boston: Houghton Mifflin, Figure 17.5

(iii) Determine level of demand and analyse the relationship with cost and profit

Companies need to consider how many of an item will be purchased at different price levels. This involves analysing the elasticity of demand, i.e. the effect of a small price change on numbers purchased (see Figure 27.1). The price elasticity of demand is calculated using the following formula:

Price Elasticity of Demand = % Change in Number Demanded

% Change in Price

For items which have highly inelastic demand, a shift in price leads to a very small change in quantity demanded.

For items which have highly inelastic demand, a shift in price leads to a very small change in quantity demanded.

Understanding the relationship between profit, revenue and costs is essential if realistic prices are to be set.

Calculating total costs determines the minimum price which can be charged to ensure profitability.

P (Profit) = R (Revenue) − C (Total Costs)

TC (Total Costs) = FC (Fixed Costs) + VC (Variable Costs)

Fixed costs are costs which remain constant irrespective of the number of items produced, such as rent and rates. Variable costs, such as raw materials and wages, do change as the number of items produced alters. Usually the variable cost of producing an item is the same for each item.

Marginal cost (MC) is the additional cost a company incurs when one more item is produced.

The point at which total costs are equal to the revenue generated is termed the *break-even* point. Calculating the break-even point at a number of different pricing levels allows a company to understand better the relationship between costs and revenue, and indicates the likely impact of different pricing alternatives.

$$\text{Break-even point} = \frac{FC}{P - VC}$$

(iv) Evaluate competitive pricing

Understanding how competitors set prices for their products, and knowing their prices, helps companies determine the parameters within which price levels should be set. Such understanding also indicates the importance which customers place on price and highlights key direct competitors. This is a particularly important consideration in markets where price competition is common.

(v) Choose a pricing policy

The selection of pricing policy is intrinsically linked to corporate objectives. The options include:

– Market Penetration Pricing
  Setting low prices relative to key competitors in order to gain large market share as quickly as possible. Companies sometimes adopt this approach with the intention of raising prices once a particular product has gained market acceptance. Success is partly dependent on the price sensitivity of the market and the company's ability to meet demand.
– Price Skimming
  The use of very high prices in order to maximise profit in the short term. This policy is only applicable for highly innovative products, with limited or no obvious competitors, and allows companies to re-coup research and development costs quickly. Despite the attractions of this approach, companies usually have to exit the market once competition becomes intensive.
– Psychological Pricing
  Price levels are determined for psychological rather than rational reasons. Perceived value pricing is based on what buyers believe the product to be worth. For example, customers would expect the price of a full English breakfast at a five-star deluxe hotel to differ from that at a transport café, although the basic offering may be similar. Odd-even pricing involves trying to attract customers using odd number prices.

The idea is that more customers will purchase an item priced at £9.99 than at £10.00.

- Promotional Pricing
This approach to pricing involves the use of special price levels to increase sales in the short term. This can involve the use of special-event pricing, linked perhaps to a national holiday. In other circumstances companies, such as retail outlets, use a small number of low-priced items (price leaders or loss leaders) to attract custom.

(vi) Select a pricing method

This refers to the mechanical process through which price is set.

- Cost-Driven Pricing
Cost-plus pricing: prices are set at a level to allow a certain percentage profit once all costs have been met.
- Competition-Driven Pricing
Going-rate pricing: prices are fixed after consideration of competitors' pricing levels. Decisions about whether to price above, below or at the same level as competing brands can then be made. In very competitive markets, where one or a small number of companies dominates, there may be a standard or 'going-rate' price.
- Demand-Driven Pricing
Variable pricing: commonly used in markets where demand is variable over time. This approach allows companies to make extra profits at peak times while ensuring some sales when demand is low. Leisure attractions, such as Madame Tussaud's, commonly adopt such an approach.

(vii) Decide on a specific price

The price which is ultimately set will depend on how companies manipulate their overall marketing mixes. This element of the mix – *price* – has more flexibility than other aspects because it can be altered very quickly.

5 USEFUL REFERENCES

Bennett, P.D. (1988) *Marketing*, New York: McGraw-Hill.
Dibb, S., Simkin, L., Pride, W. and Ferrell, O.C. (1991) *Marketing: Concepts and Strategies*, **Boston: Houghton Mifflin.**
Dunlop, J. (1986) *Q&A Marketing: Economics for Marketing*, London: Financial Training Publications.
Lancaster, G. and Massingham, L. (1988) *Essentials of Marketing*, **Maidenhead: McGraw-Hill.**
Lusch, R.F. and Lusch, V.N. (1987) *Principles of Marketing*, Belmont, California: Kent.
Monroe, B.K. (1979) *Pricing: Making Profitable Decisions*, **New York: McGraw-Hill.**

Chapter 28

Marketing communications (promotional activity)

I THE MARKETING COMMUNICATIONS PROCESS

Effective marketing depends on the exchange of goods, services and ideas, and thereby is heavily dependent on effective communications. In marketing, marketing communications is defined as the communication of information which facilitates or expedites the exchange process.

The communications process is instigated by the *source*, which will be the company with the product or service to offer. The source develops a *coded message* (a promotional campaign), which passes through a chosen *medium* of transmission (e.g. print, broadcast, personal selling etc.), through to the *target audience* or receiver of the message. In marketing, the elements of the *promotional mix* are used to facilitate the communications process: advertising; personal selling; PR and publicity; and sales promotion.

In any market there will be a mix of consumers in terms of *product adoption.* The *innovators* who are the minority of consumers first to take a new product or idea, through the *early adoptors,* the *early majority,* the *late majority* and finally to the *laggards.* Promotional activity and communications effort aimed at the innovators and early adaptors must explain the nature of the product and create a market, as such consumers will have no previous experience or information of such products. By the time, at the other extreme, the laggards in the market are seeking to make a purchase, overall market size will be quite large and awareness of such products high.

2 PRODUCT ADOPTION AND PROMOTION

The position of the product in terms of its adoption is important in determining overall promotional strategy and the tactics will change as the level of adoption progresses. Consumers must first be *aware* of a product or service, develop an *interest* so as to wish to *evaluate* it against competing product offers, before *trying* the product or service in order to fully *adopt* (purchase) the product in question (see Figure 28.1).

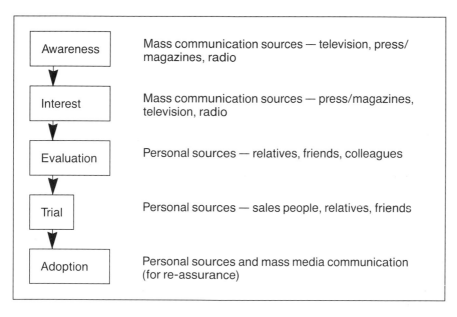

Figure 28.1 The stages of product adoption and promotion

3 FIVE COMMUNICATIONS EFFECTS

Key workers in the area of marketing communications, such as Rossiter and Percy, define five key communications effects:

Category need: it is important for consumers to understand that there is a market, with products in existence, to meet perhaps previously un-realised consumer needs. They must want the general product category.

Brand awareness: once consumers realise there is a need for a particular category of product, marketers must concentrate promotional effort on enforcing specific brand awareness.

Brand attitude: there will be numerous competing brands on offer, so not only must consumers be made aware of a brand but they must have a favourable attitude to the brand to keep their interest.

Brand purchase intention: the favourable attitude to a brand must actually be stimulated so as to encourage consumers to experience the product and consider making a purchase.

Purchase facilitation: having created a need for a product, brand awareness, favourable brand attitude and encouraging consumers to evaluate the specific brand, the elements of the marketing mix other than promotion must play an important role in making the product or service available for purchase/consumption.

4 THE PROMOTIONAL MIX

The four key elements of the promotional mix are advertising, personal selling, sales promotions, PR and publicity (including sponsorship).

4.1 Advertising

A paid form of non-personal communication about an organisation and/or its products that is transmitted to a target audience through a mass medium.

4.1.1 Advertising uses

These are numerous:

- to promote products and organisations
- to stimulate primary and selective demand
- to off-set competitors' advertising
- to aid sales people
- to increase uses of a product
- to remind and enforce attitudes
- to reduce sales fluctuations

Advertising can target a large audience or specific group (by carefully selecting media). It is generally the most expensive element in a company's marketing budget, but because it tends to be through mass media and hits a large number of people, it is a relatively low per capita cost. However, actual expenditure in real terms is very high. Feedback is slow and its effectiveness is hard to measure.

4.2 Personal selling

Personal selling is a process of informing customers and persuading them to purchase products through personal communication in an exchange situation.

It is the passing on of information and persuasion with face-to-face communication, and can be narrowly focused at a few individuals, with immediate feedback. It is expensive (salesforce time and salaries), but significantly more specific and has greater impact than advertising. Personal selling depends heavily on language:

- verbal
- kinesic (body language)
- proxemic (distance)
- tactile (physical contact)

4.2.1 The personal selling process

(i)   prospecting and evaluating
(ii)   preparation
(iii) approaching the customer
(iv)   making the presentation
(v)   overcoming objections
(vi)   closing the deal
(vii) following up

4.3 PR and publicity

Public relations is the planned and sustained effort to establish and maintain good will and mutual understanding between an organisation and its publics. Publicity is non-personal communication in news story form, regarding an organisation and/or its products, which is transmitted through a mass medium at no charge.

No charge is perhaps a little misleading. Whereas with advertising there is an overt charge for column centimetres in the press or seconds of air time on TV or radio, PR releases and material are used in news bulletins and the media with no obvious cost. However, there is an associated cost in resources (using a PR agency, or internal PR manager), and very often publications using PR material expect an organisation to support it with the placing of its advertisement in the same publication.

4.3.1 Types of publicity

- Press release: one page, less than 300 words, contact name
- Feature article: 1,000 words for specific publication
- Captioned photograph
- Press conference
- Editorials
- Films and tapes
- In-company publications
- Interview techniques

- VIP links
- Visits/seminars/meetings

4.3.2 Uses

- Awareness of products, brands, activities, personnel.
- Maintain level of positive public visibility.
- Enhance/shift a particular image/perception.
- Overcome negative imagery/publicity.

4.3.3 Golden rules for PR

- Must be a continuous programme.
- Person/department/agency accountable.
- On-going working relationships with media personnel.
- Well-produced material matching target media's exact requirements.

Good PR does not happen overnight. It is a continuous activity, requiring clear policies, commitment, accountability, the development of long-term links with journalists and the media, and the understanding of targeted media's publication/broadcast criteria and requirements.

4.3.4 PR in Crisis management

- Identify key targets to receive message.
- Do not cover up: have a policy ready to implement.
- The company should report facts itself.
- Do not discourage news coverage: give immediate access.

If the media deems a story newsworthy it will be featured whether or not a company co-operates with journalists. It is preferable to be 'in control'; to identify who needs to hear the company's account (specific media, certain customers, distributors, regulatory bodies etc.); to present selected facts and to 'assist' journalists. In this manner there is far greater opportunity to input into (slant) the story, and therefore for 'damage limitation'.

4.4 Sales promotion

Activity and/or material inducing sales through added value or incentive for the product to resellers, sales people, or consumers.

Sales promotions on the whole do not grow a market. Through their nature, they are usually offering an incentive (price reduction, free merchandise, give-away, competition, or whatever) and therefore persuade regular purchasers of the particular brand to simply bring forward their purchase. It is therefore a very useful technique for evening-out sales troughs and/or helping short-term cash flow problems.

4.4.1 Types of sales promotion

- Sales force promotion, from manufacturer to sales force.
- Trade promotion, from manufacturer to distributors.
- Consumer promotion, from manufacturer to end-user consumers.
- Retail/distributor promotion, from distributors to consumers.

4.4.2 Examples of sales promotion

Consumer: coupons, free samples, demonstrations, competitions.

Trade: (at wholesalers, retailers and sales people): sales competitions, free merchandise, point of sale displays, trade shows and conferences.

The UK spends half as much on sales promotions as advertising, and therefore sales promotions are very important marketing activities. Sales promotions are usually instigated to supplement personal selling or advertising, and are rarely used in isolation. Because they induce sales, sales promotions are irregular in use, aimed at short-term sales increases.

5 SELECTING A PROMOTIONAL MIX

These are the key considerations:

- Companies' objectives:
  awareness/education/heavy sales
- Budget and resources
- Type of market:
  FMCG/consumer/industrial/service
- Policy:
  push or pull

Under a 'push' policy, each member of the marketing channel promotes to the next member of the marketing channel with the intention of pushing a product or service down through the marketing channel. Under a 'pull' policy, promotion is aimed directly at the end-user of the particular product or service with the intention of the end-user demanding distributors to stock the particular product. In most markets, the two policies are *not* mutually exclusive: using different promotional techniques and campaigns, they are often tackled simultaneously.

- Nature of the target market:
  size, geographic spread, demographics
- Product characteristics:
  industrial/consumer/service; seasonality; price; product life cycle; product use
- Market coverage:
  intensive/selective/exclusive [cf. Chapter 26]
- Cost and availability of media slots

6 USEFUL REFERENCES

Burnett, J.J. (1993) *Promotion Management,* **Boston: Houghton Mifflin.**

Coulson-Thomas, C.J. (1983) *Marketing Communications,* London: Heinemann/ CIM.

Davis, M.P. (1990) *Business to Business Marketing and Promotion,* London: Century Hutchinson.

Douglas, T. (1988) *The Complete Guide to Advertising,* London: Macmillan.

Jefkins, F. (1988) *Public Relations Techniques,* **London: Heinemann.**

Rapp, S. and Collins, T. (1987) *MaxiMarketing,* New York: McGraw-Hill.

Rossiter, J.R. and Percy, L. (1987) *Advertising and Promotion Management,* **New York: McGraw-Hill.**

Weilbacher, W.M. (1984) *Advertising,* New York: Macmillan.

Chapter 29

Services marketing

1 DEFINITION

A service is the result of applying human or mechanical efforts to people or objects. *Services* are intangible products involving a deed, a performance or an effort which cannot be physically possessed.

(Dibb *et al.*, 1991)

The marketing of consumer goods, and to some extent industrial goods, is made simpler by the fact that there is a tangible product, be it a tin of Heinz Baked Beans, a Porsche sportscar or a JCB backhoe loader (digger). However, for a fast food restaurant what exactly is the product? Is it the burger in a bun, the environment, or the provision of a meal? Is it the service level, friendliness, atmosphere or efficiency with which food is delivered to the consumer? Similarly, for travel, tourism, leisure, financial services, consultancy, health care, education, the public sector and charities, exactly what is the product? For most services, the product is somewhat intangible and therefore more difficult both to brand and to market.

2 CLASSIFICATION OF SERVICES

- Profit-making services (financial, tourism etc.)
- Non-profit (voluntary organisations, charities etc.)
- Public utilities/services (health, and in most countries telecommunications and power)

3 IMPORTANCE OF SERVICES

GDP	% of services
Europe	58%
USA	67%
Japan	58%

Employment in services

Europe	60%
UK	67%

4 REASONS FOR GROWTH OF THE SERVICE SECTOR

The reasons are mainly affluence and more leisure time, with demographic and psychographic factors. There is a desire to avoid fixed costs and to delegate tasks to specialists.

- Marginal utility of goods has declined (particularly of food, many consumer durables). After World War II many now 'basic' goods and services were seen as luxuries. In the 1990s, the consumer's desire is for more interesting and leisure-orientated products.
- Smaller families (more time, greater disposable income).
- More leisure: services consume time and are actively sought (particularly in the entertainment/tourism sectors).
- There is a desire for self-fulfilment: experience rather than ownership, therefore people buy-in outside services.
- Affluence: mundane activities are contracted out.
- Technology: there is a need for specialist services to maintain many everyday household and office objects.
- Political: there is electoral competition to offer better claimed levels of services.

For non-consumer services there are three key reasons why, in business situations, service provision has grown in the economy:

- Specialisation: delegation of non-core tasks (e.g. advertising, marketing research, head-hunting etc.).
- Technology: the need for knowledgeable organisations (e.g. consultants, IT advisers etc.).
- Flexibility: the need to avoid fixed overheads (e.g. marketing research bought-in on an ad hoc basis, maintenance and cleaning contracts).

5 THE FOUR KEY BASIC SERVICE CHARACTERISTICS

- *Intangibility*
  Services cannot be touched, stored or acquired. They are an experience or process.
- *Direct Organisation – Client Relationship*
  The buyer generally meets the company's representative. Therefore, very often the production of the service and its consumption are inseparable.
- *Consumer Participates in the Production Process*
  Service quality depends partly on the knowledge and co-operation of the consumer.

– *Complexity*

Service management has to cope with complex systems, largely through the importance of the direct interface with customers and the role of an organisation's personnel.

For the full discussion of the ramifications of these characteristics see Donnelly and George (1981) or Lovelock (1984).

6 IMPLICATIONS FOR MARKETING

6.1 Revised marketing mix for services

The standard marketing mix is:

product
price
place (distribution)
promotion

This is no longer adequate for services. In addition to the above '4Ps', researchers of services marketing have added '3Ps':

people
physical evidence/ambience
process

People

In a bank the clerk is very much part of the product; in a restaurant the chef and the waiter are fundamental to the offer of the service. Operational staff often perform the task and sell the product. Employee selection, training and motivation are crucial. The famous quote by Leo Burnett of Leo Burnett Advertising Inc. sums up the importance of this additional element of the marketing mix:

Every evening, all our assets go down the elevator.

Physical Evidence

The environment (decor and 'feel') and ambience are very much a part of the product offer; as are facilities in the restaurant, hospital, sports club or whatever; as are cleanliness and upkeep.

Process

Friendliness of staff and flows of information affect the consumer's perception of the product offer. Appointment/queuing systems become part of the product offer. All are operational matters which *directly* affect customer perceptions and are important marketing elements.

The implications are that there are problems in creating a differential advantage or competitive edge in services marketing – more so than in the marketing of consumer or industrial products – owing to the characteristics of services, the intangibility of the product and the extended marketing mix.

6.2 Problems in creating a differential advantage

The aim of marketing is seen as achieving product/brand differentiation with a real or perceived differential advantage/competitive edge [cf. Chapter 18]. For any product this is difficult, but in services it is even more difficult. Once achieved, it is hard to sustain. The reasons are simple but varied:

- No product differentiation.
- No patent protection.
- Few barriers to entry: easy for competitors to enter and to copy.
- Difficult to control customer interface.
- Problems of growth (key personnel can only be spread so far).
- Irregular service quality.
- Difficult to improve productivity and lower the cost to the consumer.
- Problems in innovation (easily copied and often 'people' based).
- Restrictive regulations (particularly in the professions).

The key implication is that marketing in services has had to adopt all the key practices from consumer and industrial marketing. In particular there has been significant work in developing branding in services and clear product differentiation, through promotional imagery and brand identity. This has been true for many years in the financial services sector and tourism industry, but is growing in other sectors, ranging from leisure and health through to education and government units.

7 USEFUL REFERENCES

Cowell, D. (1984) *The Marketing of Services*, London: Heinemann/CIM.
Dibb, S., Simkin, L., Pride, W. and Ferrell, O.C. (1991) *Marketing: Concepts and Strategies*, Boston: Houghton Mifflin.
Donnelly, J.H. and George, W.R. (1981) *Marketing of Services*, AMA Proceedings Series, Chicago: American Marketing Association.
Lovelock, C.H. (1988) *Managing Services*, Englewood Cliffs: Prentice-Hall.
—— (1984) *Services Marketing*, Englewood Cliffs: Prentice-Hall.

Chapter 30

Industrial marketing

1 DEFINITION

An industrial market consists of individuals, groups and organisations that purchase a specific kind of product for direct use in producing other products or for use in day-to-day operations.

Industrial marketing involves activities – exchanges – between industrial or business customers of industrial products. Companies produce goods which are used by other companies to produce other products. Customers are companies, government departments or institutions, not the general public as consumers.

2 PRODUCTS

Raw materials:	cotton, crude oil, iron ore etc.
Major equipment:	installations, heavy equipment, plant.
Component parts:	manufactured materials and parts used as components in subsequently produced products/services.
Accessory equipment:	PCs, desks etc.
Process materials:	used in the production of other goods: supplies, materials, ingredients.
Supplies/services:	maintenance, repair, cleaning, legal, consultancy etc.
Consumable supplies:	paint, cleaning fluids, pencils, photocopying paper etc.

3 TARGET MARKETING

This is relatively straightforward. In most countries there is significant industrial census data collected for government purposes, known in the UK and USA as SIC (Standard Industrial Classification) data. With this information it is possible to identify for any product the number of units sold, and to which markets (customer groups), all coded through SIC codes. It is therefore possible to estimate market sizes, potential market sizes, key customer groups, and major competitor organisations. It is also possible to determine purchase potential by:

(i)   gaining number of units sold from SIC data, and
(ii) producing such information as a ratio to the number of customers in a market (from the entries in a trade directory).

4 MARKETING MIX VARIATIONS

Compared with the marketing of consumer products, there are relatively few variations in the marketing practices for industrial products. Whereas with services marketing, owing to the nature of the intangible product, there is a more convuluted and extended marketing mix, the core marketing mix (4Ps) holds firm for industrial marketing but with important caveats.

4.1 Product

The product is more broadly defined than the actual component or finished good being sold on from one company to another. Very often service – as part of the product package offer – is very important. Key elements, in addition to the core product, of importance in industrial marketing are:

- On-time delivery
- Quality control
- Custom/bespoke design
- Parts distribution
- Technical advice before a sale:
     product specification
     installation
     application

4.2 Distribution/channels

There are mainly direct marketing channels or carefully selected distributors: often because significant levels of technical advice are required during the product specification stage, supply, process and installation. Occasionally agents are used in order to field enquiries and handle general administration, particularly for seasonal products. However, many industrial companies prefer to control the channel directly as quality control for agents (and distributors) can be a problem. Distributors fulfil similar roles to agents, but they sell under their own name, carry stocks and have their own expert staff; they may not be totally dependent on the one supplying company.

4.3 Promotion

This is very different from consumer marketing.

Personal selling

This is the dominant element of the promotional mix:

- Fewer customers; often making mass media communications financially unviable, and direct contact more feasible.
- Technical products often require detailed explanations.
- High cost products require a re-assurance element from the personal selling process.
- Repeat purchases are common, and the sales force follows up leads/builds rapport with regular customers.

However the cost of personal selling is high (salaries, expenses, cars etc.), so recently *telemarketing* (telephone selling) has emerged as a significant element in the promotional mix in industrial marketing.

Advertising

There is relatively little (compared with consumer marketing), but it is used to create general awareness prior to a personal selling effort/sales promotion campaign. However, through technical journals, trade directories and trade associations, advertising can be quite specifically targeted. Trade adverts tend to be 'wordy' and detailed. They tend not to be the persuasive/emotive advertisements as typified by consumer products.

Sales Promotion

This is very important in industrial marketing, particularly through catalogues and print material, sample merchandising and trade shows. Again, it is typically tied to personal selling and the sales force.

4.4 Price

Legal and economic constraints are quite prevalent (EC agreements for instance). Low pricing used to be the fundamental selling platform in industrial marketing, but now the need to create a differential advantage [cf. Chapter 18] is the focus, which may help justify an above-average market price. The common pricing methods are:

- preset or administered pricing
- bid pricing
- negotiated pricing

5 DIFFERENTIAL ADVANTAGE

Increasingly, marketers for industrial products are seeing the need to develop marketing strategies similar in complexity to those instigated by FMCG and consumer goods companies. Industrial companies are no longer in the market simply to supply raw materials/components/services to other producing/service businesses as a base price operation. There is a need to steal an edge in terms of product innovation and selling techniques over competitors, and to perpetually update positioning and product imagery. The creation of a differential advantage, either through selling/distribution methods or through product innovation, is very much a focus for most industrial companies.

6 USEFUL REFERENCES

Chisnall, P.M. (1985) *Strategic Industrial Marketing,* **London: Prentice-Hall.**
Choffray, J.M. and Lilien, G.L. (1980) *Marketing Planning for New Industrial Products,* New York: John Wiley.
Hutt, M.D. and Speh, T.W. (1992) *Business Marketing Management: Strategic View of Industrial and Organisational Markets,* **Fort Worth: Dryden Press.**
Moriarty, R.T. (1983) *Industrial Buying Behaviour,* Lexington: Lexington.
Powers, T.L. (1991) *Modern Business Marketing,* **St Paul, Minnesota: West.**
Webster, F.E. (1991) *Industrial Marketing Strategy,* New York: John Wiley.

Chapter 31

Marketing planning

1 DEFINITIONS

Marketing Planning is a systematic process involving assessing marketing opportunities and resources, determining market objectives, and developing a plan for implementation and control.

The *Marketing Plan* is the written document or blueprint for implementing and controlling an organisation's marketing activities related to a particular marketing strategy.

2 THE MARKETING PLANNING PROCESS

There is a logical and straightforward approach to marketing planning:

(i) Analysis of markets and the trading environment
(ii) Determination of core target markets
(iii) Identification of a differential advantage
(iv) Statement of goals and desired product positioning
(v) Development of marketing programmes to implement plans

The analysis of target markets [cf. Chapter 23], of key competitors – current plus up and coming players – [cf. Chapter 24], and of the marketing environment [cf. Chapter 19] creates a firm foundation for decision-making. Without an understanding of customer segments, trends and competitors, the marketing programme is based on no clear strategy. The marketer must determine a basis for competing or a differential advantage [cf. Chapter 18] in each of the targeted market segments. The selection of target markets and the determination of a differential advantage must take into account the company's marketing assets, and its strengths and weaknesses. Marketing assets can be *customer*-based, including the strength and reputation of the brand; *distribution*-based, such as channel control and distribution coverage; or *internal* assets, including skills and resources.

To implement the planned strategy, a marketing programme must be formulated which – through the elements of the marketing mix – takes the product or service to the targeted customers in the most beneficial and clear manner. The marketer must calculate the costs associated with implementing this marketing programme and justify them with accurate sales forecasts [cf. Chapter 22].

2.1 The process

Analysis of customers' needs and perceptions; market segmentation and brand positioning.

Analysis of the marketing environment and trends.

Analysis of competition and competitors' strategies.

Analysis of market opportunities/trends.

Analysis of company's strengths, weaknesses, opportunities and threats – SWOT.

Determination of core target markets; basis for competing/differential advantage; desired product positioning.

Specification of sales targets and expected results.

Specification of plans for marketing mix programmes:
- products
- promotion
- distribution
- service levels
- pricing

Specification of tasks/responsibilities; timing; costs; budgets.

2.2 The planning cycle

As Figure 31.1 depicts, marketing planning never ceases: it is an on-going analysis/planning/control process or cycle. Many organisations update their marketing plans annually, presenting the key recommendations to all senior managers.

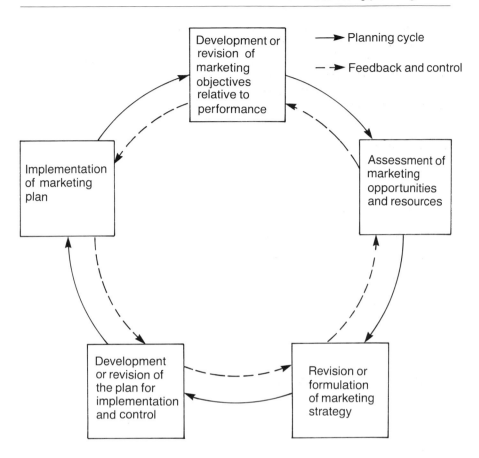

Figure 31.1 The marketing planning cycle
Source: Dibb, S., Simkin, L., Pride, W. and Ferrell, O.C. (1991) *Marketing: Concepts and Strategies*, Boston: Houghton Mifflin, Figure 18.11

3 THE MARKETING PLAN REPORT

Presentations to marketing colleagues and to senior directors may complete the planning process, but the written report is the subsequent action plan and reference point. This document must be well written and clear, with full supporting evidence in the analysis to explain its conclusions and recommendations. There are various formats, but a popular structure is:

Section Title	Typical Pages
1 Management Summary	2–3
2 Objectives	1
Company mission statement	
Detailed company objectives	
Product group goals	
3 Product/Market Background	2–3*
Product range and explanation	
Market overview and sales summary	
4 Situation or SWOT Analysis	1–2*
Scene-setting overview	
5 Analysis	8–12*
Marketing environment and trends	
Customers	
Competition and competitors' strategies	
6 Strategies	3–4
Core target markets	
Basis for competing/differential advantage	
Desired product positioning	
7 Statement of Expected Results/Forecasts	1–2
8 Marketing Programmes	8–12*
Marketing mixes	
Tasks and responsibilities	
9 Financial Implications/Budgets	1–2
10 Operational Implications	1–2
11 Appendices	20+
SWOT details	
Background data and information	
Research findings	
References	

*Likely to be supported with material in appendices

4 NOTES ON THE REPORT DOCUMENT

Management Summary, or *Executive Summary*, should be a concise overview of the entire report, including key aims, overall strategies, fundamental conclusions and salient points regarding the suggested marketing programmes (mixes). Not many people read an entire report, tending to 'dip in' here and there, so the Management Summary should be good, punchy and informative.

Objectives are for the benefit of the reader, to give perspective to the report. Aims and objectives should be stated briefly.

Product/Market Background is a necessary section. Not everyone will be fully familiar with the products and their markets. This section 'scene-sets', aiding the reader's understanding of the marketing plan.

The *SWOT* or *Situational Analysis* is an important foundation for any marketing plan, helping to produce realistic and meaningful recommendations. The section in the main body of the report should be kept to a concise overview, with detailed market by market or country by country SWOTs – and their full explanations – kept to the appendices.

The *Analysis* section is the heart of the marketing planning exercise: if incomplete or highly subjective the recommendations are likely to be based on an inaccurate view of the market and the company's potential. This section gives a sound foundation to the recommendations and marketing programmes. It includes analyses of the marketing environment, market trends, customers, competitors, competitor positions and competitors' strategies.

Strategies should be self-evident if the analyses have been objective and thorough: which target markets are most beneficial to the company, what is to be the differential advantage or competitive edge in these markets, and what is the desired product positioning. This strategy statement must be realistic and detailed enough to action.

Having highlighted the strategic thrust and intention, it is important to explain the *Expected Results* and sales volumes, to show why the strategies should be followed.

Marketing Programme Recommendations are the culmination of the various analyses and statement of strategies: exactly what needs to be done, how and why. This is the detailed presentation of the proposed marketing mixes designed to achieve the goals and implement the strategies.

The full picture may not be known, but an indication of required resources, the *Financial Implications* must be given.

These strategies and marketing programmes may have ramifications for other product groups, sectors or territories, for R&D, for engineering etc. The *Operational Implications* must be flagged up.

The report should be as concise as possible. The document must, though, tell the full story and include evidence and statistics which support the strategies and marketing programmes being recommended. The use of *Appendices* – so long as they are fully cross-referenced in the main body of the report – helps to keep the report concise and well focused.

5 SWOT OR SITUATION ANALYSIS

The SWOT (or TOWS) analysis is one of the most commonly implemented analyses in marketing. A simple format for presentation is illustrated in Figure 31.2. It is important the SWOT is not merely a collection of managers' hunches. It must be based on objective facts and on marketing research findings. Managers often produce SWOT grids for each leading competitor and for separate markets, revealing a company's relative strengths and weaknesses and ability to face the identified threats and opportunities.

The Situation Analysis is a slightly different approach to tackling a similar analysis, taking the four elements of the SWOT analysis and combining them into two groups: factors external to the company (opportunities and threats), and those internal or within the company (strengths and weaknesses).

Strengths	Weaknesses
– – – –	– – –
Opportunities	Threats
– – –	– – – – –

Figure 31.2 The SWOT grid

5.1 Issues: external environment – threats/opportunities

Social/Cultural
Regulatory/Legal/Political
Technological
Economic Conditions
Competition:
– Intensity of rivalry
– Ability
– Threat of entry
– Pressure from substitutions
– Bargaining power of buyers
– Bargaining power of distributors
– Bargaining power of suppliers
Market's customer needs

5.2 Issues: Internal Environment – Strengths/Weaknesses

Marketing
Product

Service
People
Pricing
Distribution/Distributors
Promotion
Branding and Positioning
Marketing Information/Intelligence

Engineering and Product Development
Often of peripheral importance, but with more formalised input from marketing (as marketing planning takes off) this changes.

Operations
Production
Sales
Marketing
Processing orders/Transactions etc.

People

R&D	Skills
Sales	Wages/benefits
Distributors	Training/development
After-Sales	Methods/conditions/
Marketing	turnover of people
Processing/Customer Service	

All central to the successful implementation of the marketing philosophy and the marketing function.

Management
A sensitive and often contentious area, but sometimes management structures and philosophies need altering to facilitate the successful implementation of a marketing plan.

Company Resources
Worthy of note, particularly:
People
Finance (Budgets)

6 USEFUL REFERENCES

Crowner, R.P. (1991) *Developing a Strategic Business Plan with Cases,* Homewood, Illinois: Irwin.

Dibb, S., Simkin, L., Pride, W. and Ferrell, O.C. (1991) *Marketing: Concepts and Strategies,* Boston: Houghton Mifflin.

Lehmann, D.R. and Winner, R.S. (1988) *Analysis for Marketing Planning,* Plano: Business Publications.

McDonald, M.H. (1989) *Marketing Plans,* Oxford: Butterworth-Heinemann.

Chapter 32

International marketing

1 DEFINITION

International marketing is marketing activities performed across national boundaries.

(Terpstra, 1978)

2 LEVELS OF INVOLVEMENT IN INTERNATIONAL MARKETS

Companies become involved in international marketing for a variety of reasons. In some cases involvement derives from a positive and planned desire to engage in activities beyond domestic markets. At the other extreme, exporting is an unplanned activity, occurring almost by accident. Appreciating the reasons for these exporting activities is important if the degree to which companies are *internationalised* is to be properly comprehended.

Casual exporting

Orders are only taken beyond domestic boundaries on an occasional, unplanned basis. It is unlikely that the product and marketing effort will be modified for the specific market.

Active exporting

Here the level of commitment to marketing internationally is higher. Some planning of activities takes place, and exporting is seen as positively contributing to sales. It is unusual for major modifications to the product and marketing effort to be undertaken at this level of international marketing.

Full-scale international commitment

Marketing across national boundaries is seen as an essential part of the company's marketing strategy, and this is fully reflected by resource levels.

Level of planning is high, and product and marketing effort are carefully tailored for the particular international market being targeted. For instance, product design would consider cultural and regional requirements.

Globalised markets

Companies which attempt to treat all international markets as one are adopting a *globalised marketing strategy*. In its purest form, each element of the marketing mix is standardised for all markets, irrespective of national boundaries and cultural differences.

3 ARRANGEMENTS FOR HANDLING INTERNATIONAL MARKETING

There is a range of ways in which organisations can become involved with international sales and markets. Which approaches they choose will depend upon their level of involvement in a particular market.

3.1 Exporting

This approach to international marketing is low risk and low involvement: the exporting company is not required to directly invest in the foreign market. It also gives the exporting company a high degree of flexibility.

Exporting can be handled indirectly, engaging the services of different types of marketing intermediaries, or managed directly by the company itself. Using intermediaries to manage the exporting arrangements is advantageous in limiting the commitment and risk which the company needs to take, but disadvantageous in the way it restricts the company's control over the foreign market.

A range of intermediary types can be used: export agents and export merchants buy a diversity of products from many different manufacturers. Their role is to arrange sales between buyers and sellers in exchange for commissions. Trading companies are not involved in manufacturing, but do take title to the products they export. They also actively assist manufacturers by offering a range of services, such as consultancy, research and development, promotions, legal advice, warehousing, financing etc., which help them become involved internationally.

Direct exporting tends to be much more expensive and risky than the indirect approaches. The benefits are seen in the additional control which the organisation has over the marketplace and its sales, distribution and marketing (including branding) activities.

3.2 Joint ventures

International joint ventures are a partnership between a domestic company and a foreign organisation or government. These arrangements are especially attractive in industries where a particularly high level of investment is required and may allow a domestic company to operate manufacturing facilities in a foreign market.

In some circumstances a joint venture is attractive because it offers clear cost benefits to companies in markets with which they are not familiar. In other cases political trade constraints require that foreign companies entering a particular market do so via a liaison with a local organisation. Joint ventures vary in the split of control between domestic and foreign partners and may include licensing, franchising or contract manufacturing agreements.

3.3 Licensing

Under certain circumstances licensing may be an appropriate alternative for companies which do not wish to invest directly in foreign markets. These temporary agreements allow a licensee to pay royalties or fees to a licensor (a foreign manufacturer not yet ready to enter a territory directly) in return for permission to use a brand, patent or manufacturing process. Some sharing of management and production expertise may also be part of the arrangement.

The benefits of a licensing approach are that companies can minimise the risk associated with entering a new market – for example, when required investment is high or in cases of political uncertainty – while increasing their international trade. The drawbacks are that the licensing manufacturer has little control over the actions of the licensee and potentially may be damaged if the licensee performs poorly.

Franchising is a form of licensing agreement. In this case, it is the responsibility of the manufacturer to provide certain components for use in manufacturing, or the retailer to develop a trading concept, merchandise and systems.

3.4 Direct investment

In this instance, the company buys into or builds manufacturing facilities in the overseas market. This approach implies a major and long-term commitment and is used by organisations requiring maximum involvement. In some circumstances the company may permit the management of a wholly owned subsidiary to operate independently so that maximum flexibility to the local market can be maintained. This level of involvement can prove especially problematic and risky in times of political turbulence.

4 MANAGING INTERNATIONAL MARKETING PROGRAMMES

Standardising marketing programmes on a global basis offers companies obvious benefits of scale economies. However, the reality of numerous local environmental differences, such as economic, cultural, social and political factors, in most cases makes a standard, global, marketing mix difficult to implement.

4.1 Product

Three options exist for companies selling products outside their domestic market:

- Offer the same product in domestic and foreign market(s).
- Adapt the product to suit each foreign market.
- Design a new product for the foreign market(s).

While the first option is the most attractive in terms of the scale economies which can be achieved, adapting the product to appeal to the tastes of different markets, and thus taking into consideration varying local conditions, may be the most realistic approach.

4.2 Promotion

It is rarely possible to globally standardise promotional programmes. For instance, even though a company may choose a common concept and

	PRODUCT		
	Do not change product	*Adapt product*	*Develop new product*
Do not change promotion	1. Product and promotion same world-wide	3. Product adaptation only	5. Product invention
PROMOTION			
Change promotion	2. Promotion adaptation only	4. Product and promotion adaptation	

Figure 32.1 International product and promotional strategies

Source: adapted from Keegan, W.J. (1989) *Global Marketing Management*, Englewood Cliffs: Prentice-Hall; 378–82

message, local differences in language, culture and even media may mean that an identical approach is impossible. Furthermore, the interpretation of advertising messages can also create difficulties, with different cultures placing very different meaning on key phrases and slogans. Local buyer behaviour, such as where, when and how the population chooses to shop, will also impact on the nature of the promotional campaign.

Promotional programmes are inextricably linked to the product element of the marketing mix. Figure 32.1 shows the different strategies which can be followed by companies seeking to adapt products and promotion across national boundaries.

4.3 Price

Prices for products are generally different in domestic and foreign markets. This is partly because of the increased cost of moving the product to the new market and partly due to a host of local factors which impact on product prices in different markets. For instance, local competition, taxes, inflation and transport costs must all be taken into consideration. Some countries engage in dumping activities in order to gain a foothold in foreign markets. This is when products are sold in non-domestic markets for lower than the domestic price. In some markets tariffs are used to prevent this practice and protect local manufacturers.

Fluctuations in exchange rates can also serve to alter the value of sales in particular currencies. Recent instability in the exchange markets has caused price changes on a daily basis, making this a particularly important factor in determining price levels.

A cost-plus approach to pricing [cf. Chapter 27] is commonly used when determining prices internationally. This allows companies to cost in the expenses involved in moving products from their country of origin.

4.4 Distribution

Companies can sell their products through existing distribution channels or attempt to develop new international channels. When making decisions about this area of the marketing programme, thought must be given to distribution both between and within the foreign markets. The choice between new or existing channels will be based both on the ability of any existing structures to carry out the necessary marketing activities and on the ease of developing new ones. If existing channels are to be used, which are chosen will depend on the capability of local channel members, such as agents, wholesalers and retailers, to carry out marketing functions across and within national boundaries.

It is often preferable to develop new distribution structures in cases where the need for after-sales service, training and information make it desirable for companies to maintain as much control as possible of the distribution of their products. In general though, companies tend to develop their own distribution in markets which are perceived to be similar to the domestic one, using independently owned channels where they are very dissimilar.

Whichever approach to distribution is adopted, companies must keep a close eye on any changes in the local environment (such as political upheaval) which may put the distribution channels into jeopardy.

5 USEFUL REFERENCES

Buzzell, R.D. and Quelch, J.A. (1988) *Multinational Marketing Management.* Reading, Massachusetts: Addison-Wesley.

Jain, S.C. (1984) *International Marketing Management,* Boston: Kent.

Keegan, W.J. (1989) *Global Marketing Management,* **Englewood Cliffs: Prentice-Hall.**

Kirpalani, V.H. (1985) *International Marketing,* New York: Random House.

Majaro, S. (1982) *International Marketing,* Boston: Unwin.

Terpstra, V. (1978) *International Marketing,* **Hinsdale, Illinois: Dryden Press.**

Glossary

Key terms from Part III, Theory notes, with page references.

Advertising – A paid form of non-personal communication, about an organisation and/or its products or services, that is transmitted to a target audience through a mass medium (p. 226).

Base Variables – In Market Segmentation these are variables used to form the basis for identifying homogeneous groups of consumers in a market: *demographic, geographic, psychographic* and *behaviouralistic* variables in consumer markets; *geographic location, type of organisation, customer characteristics, product usage* in organisational markets (p. 191).

Brand – Established product name, term, symbol, design, wholly of a proprietary nature, usually officially registered. There are three types: *Manufacturer, Private/Own Label,* and *Generic* (p. 207).

Brand Awareness – Once Category Need is established, consumers must be aware of the specific brand if they are ever to adopt the particular brand (p. 225).

Brand Extension – A newly launched product or service is given the identity or name of an existing product, but only if the product has an affinity with the new product (p. 208).

Brand Management – Product Management (p. 205).

Break-Even Point – When total costs are equal to the revenue generated from a product or service (p. 222).

Buyer Behaviour: Consumer – The decision processes and acts of individuals involved in buying and using products or services (p. 165).

Buyer Behaviour: Organisational – The purchase behaviour of producers, re-sellers, government units and institutions (p. 169).

Buyer Behaviour Influences – *Consumer*: person specific, psychological, social. *Organisational*: business environment, company aims/policies/resources, personal relationships, characteristics of personnel (p. 167).

Buyer Behaviour Process: Consumer – Problem recognition; information search; evaluation of alternatives; purchase; post-purchase evaluation (p. 165).

Buyer Behaviour Process: Organisational – Problem recognition; product specification; product/supplier search; evaluation of options; selection of product/supplier; evaluation of product/supplier performance (p. 170).

Campaign – Organised course of action, planned carefully to achieve predetermined goals. Can relate to sales drives or any part of the Promotional Mix, but typically is applied to Advertising (p. 224).

Campaign – The weekly trade magazine published in London by Haymarket Publishing; news and features primarily from the advertising industry, with updates on the rest of the marketing communications industry (p. 160).

Category Need – To be potential customers, consumers must first realise a particular product or service exists and that they have a need for such a market (p. 225).

Causal Forecasting – This set of techniques includes *Barometric, Surveys of Buyer Intentions, Regression Analysis*, and various *Econometric Models*. These tools examine changes in sales due to fluctuations in one or more market variables (p. 186).

Channel – A *Marketing Channel* is a channel of distribution, a group of interrelated intermediaries which direct products to consumers (p. 215).

Communications Effects – *Category Need*; *Brand Awareness*; *Brand Attitude*; *Brand Purchase Intention*; *Purchase Facilitation* (p. 225).

Competitive Edge – Differential Advantage (p. 159).

Competitive Positions – *Warfare Strategy* believes an organisation must know its position in a market relative to its competitors. A **Market Leader** has market share leadership in a market and must grow its market by finding new applications for its products or services, by market development, or by market penetration, while defending its position against rival challengers. A **Challenger** is aggressively attacking the market and the market leader to gain market share. A **Market Follower** has low market share and few resources to contend for market leadership. A **Nicher** specialises in terms of market/product/customers by finding a small, safe, non-competitive niche (p. 200).

Competitors – These are generally viewed by an organisation as those rival organisations which market similar or substitutable products or services to the same Target Market (p. 197).

Costs: Fixed – Costs which remain constant irrespective of the number of items produced, such as rent and business rates (p. 221).

Costs: Marginal – The additional cost an organisation incurs when one more item is produced (p. 222).

Costs: Variable – Costs, such as raw materials and labour, which vary as the number of items produced fluctuates (p. 221).

Differential Advantage – If a Marketing Mix is developed which is exactly in line with the targeted consumers' needs and expectations, which is a superior marketing mix to those offered by direct competitors, then there is a real or perceived *differential advantage*: something a product or an organisation has, desired by consumers and not matched by competitors (p. 159).

Direct Marketing – The use of non-personal media to introduce products or services by *mail* or *telephone* (p. 225).

Distribution – In the Marketing Mix, the 'Place' element; the selection and control of a *Marketing Channel* (p. 214).

Environmental Scanning – The process of tracking information about the *Marketing Environment* from observation, secondary sources and primary research (p. 161).

Family Branding – Three choices for an organisation naming and branding its products or services: *Individual Brand Names* for each separate product; *Blanket Family Name* across the portfolio; *Company Name* combined with *Individual Brand Name* for each product or service (p. 208).

Focus Group – Between 6 and 8 people, usually single sex, who – for a small fee or product sample – take part in two- or three-hour group discussions. These discussions commence generally, before focusing on a specific product field, brand or advertising application (p. 178).

Forecasting – Predicting future events on the basis of historical data, opinions, trends, known future variables. Principally there are three categories of forecasting models in marketing: *Judgemental, Time Series Projections,* and *Causal* (p. 181).

Industrial Market – An *Industrial Market* consists of individuals, groups, organisations which purchase a specific kind of product for direct use in producing other products or for use in day-to-day operations (p. 235).

Intermediaries – In *Marketing Channels*, these are agents or brokers, wholesalers or retailers for consumer goods, and agents or distributors for industrial goods. They *sort out, accumulate, allocate goods* (p. 214).

International Marketing – Marketing activities performed across national boundaries (p. 246).

Intuition – In many situations managers have neither time nor resources to access Marketing Intelligence or commission Marketing Research in order to address a problem; instead they make decisions based on their experience and understanding of their market (p. 175).

Judgemental Forecasting – Subjective opinions of managers, aggregated and averaged: *Sales Force Composite* seeks the views and predictions from the fieldforce; *Expert Consensus* includes the opinions of industry experts; *Delphi* attains forecasts from the fieldforce, centrally collates and revises them before returning the updated forecasts to the fieldforce for further modification and opinion (p. 182).

Market Coverage – the Intensity of Market Coverage presents three options: *Intensive* with many distribution outlets; *Selective* with fewer outlets but with larger catchments; *Exclusive* with deliberately restricted and limited distribution (p. 214).

Market Segmentation – The identification of target customer groups where customers are aggregated into groups with similar requirements and buying characteristics (p. 189).

Market Segmentation Process – *Segmentation*; *Targeting*; *Positioning*. How does the market break down? Which segment should be targeted? How should the product be offered to the targeted market; how should it be positioned relative to competitors' products? (p. 189).

Marketing – Marketing consists of individual and organisational activities that facilitate and expedite satisfying exchange relationships in a dynamic environment through the creation, distribution, promotion and pricing of goods, services and ideas. It is the management process responsible for identifying, anticipating and satisfying customer requirements profitably (p. 155).

Marketing – The weekly trade magazine published in London by Haymarket Publishing; news and features from the world of practising marketers (p. 160).

Marketing Assets – Properties or features which can be used to advantage in the marketplace: *Customer-based*, such as image and reputation, brand name; *Distribution-based*; *Internal Assets*, including skills and experience, economies of scale, technology (p. 239).

Marketing Audit – A systematic examination of the objectives, strategies, organisation, and performance of an organisation's marketing unit (p. 240).

Marketing Communications – The communication of information which facilitates or expedites the exchange process (p. 224).

Marketing Environment – Those external forces that directly or indirectly influence an organisation's acquisitions or inputs and generation of outputs. The *macro marketing environment* includes legal, regulatory, political, societal, technological and economic forces. The *micro marketing environment* includes direct competition, substitute competition, supplier influences, the company's resources, customers' requirements and perceptions (p. 161).

Marketing Information System (MIS) – This is a *framework* for managing and accessing internal and external data, including Marketing Intelligence and Marketing Research information (p. 174).

Marketing Intelligence – The data and ideas available within a system, such as a marketing department (p. 174).

Marketing Mix – The tools available to the marketing manager, often referred to as 'the 4Ps': *product, place (distribution), promotion,* and *pricing* (p. 156). For the marketing of services, the 4Ps are extended to 'the 7Ps', with the addition of *people, process,* and *physical environment (ambience)* (p. 233). Increasingly, marketers of consumer goods and industrial products are including aspects of the *extended marketing mix* in their work (cf: Chapter 29).

Marketing Plan – The written document or blueprint for implementing and controlling an organisation's marketing activities related to a particular marketing strategy (p. 239).

Marketing Planning – A systematic process involving assessing marketing opportunities and resources, determining market objectives, and developing a plan for implementation and control (p. 239).

Marketing Research – A formalised means of obtaining/collecting information to be used to make sound marketing decisions in addressing specific problems (p. 173).

Marketing Research Process – Define and locate the problem (task); develop hypotheses; collect data; analyse and interpret findings; report research findings and conclusions (p. 175).

Marketing Strategy – A plan for selecting and analysing a Target Market; developing and maintaining a Marketing Mix (p. 158).

Marketing Week – The weekly trade magazine published in London by Centaur Communications; news and features from the marketing and agency world (p. 160).

Medium/Media – Choice of *medium of transmission* for a promotional campaign: print, TV/radio, cinema, posters, personal selling, etc (p. 224).

Multi-Branding – Each product or service in an organisation's portfolio is given its own unique name and brand identity (p. 208).

New Product Development (NPD) – As products or services are deleted from the Product Mix, replacement products must be launched. The **NPD Process** includes: *Idea Generation*; *Idea Screening*; *Business Analysis*; *Product Development*; *Test Marketing*; *Commercialisation* (p. 212).

Perceptual Maps – Based on a variety of mathematical and qualitative research tools, *Perceptual Mapping* describes consumers' perceptions of brands or products, and their attributes, on 'spatial maps' (p. 196).

Personal Selling – A process of informing customers and persuading them to purchase products through personal communication in an exchange situation (p. 226).

Porter's Competitive Strategies – The competitive arena is affected by outside forces: *bargaining power of suppliers*; *bargaining power of buyers*; *threat of substitute products or services*; *threat of new entrants* (p. 197).

Porter's Generic Strategies – Three generic strategies resulting in success for organisations competing for position in any particular market: *Cost Leadership*; *Differentiation*; *Focus* (p. 199).

Positioning – Part of the Market Segmentation process. *Product Positioning* refers to decisions and activities intended to create and maintain a firm's product or service concept in customers' minds. *Market Positioning* arranges for a product or service to occupy a clear, distinctive and desirable place – relative to competing products or services – in the minds of targeted customers (p. 194).

Price – As an element of the Marketing Mix, *Price* is a value placed on anything which is exchanged; a good, service or idea. *Price* is influenced by the competitive situation, the Marketing Environment, organisational policies, objectives, cost structures, the other elements of the Marketing Mix, and consumer needs and expectations (p. 218).

Primary Data Collection – In Marketing Research this is the act of collecting bespoke information for specific research requirements. There are two types: observation (mechanical or personal) and surveys (mail/postal, telephone or personal) (p. 176).

Product – Everything (both favourable and unfavourable) received in an exchange: a product is a complexity of tangible and intangible attributes, including functional, social and psychological utilities or benefits. A product may be a good, service or an idea (p. 205).

Product Adoption Process – *Awareness*; *Interest*; *Evaluation*; *Trial*; *Adoption* (Purchase and Consumption) (p. 225).

Product (Brand) Management – A form of marketing management where the marketing function is orientated around individual products/brands or product portfolios. *Product Management* is proactive, taking responsibility for both Marketing Strategy and the implementation of Marketing Mixes; it is not marketing as a service or ancillary resource (p. 205).

Product Deletion – *Phase Out, Run Out* or *Immediate Drop*; through whichever mechanism, products and services reach obsolescence and need to be deleted from the Product Mix (p. 212).

Product Life Cycle (PLC) – *Introduction*; *Growth*; *Maturity*; *Decline*. Most products, services and markets pass through this sequence. Marketing Strategies must be altered accordingly (p. 210).

Product Mix – The range of products controlled by one organisation. Often broken into product categories when the organisation is active in numerous, unrelated markets (p. 210). The *Product Mix* is dynamic and requires manipulation: *Product Deletion*; *Product Modification*; *New Product Development.*

Product Modification – Products need revising and updating periodically to remain competitive and in the Product Mix (p. 211).

Product Portfolio – The *Portfolio* approach to marketing attempts to manage the Product Mix so as to balance short-term gains with longer term profitability. There are various analytical tools available to assist in this management process: *The Boston Consultancy Group* (**BCG**) *Growth-Share Matrix* and the *Directional Policy Matrix* (**DPM**) are the most popular for analysing the relative attraction and positions of an organisation's various products or brands (p. 210).

Products: Consumer – Goods consumed by the general public; consumers as individuals: *Convenience Goods, Shopping Goods, Speciality Goods, Unsought Goods* (p. 206).

Products: Industrial – Supplies used in the manufacture of other products: *Raw Materials, Component Parts, Capital Items, Accessory Equipment, Consumable Supplies, Ancillary Services* (p. 206).

Products: Services – Service products tend to be intangible, requiring the participation of the consumer in their production and consumption:

Tourism/Catering, Travel, Health, Leisure/Entertainment, Education, Financial, Consultancy, Retailing, Government/Administration, Non-Profit/Voluntary/Charitable (p. 206).

Promotional Mix – The core elements of promotional activity: traditionally *Advertising, Sales Promotion, Personal Selling* and *Public Relations/Publicity*, with the more recent additions of *Sponsorship* and *Direct Marketing* (p. 226).

Publicity – Non-personal communication in news story form, regarding an organisation and/or its products or services, which is transmitted through a mass medium at no charge (p. 227).

Quali-Depth Interviews – A relatively new Marketing Research approach: 20–25-minute interviews conducted in halls or meeting rooms close to, for example, a high street (p. 178).

Qualitative Research – Deals with information too difficult or expensive to quantify; value judgements typically involving group discussions or personal interviews (p. 176).

Quantitative Research – Research findings which can be analysed and expressed numerically; often large sample surveys from mailed questionnaires or telephone interviewing, or analysis of sales data and market forecasts (p. 176).

Sales Promotion – Activity and/or material inducing sales through added value or incentive for the product to resellers, sales people or consumers. There are *Trade Promotions, Consumer Promotions* and *Retail/Distributor Promotions* (p. 228).

Sampling – In Marketing Research, except in industries with few customers or competitors, it is not cost effective to survey populations. Instead, samples are selected which represent their total populations or target markets. **Probability** sampling can be *random, stratified* or *area.* **Judgemental** sampling is more subjective and often is *quota* based (p. 179).

Secondary Data – In Marketing Research this is 'second-hand' information previously collected or published for another purpose, but readily available to consult. There are two types: internal sources (information within an organisation) and external sources (in libraries, publications) (p. 176).

Selling – A process of persuasion leading to a continuing trading arrangement, initiated and perpetuated at either a personal or an impersonal level but commonly confined to oral representation supported by visual aids. The focus is off-loading goods, services or ideas; is one-way with no customer feedback into the marketing mix (p. 157).

Services – A *Service* is the result of applying human or mechanical efforts to people or objects. Services are intangible products involving a deed, a performance or an effort which cannot be physically possessed or stored (p. 231).

Services Marketing Mix – This is extended from 'the 4Ps' to 'the 7Ps': *Product, Price, Place (Distribution), Promotion*; plus, *People, Physical Evidence (Ambience), Process* (p. 233).

Shopping Mall Intercept – Typified by the market researcher on a street corner or in a shopping centre, with a clipboard and three or four minutes' questions (p. 178).

Situational Analysis – Takes the four elements of the *SWOT Analysis* and combines them into just two sets of issues: factors external to the organisation, and those within the organisation – opportunities and resources (p. 244).

Sponsorship – The financing or partial funding of an event, personality, activity, programme or product in order to gain consumer awareness and media coverage from the association; most commonly in sports, the arts and entertainment (p. 226).

SWOT Analysis – Central to Marketing Planning, the *SWOT* is an analysis of an organisation's *S*trengths, *W*eaknesses, *O*pportunities and *T*hreats, product group by product group. The Strengths/Weaknesses are internal considerations, while the Opportunities/Threats relate to the market and the Marketing Environment (p. 243).

Target Audience – Group of people or a market segment at which a specific Promotional Campaign is aimed (p. 224).

Targeting – Part of the Market Segmentation process, *Targeting* is the act of identifying which market segments (or sectors) on which to concentrate resources and marketing activity: *mass marketing, single segment,* or *multisegments* (p. 193).

Time Series Forecasts – A set of observations, such as monthly or annual sales returns, examined and extrapolated to produce predictions for future figures. The main approaches are: *Naive, Moving Averages, Exponential Smoothing, Statistical Trend Analysis,* and *Box Jenkins* (p. 184).

Warfare Strategies – The analysis of competition linked to military warfare strategies. These include: *principles of Defensive Warfare*; *principles of Offensive Warfare*; strategies for *Market Leaders, Challengers, Followers, Nichers* (p. 200).

Bibliography

Assael, H. (1991) *Consumer Behaviour and Marketing Action*, Boston: Kent.

Baker, M.J. (1991) *Marketing, An Introductory Text*, London: Macmillan.

—— (ed.) (1987, 1991) *The Marketing Book*, London: Heinemann/CIM.

Bennett, P.D. (1988) *Marketing*, New York: McGraw-Hill.

Birn, R. (1990) *The Effective Use of Marketing Research*, London: Kogan Page.

Breen, G. and Blankenship, A.B. (1982) *Do It Yourself Marketing Research*, New York: McGraw-Hill.

Burnett, J.J. (1993) *Promotion Management*, Boston: Houghton Mifflin.

Buzzell, R.D. and Quelch, J.A. (1988) *Multinational Marketing Management*, Reading, Massachusetts: Addison-Wesley.

Chisnall, P.M. (1985) *Strategic Industrial Marketing*, London: Prentice-Hall.

—— (1992) *Marketing Research*, London: McGraw-Hill.

Choffray, J.M. and Lilien, G.L. (1980) *Market Planning for New Industrial Products*, New York: John Wiley.

Clifford, D.K. and Kavanagh, R.E. (1985) *The Winning Performance: How America's High Growth Companies Succeed*, New York: Bantam Books.

Coulson-Thomas, C.J. (1983) *Marketing Communications*, London: Heinemann/CIM.

Cowell, D. (1984) *The Marketing of Services*, London: Heinemann/CIM.

Crowner, R.P. (1991) *Developing a Strategic Business Plan with Cases*, Homewood, Illinois: Irwin.

Davidson, J.H. (1972) *Offensive Marketing*, New York: Penguin.

Davies, G.J. and Brooks, J.M. (1989) *Positioning Strategy in Retailing*, London: Paul Chapman.

Davis, M.P. (1990) *Business to Business Marketing and Promotion*, London: Century Hutchinson.

Dibb, S., Simkin, L., Pride, W. and Ferrell, O.C. (1991, 1994) *Marketing: Concepts and Strategies*, Boston: Houghton Mifflin.

Donnelly, J.H. and George, W.R. (1981) *Marketing of Services*, AMA Proceedings Series, Chicago: American Marketing Association.

Douglas, T. (1988) *The Complete Guide to Advertising*, London: Macmillan.

Drucker, P. (1981) *Management in Turbulent Times*, London: Heinemann/Pan.

—— (1992) *Peter Drucker in the Harvard Business Review*, Harvard Business Review Paperback Books Series, Boston: Harvard Business School Press.

Dunlop, J. (1986) *Q&A Marketing: Economics for Marketing*, London Financial Training Publications.

Engel, J.F., Blackwell, R.D. and Miniard, P.W. (1992) *Consumer Behaviour*, Chicago: Dryden Press.

Fernie, J. (ed.) (1990) *Retail Distribution Management: Strategic Guide to Developments and Trends*, London: Kogan Page.

Frank, R. and Wind, Y. (1971) *Market Segmentation*, Englewood Cliffs: Prentice-Hall.

Gattorna, J. (ed.) (1983) *The Physical Distribution Handbook*, Aldershot: Gower.

Handscombe, R. (1989) *The Product Management Handbook*, London: McGraw-Hill.

Harvard Business Review Paperbacks Series (1991) *Accurate Business Forecasting*, Boston: Harvard Business School Press.

Hutt, M.D. and Speh, T.W. (1992) *Business Marketing Management: Strategic View of Industrial and Organisational Markets*, Fort Worth: Dryden Press.

Jain, S.C. (1984) *International Marketing Management*, Boston: Kent.

Jefkins, F. (1988) *Public Relations Techniques*, London: Heinemann.

Keegan, W.J. (1989) *Global Marketing Management*, Englewood Cliffs: Prentice-Hall.

Kirpalani, V.H. (1985) *International Marketing*, New York: Random House.

Kotler, P. (1991) *Marketing Management*, Englewood Cliffs: Prentice-Hall.

Lancaster, G. and Massingham, L. (1988) *Essentials of Marketing*, Maidenhead: McGraw-Hill.

Lehmann, D.R. and Winner, R.S. (1988) *Analysis for Marketing Planning*, Plano: Business Publications.

Lilien, G.L. and Kotler, P. (1983) *Marketing Decision Making*, New York: Harper and Row.

Lovelock, C.H. (1984) *Services Marketing*, Englewood Cliffs: Prentice-Hall.

—— (1988) *Managing Services*, Englewood Cliffs: Prentice-Hall.

Lusch, R.F. and Lusch, V.N. (1987) *Principles of Marketing*, Belmont, California: Kent.

McCarthy, E.J. and Perreault, W.D. (1990) *Basic Marketing*, Homewood, Illinois: Irwin.

McDonald, M.H. (1989) *Marketing Plans*, Oxford: Butterworth-Heinemann.

Majaro, S. (1982) *International Marketing*, Boston: Unwin.

Marketing Q&A Series (1986) London: Financial Training Publications, 1986.

Monroe, B.K. (1979) *Pricing: Making Profitable Decisions*, New York: McGraw-Hill.

Moriarty, R.T. (1983) *Industrial Buyer Behaviour*, Lexington: Lexington.

Naert, P. and Leeflang, P. (1978) *Building Implementable Marketing Models*, Leiden: Martinus Nijhoff.

Parasuraman, A. (1991) *Marketing Research*, Reading, Massachusetts: Addison-Wesley.

Peter, J.P. and Olson, J.C. (1987) *Consumer Behaviour*, Homewood, Illinois: Irwin.

Porter, M.E. (1979) 'How competitive forces shape strategy', *Harvard Business Review* 47 (March–April): 137–45.

—— (1980) *Competitive Strategy: Techniques for Analysing Industries and Competitors*, New York: Free Press/Macmillan.

Powers, T.L. (1991) *Modern Business Marketing*, St Paul, Minnesota: West.

Rapp, S. and Collins, T. (1987) *MaxiMarketing*, New York: McGraw-Hill.

Ries, A. and Trout, J. (1981) *Positioning: The Battle for Your Mind*, New York: McGraw-Hill.

Rossiter, J.R. and Percy, L. (1987) *Advertising and Promotion Management*, New York: McGraw-Hill.

Saunders, J. (1987) 'Marketing and competitive success', in M. Baker (ed.) *The Marketing Book*, London: Heinemann/CIM.

Shipley, D. (ed.) (1989) 'Industrial distribution channel management', special edition, *European Journal of Marketing* 23(2), Bradford: MCB.

Terpstra, V. (1978) *International Marketing*, Hinsdale, Illinois: Dryden Press.

Tull, D.S. and Hawkins, D.I. (1990) *Marketing Research*, New York: Macmillan.

Webster, F.E. (1991) *Industrial Marketing Strategy*, New York: John Wiley.

Weilbacher, W.M. (1984) *Advertising*, New York: Macmillan.

Weitz, B.A. and Wensley, R. (1988) *Readings in Strategic Marketing*, Chicago: Dryden Press.

Wind, Y. (1982) *Product Policy: Concepts, Methods and Strategy*, Reading, Massachusetts: Addison-Wesley.

Index

Note: Page references in *italics* indicate tables and figures; those in **bold** indicate the glossary. Italics are also used for the names of companies treated in full in the case studies.